Photographs by

JANIS NICOLAY

From Baby's First Foods to Wholesome
Family Meals: Over 120 Delicious Recipes
for Clean Eating and Healthy Living

LEAH GARRAD-COLE

It
All
Begins
with
Food

♥

appetite
by RANDOM HOUSE

Appetite by Random House® and colophon are registered trademarks of Penguin Random House LLC.

Library and Archives of Canada Cataloguing in Publication
is available upon request.
ISBN: 9780147529992
eBook ISBN: 9780147530004

Book and cover design by Kelly Hill
Cover and author photograph by Janis Nicolay
Front cover: North Arm Farm, Pemberton, BC

Printed and bound in China

Published in Canada by Appetite by Random House®,
a division of Penguin Random House Canada Limited.

www.penguinrandomhouse.ca

10 9 8 7 6 5 4 3 2

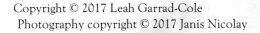

appetite
by RANDOM HOUSE

Penguin
Random
House

For my children, Poppy and Cameron.
With so much love.

Contents

Foreword

As a mama and a holistic nutritionist, I can say food is both my passion and my job! When it came to introducing foods to my baby girl, Vienna, my goal was to feed her only whole, organic food—and homemade as often as possible. With this in mind, I found myself on the hunt for a resource for how best to do this that really spoke my language while also being evidence-based. There was a lot of conflicting information online, and much of it just didn't resonate with me. I mean, it just didn't feel right to introduce rice cereal as a first food when there are far more nutritious foods like avocado and sweet potato!

One day, while stocking up on basics to make baby food at my favorite health food store, I came across a whole shelf devoted to a brand called Love Child Organics. The first thing I did was read the ingredients in the fruit and vegetable puree. I was pleasantly surprised to see that not only was it all organic but it was made from only whole foods in a BPA-free squeezy bottle too. I bought some purees and Teefies and felt good that I had finally found a brand that gets it—hurray for real food!

Vienna tried both and loved them (the Teefies were her favorite teething cookies). I felt confident knowing that even though I make 95% of her food, I had a safe, healthy backup if I needed it. As it turns out, the amazing mama who created this brand is also the author of this wonderful book, which is an incredible resource for all parents who want to feed their family nourishing, delicious food.

After reading this whole book and drooling over all the wonderful recipes, I felt inspired and excited that parents will have access to this valuable, and much-needed, information!! I love all the tips for growing adventurous eaters like taking your babe to a farmers' market and eating together as a family but not to beat yourself up if that doesn't happen every meal either—Leah gets it, because she's a mom too.

And the "favorite first single foods at a glance" chart is a total gem! I wish I had had this book when I was introducing foods to Vienna, because it is super handy for trying to figure out the best way to cook certain fruits and vegetables. For me personally, it helps me be more creative in the kitchen. It's easy to get stuck in a rut making the same meals you know your little one will love, but Leah makes it easy to try new foods and new recipes.

One of the most common questions people ask me at my public lectures is "Joy, what is one thing I can do to improve my health and my family's health?" I love this question, and my answer has been the same for years: COOK YOUR OWN FOOD. And *It All Begins with Food* can help you do that. The recipes in this book are straightforward and quick to prepare—making them ideal for busy parents—and ooze with nourishment, love, and joy. I can't wait to get in the kitchen and whip up another batch of quinoa bites and prune muffins!

Joy McCarthy
Holistic Nutritionist, CNP

Introduction

Hello and Welcome!

When we become parents, the life we knew before is suddenly turned on its head. Many elements of our lives are forever altered, including how we think about and approach food. Now that we have a family to feed, there are so many things to consider—but where is a new parent to start? Welcome to *It All Begins with Food*, a book dedicated to clean, whole-food recipes for your entire family. Moms and dads, you will love the ingredients, and your children will love the taste! From one health-conscious parent to another, this is more than just a cookbook. It is essentially a one-stop shop of nutrient-dense recipes and helpful information to support you as you cook nutritious food for your growing family, right from their very first bites.

Unfortunately, feeding children tasty, healthy food isn't always as easy as it should be. There is an overabundance of information out there, and it can make the task of feeding your family really confusing and overwhelming. We all want our children to eat well, but it's hard to know where to start, and with our busy lives, it's really difficult to find the time to make it happen. When I think back to not that long ago when my children were babies, I wish I'd had one trusted resource that I could rely on as I navigated my way through the choppy waters of baby feeding and cooking family foods. We all want to do the right thing by our children, but how do we know which advice to trust when the theories on how and what to feed babies, and which foods are healthy and which ones are not, seem to come from completely opposing teams? With plenty of encouragement, plus helpful tips and tricks along the way, this cookbook is here to help! I'll share with you up-to-date information about everything you need to know, from how to get started with solids, to understanding organics and GMOs, to stocking your pantry with nutritious ingredients that will set you and your little ones up for success. As for recipes, I've got you covered right from the baby stage, with purees, finger foods, and advice on how to make it all happen. And as your little ones grow, this cookbook will grow along with them, bringing your children running to the table for everything from super-powered breakfasts to healthier birthday party food (that still feels and tastes like a treat!) to enticing family meals that moms and dads will enjoy too. What if your family has special dietary requirements? You'll be pleased to see that there are plenty of recipes in here for you too, and suggestions for ways to adapt ingredients to fit your personal needs. (See page 13 for an explanation of the icons used in each recipe.)

With an unwavering focus on replacing ingredients that have little nutritional value with ones that are nutritionally dense, *It All Begins with Food* ensures that every bite counts while making sure that the end result is pleasurable and the ingredients are easy to find. Now, it's true that the wholesome foods in this book don't taste exactly like the foods that we ate as children. No amount of butternut squash will ever recreate the richness of a classic mac and cheese, and bread made from whole-grain spelt flour will never be the soft, sugary bread of our youth. But here's the good news: whole and unprocessed food tastes different for sure, but it also tastes amazing! And do you know what's even better? Our children won't think they're missing out on anything. If we make clean, nutrient-rich food part of their everyday lives, it will be their norm, and they'll live healthier lives because of it. Come along with me, and together we can get cooking!

With LOVE,

Leah

My Story

I come from a long line of foodie women who love creating in the kitchen. My mother is an excellent home cook, and she's always made everything from scratch. My Russian grandmother could rarely be found outside the kitchen, and her borscht is still the best I've ever tasted. Over the years, even my father has escaped his rather un-foodie roots and become quite adept at making some really delicious and exotic dishes that have become family staples. The love of real home-cooked food surrounded me from the beginning and has shaped who I am as a food-loving adult.

My own fascination with cooking came into its own in my early twenties (I'd moved out and didn't have my mother to cook for me anymore) when I found myself tired, a bit depressed, and approximately 30 pounds overweight. I just didn't feel good, and I didn't look my best either. I knew intuitively that the white-carb-rich food and the huge amounts of sugar I'd begun to eat so much of shortly after high school, when I was first out on my own, weren't helping my body to thrive. I was at a crossroads, and I came to the realization that it was up to me to take responsibility for how I was looking and feeling, and to do something about it if I wanted to enjoy my adult life. For me, that meant going back to my roots by getting in the kitchen and creating delicious food that I would love to eat but that wouldn't bring me down. I started adapting recipes, replacing empty ingredients like white flour and refined sugar with more healthful and colorful options, and including ingredients that are known to be nutritionally rich, superfoods like quinoa, flaxseed, kale, and sweet potatoes. My quest to get healthy and learn to cook for myself turned into a full-fledged hobby, and I spent much of my free time in my twenties in the kitchen concocting healthy recipes for one, and eventually, once I met my husband, for two. As my confidence grew, I found I really enjoyed cooking for friends and family. I started to truly believe that I wasn't too bad at this whole cooking thing.

Back in my previous life, before I had children, I was a teacher and administrator, mostly working with children in inner-city schools who often dealt with issues of food security. They simply didn't have much access to clean, nutrient-dense food, and sadly, a significant portion of their diet was based on foods that were sugary, high in sodium and unhealthy fats, and pumped up with artificial colors, flavors, or preservatives. I saw firsthand that these substances certainly weren't helping my students overcome challenges with learning, attention, and behavior; in all likelihood, junky food was making their outcomes worse. This was never more evident than when I worked in a respite school for young teens who'd been experiencing issues managing their behavior at school. I regularly witnessed that there was nothing quite like no breakfast and a junk-fueled stop at the convenience store on the way to school to cause a massive behavioral incident at 10 a.m. Meanwhile, as I completed my master's in special education, I had the opportunity to study the impact of chemical-laden foods on children's ability to focus and to control their impulsiveness.

> It became very clear to me that certain substances do not belong in children's bodies and that they significantly interfere with learning and behavior.

It became very clear to me that certain substances do not belong in children's bodies and that they significantly interfere with learning and behavior.

When I had my first baby, my interest in food additives became personal, and I started paying even more attention to the labels at the supermarket. I was absolutely shocked and frustrated by the number of preservatives, fillers, artificial colors, refined sugars, and over-processed oils that could be found in foods commonly eaten by children, and worse, that are marketed as "healthy." This made me more determined than ever to ditch processed food for good, to eat local and organic (whenever my budget allowed), and to make as much homemade food as I could. Of course, I still buy plenty of foods from the supermarket (with juggling family life, work, friends, pets, and all our other grown-up commitments, we all need easy ready-made options when homemade feels unattainable), but I have become much pickier about what I'll put in my cart and what I'll put in the mouths of my family.

This heightened passion for what is currently termed "clean" food coincided with a critical point in my life, when I had moved back to Canada from the UK (I am Canadian and my husband is from England) and was finishing my maternity leave with my baby Poppy. I needed to decide whether to stay in teaching or to take a risk and try something new.

With my passion for children and food and my husband's keen business sense, we decided to create our own children's food company, and Love Child Organics was born. Of course, it wasn't quite *that* simple. It took 18 months of research and planning, problem solving, and a breathtaking ride on a roller coaster of emotions to launch our first products. But from our first six organic purees to the many more products we have on shelves in supermarkets today, our values have remained rooted in our belief that food for children should be the best possible quality. At Love Child Organics, we believe it is our responsibility to choose ingredients that are kind not only to little growing bodies but also to the Earth. All of our organic recipes are packed with nutritious organic ingredients and are absolutely free from preservatives, fillers, refined sugars, pesticides, GMOs, and anything artificial. We are so proud and honored that our food is available all across the country and that thousands of babies and children are eating it each and every day. We know that we have been entrusted with an incredible privilege, and as parents ourselves, we feel that responsibility to our core.

So, if my business was built on selling ready-to-eat healthy, nutritious foods, why am I writing this cookbook? There are two reasons. The first, in a word, is choice. Love Child Organics already offers you the choice of buying healthy food for little ones that's ready to eat on those days when 48 hours still wouldn't be enough for you to get everything done. I *also* want to offer you the choice of spending some time in the kitchen exploring your *own* food preferences and finding out what works for you and your children. But people have asked me, "Why are you writing a cookbook with baby food in it? Don't you want people to just buy Love Child Organics?!" Well, of course I want people to buy Love Child, but I also truly want to empower new parents to cook homemade baby food if they'd like to try, and the reality is that for convenience's sake, most parents do use a combination of homemade and prepared baby food. So, if you choose to make your own baby food, this book is here to help, and if you just want to buy it at the store, that is absolutely OK too! Obviously I hope you'll choose Love Child Organics now that you know a bit more about our story and philosophy!

However, the baby food stage is very short (even though it may not feel that way at the time!), and eventually parents—that's you!—will need to get in the kitchen and cook, even if they avoided it during the baby stage. This book has everything you'll need to cook not only for the baby stage, but also for the many years of family eating to come. And the philosophy I drew upon when creating these recipes for families is exactly the same as the philosophy I apply when developing Love Child products: Include high-quality, nutrient-dense superfood ingredients as much as possible, avoid empty, nutrient-poor ingredients, and make the end result enticing and delicious. It's as simple as that! Every single recipe in this book was built on this philosophy and has been personally developed by me in my home kitchen and tested out on my own young family.

And this brings me to my second reason for writing this book: I believe in the power of homemade food, particularly food that centers on healthy whole-food ingredients, and I want to help parents to make it a part of their family life. But there is a caveat to this: I want to encourage parents to cook for their families in a way that is realistic and achievable, rather than prescribe something that will ultimately just make them feel more stressed about what they think they should be doing and all the things they are inevitably not doing perfectly.

Let me tell you a little story about a conversation I had with some moms that really drove this point home for me. I was out for dinner with five women, one of whom I knew very well, and four others whom I'd met a handful of times. We had a bit of wine and got into quite a bit of sharing about the intricacies of our family lives. They all talked at length about how stressful mealtimes are for them and the pressure they felt to get a nutritious homemade meal on the table. They were all trying to eat dinner together with their young families, for the most part, every night. They worked outside the home, arriving back at the house around 6 p.m. after picking their children up from day care. They felt like they had to have dinner with the kids because they hadn't seen them all day, and that the evening meal together was something that they couldn't miss. But none of them were enjoying these dinners, and the amount of resentment and negativity they had about the whole process was taking away from the special family time together that they so badly wanted to create.

I know what it's like to be a mom who wears lots of hats—one of which is to cook for a family—and I understand the quandary of wanting them to "just eat" and wanting them to eat something nutritious. And then, of course, there's the infamous, inescapable "mom guilt" and the pressure we put on ourselves to cook something homemade and eat together regularly at the family table, despite our incredibly busy lives. The issue is that life inevitably gets in the way of this, and the pressure to cook homemade food and all eat together can cause significant stress for parents who feel trapped by the idea that they must make one meal for everybody and eat dinner together each night.

My personal feeling is that while we can strive to eat together whenever possible, for all sorts of reasons, we can't always eat the same thing at the same time, particularly when children are very little. As a mom of two small children I know this firsthand, and while I've certainly had my moments of mom guilt, I've come to terms with the reality of raising a busy family of individuals, who from time to time each have different needs relating to types of food and times that food is best eaten. We make it a goal in our family to eat one meal per day together as often as we can (and it doesn't always have to be dinner—a family breakfast is just as good). Some days, I'll quickly pull something together that works just for my little ones. The reality is that it's best for everyone if we are flexible about how we approach food, and that putting pressure on ourselves to do things in a certain way, even if we know deep down it isn't working, just isn't worth it.

Now, I'm sure you've worked this out already, but let me assure you that this book was not written by, and is not aimed at, professional chefs or nutritionists. It's written for parents who care by a mom who's been there. I am not a certified nutrition expert, nor do I have any formal culinary training. What I am is a passionate family cook who, over the last several years, has been immersed in learning about organic and better-quality foods, making food for babies and children, and (I say with a sigh), until the day he becomes motivated to cook, keeping my husband fed too.

This book is written from my personal experience of all these challenges, and I hope, from one parent to another, it supports you and your family on your food journey.

The pressure to cook homemade food and all eat together can cause significant stress for parents who feel trapped by the idea that they must make one meal for everybody and eat dinner together each night.

How to Use This Book

My dream for this book is that it will be a source of support to all parents of young children who strive to feed their children a healthy diet full of clean, nutritious whole-food ingredients. We all know the expression "you can't please everyone," but I couldn't help but try.

Earlier, I mentioned my belief in the importance of being flexible when it comes to food, and you'll notice that the recipes in this book accommodate a wide variety of dietary needs. This is intentional. From my experience with my own family, my friends' families, and my food business, I have become very aware of individual dietary needs due to allergies, intolerances, and personal preferences. It's not uncommon for a family to have one child who can eat everything, another who is allergic to eggs, a mom who's off gluten, and extended family members who follow a plant-based diet. In fact, my family is one of those families, and as the "mom chef," I'm always juggling ingredients so that the food we eat works for everyone as much as possible. While not every recipe in this book will be free from all common allergens or be suitable for people who prefer a specific type of diet, I've tried hard to ensure that these types of needs were considered so that families who are following special diets will find many recipes that work for them, or at the very least be able to adapt recipes to make them friendly to the way they eat. This also means that if you are suddenly asked to bring grain-free muffins to a playdate, or if you're feeding guests who have different food needs from your own family's, you will be able to find recipes that will work.

Love Child Organics is a brand primarily for children aged 6 months to 6 years. This book has child-approved recipes for those early years (including lots of recipes specifically for babies and toddlers), but it also goes beyond with healthy recipes that will appeal to any age. These introductory pages contain lots of information for new and established parents, from starting solids, to understanding organics and GMOs, and even embarking on meal planning as your family grows and life becomes increasingly busy. I've also included lists of clean ingredients to keep in your pantry and special equipment to make sure you'll have everything you need to make the recipes. If you have a new baby and are about to start your first foray into solid food, I really encourage you to spend some time reading these pages carefully and looking at the single food charts on pages 68–81. They are great snapshots of useful information as you start your baby on her very first foods.

Chapter 1, "Purees and Mashes," and chapter 2, "Finger Foods," are dedicated to baby and toddler food and are a wonderful place to dive in if you are a parent to new eaters, but if your children are a bit older, don't bypass them completely. The finger food chapter has several recipes that can work for all ages, and they're all very quick and easy to make. (And you might be surprised by how many of the recipes in those chapters can be adapted for adult meals or snacks.)

From there, the book moves into recipes designed for young children (I've tested them on my own two and most of the children in my neighborhood—with great success!) but that also appeal to older kids and adults. While making food specifically for children can be fun and almost a rite of passage for new parents, cooking food everyone in the family likes to eat is definitely the way to go when it comes to time management in the kitchen. In addition to recipes for smoothies and all main meals, I've also included recipes for kitchen staples such as ketchup (page 245) and tortillas (page 240), things you would traditionally buy as processed foods.

Don't be confined by the chapter titles. Many lunch recipes will work for dinners, and vice versa, for example. So be sure to flip through all the pages, whether you're looking for a recipe for a specific purpose or simply seeking inspiration. Somewhere in this book, I hope that you'll find what you're looking for. (In the family dinner chapter, you'll see that I've included only three side dishes. This is because some of the other recipes in this book will work well as sides.)

To help you even more, I've included some icons to tell you a little bit about the recipes. As you get to know this cookbook, these little symbols will get to be your best friends.

They let you know at a glance the special characteristics of each recipe, including which common allergens a recipe is free from, whether it is plant-based, if it is good for freezing, and if it makes enough to feed a family of four. (See facing page.) And on that latter point, I'd like to explain the somewhat unconventional yields in this book. You're probably used to seeing things like "Serves 4–6" in a recipe, right? That's great for cookbooks that are generally aimed at grown-up eaters. This book, however, covers a range of ages, so I've adapted my yields accordingly. You'll see things like "Serves 2 toddlers" in some recipes, and that's because the recipe is built on the needs of the target age group. Only you know how much your children can and will eat, but these yields will serve as a guideline.

If a recipe contains an ingredient you'd prefer to avoid, or you don't have certain ingredients to hand, don't feel you need to skip to the next page or run out to the grocery store. Because the recipes are meant for busy parents, they're simple by nature and basic substitutions will result in a similar end product in most cases. Here are some basic substitutions.

1 large egg = 1 Tbsp ground chia seeds or ground flaxseed + 3 Tbsp water.

Dairy milk can almost always be substituted 1:1 with non-dairy milks like almond milk, coconut milk, and hemp milk.

Honey can be substituted for maple syrup. However, honey is slightly sweeter, so you may want to cut back the amount of honey slightly from the measurement for maple syrup.

Instead of coconut sugar, you can use an equal measurement of brown sugar.

Melted virgin coconut oil can be substituted 1:1 in most cases with melted butter, ghee, or extra virgin olive oil. Results in baking may vary slightly.

Butter can be substituted 1:1 with solid coconut oil. However, they do react somewhat differently in cooking, so results may vary, particularly in baking.

Spelt flour can be substituted 1:1 with organic whole wheat flour.

If you feel your creative juices flowing and simply want to adapt the recipes to suit your personal tastes, I really encourage you to go for it! Use the recipes as a base, then put your own twist on them. That is what fun and learning in the kitchen are all about.

And keep an eye out for special tips and anecdotes throughout the book. They're there to give you those extra tidbits of information that can really help as you navigate your way through feeding your family.

This recipe can be frozen.

Recipes with this symbol are entirely, or can be made as, plant-based (but not necessarily vegan).

Gluten-free: The recipe can be made gluten-free.

Grain-free: The recipe does not use grains.

Dairy-free: The recipe either does not call for dairy products or can be easily adapted to be made without dairy products.

Egg-free: The recipe either does not call for eggs or can be easily adapted to be made without eggs.

Will feed a family of four, based on two adults and two young children. This is my personal situation and it's how I tested the recipes and calculated the yields.

Eating with Health and the Earth in Mind

It's only fair that I give you a bit of a warning before you read this section. This is the part of the book where I climb up on my soapbox, speaking opinionatedly (but from the heart and with the best of intentions!) to anyone who will listen. I hope you'll hang in there with me as I get some things off my chest and get real with you about the food we're eating.

Here's the thing: *The quality of the food we feed our family matters.* It matters because it goes directly into our children's growing bodies. It matters because we—moms and dads—need to be in good health physically and emotionally to look after ourselves and our little people. It matters because the choices we make affect the planet we live on, and the people, animals, and plants that inhabit it. We can't eat low-quality, highly processed food (which, by the way, describes the majority of the pre-pared food we have to choose from) thinking that there aren't conse-quences for our health and the environment. When life is busy, reading ingredient lists and paying attention to where our food comes from can seem like just one more chore, but in reality, it takes only a few seconds to make small choices that will have a big impact on our children, ourselves, and the planet.

In the last several years, through my work with Love Child Organics, I have learned many things about our agriculture system and the food industry. Some days I wish I could unlearn much of it, because so much food isn't created with the best interests of people, animals, or the planet in mind. Our food system is very different than it was in the days of our grandparents—and not for the better. Generally speaking, conventional food in North America is grown and produced in the quickest and cheapest way possible, using chemicals and including synthetic ingredients that are presumed (but not known for sure!) to be safe. You'd think there would be regulations to protect against this, and yes, there are some, but they do not go nearly far enough, and food companies are at liberty to make food with a whole host of questionable ingredients. It costs a lot of money for big food companies to change the processes and ingredients that they have used for years, and until they are forced to change through regulation or they decide changing is worth it from a marketing perspective, you should keep in mind that just because something is allowed on the shelf, it absolutely doesn't mean that the ingredients are proven to be safe, never mind good for us. (Soda pop, anyone?)

Not only that, but many chemical fertilizers and pesticides used in agriculture, additives used in food, and chemicals used in cosmetics and household products are banned in the European Union and some other areas throughout the world but still permitted in North America! Generally speaking, the EU takes a more cautious approach when assessing the safety of ingredients, banning substances if there is evidence that they could be unsafe rather than requiring definitive proof that they cause harm, which is the system here. Bizarrely, many global manufacturing companies recognize the risks of these ingredients, leaving them out of products intended for the EU, but using them in or on products for the North American market! How do those companies justify such double standards?

Over the last decade or so, there has been increasing consumer demand for safer practices and products, and with some know-how, it is possible to find food and household products that are safe for your family. Many small food companies (like Love Child, I am proud to say), and now even some larger companies too, are holding themselves to a higher standard than that required by law and are making products that we can bring into our homes without concern. There is still a long way to go before we can walk into stores knowing that all the products on offer are created through safe and sustainable farming and manufacturing processes, but let's recognize progress where it's happening.

The more I've learned about food and the environment over the past few years, the wider my eyes have opened. I am forever changed in terms of the type of food and products I will bring into my home. While acting on new information can be daunting, especially if it makes you feel pressured to change your habits, it is also extremely empowering to feel educated about choices you can make for your family that really will protect them while being kinder to the environment. If you are interested in learning more about this topic and are looking for specific information to help you choose the safest products for your family and the Earth, I highly recommend that you become acquainted with the following organizations online:

- **The Environmental Working Group: www.ewg.org**
- **Healthy Child Healthy World: www.healthychild.org**

As partner nonprofit, nonpartisan organizations, staffed with experienced and knowledgeable scientists, and policy and communication experts, the EWG and HCHW provide in-depth, yet user-friendly information about how to protect your family's health and the environment from toxins. I have learned so much from them and visit their sites regularly, both as a support to the business and to learn about choices I can make to protect my family from toxins and help protect the environment. I really can't recommend them highly enough.

Let's Talk about Organic—It's about So Much More than Pesticides

Yes! We've arrived at one of my favorite topics! Simply put, choosing to eat organic food is one of the best things we can do for our families and the planet. But what does organic really mean? There are many misconceptions out there, so let's take a minute to get to the bottom of what it really is.

In Canada, the organic system is controlled by strict government regulations. The Canadian Organic Standards (you can find them easily online) are well respected the world over and cover both domestic and imported products. As the founder of an organic food company and a parent, I recognize and appreciate the value of these standards, especially since I've had the experience of meeting them as an organic business and know how robust they are.

I live and work in Canada, so my knowledge and experience of organic standards come primarily from the Canadian system. If you're in the US, take a look at the following websites (these are only two of many):
- **www.usda.gov (use the A–Z index to find Organic Agriculture)**
- **www.ams.usda.gov (click on Organic Certification)**

Essentially, the standards place restrictions on the use of synthetic fertilizers; toxic pesticides; the routine use of synthetic hormones, antibiotics, and other drugs on animals; animal cloning; genetic engineering (GMOs); irradiation; and sewage sludge. They also forbid the inclusion of artificial sweeteners, flavors, preservatives, food colors, and many other additives in processed foods. So you know that when you choose organic food, you are not only significantly reducing your exposure to toxic pesticides, but also sidestepping multiple other food additive nasties. In Canada, for a product to be certified organic and display the Canada Organic logo, it must contain a minimum of 95 percent organic ingredients. Some companies, Love Child Organics being one of them, choose to go beyond that and use 100 percent organic ingredients in many of their products.

However, the benefits of organic food are much more than simply avoiding toxins. Here are my top reasons for going organic.

Organic food is supportive of growing children's brains and bodies. The long-term health effects of pesticide exposure are not fully known, but there is evidence that chemical herbicides may be carcinogenic and cause hormone disruption. What we do know is that children who eat organically grown food are exposed to far fewer of these chemicals than children who don't. Children are small and more susceptible to the effects of toxins, so even low levels of pesticides could concentrate more highly in their bodies than in adults. More children than ever are being diagnosed with ADHD, autism, severe allergies, and even cancer, and I know I'm not alone in wondering whether what we're eating and the toxins we're exposed to in our environment play a role in this. Most experts agree that babies and children are among those who benefit most from eating organic food.

Organic farming is better for our environment and supports biodiversity. Increasingly, as consumer education on organics grows, for many people the main reason to eat organically grown and processed food is to support sustainable farming methods that are friendlier to the Earth and support greater biodiversity. Organic methods include crop rotation, composting, and natural methods to control pests that may otherwise damage crops (just like the good old days, in fact). Organic farms use far less energy than conventional farming, thereby reducing carbon emissions, and because they don't use chemical pesticides, they reduce the risks to animals like butterflies and bees, which are so important to our ecosystem.

Organic farming means safer water. Organic farmers are expected to use methods that respect surrounding water systems. Prohibiting the use of toxic chemicals means fewer toxins end up in our water. With several documented cases in the last couple of years of high pesticide residue in our water systems, supporting organic farming seems more important than ever.

Organic farms are safer for farm workers. Let's not forget that farms are powered by human beings, farm workers, who in conventional farming are exposed to high levels of toxic fertilizers and pesticides every day. Organic farming provides a much safer work environment for these farm workers and is more respectful of them as human beings.

Organic farming of animals is committed to animal welfare. The Canadian Organic Standards require that organically raised animals are not just given organic feed, but are treated with responsibility, care, and consideration so that stress, injury, and suffering are minimized. They must be given some access to the outdoors and more space per animal than in conventional livestock farming. The more I learn about the farming of animals, even organic farming of animals, the more I believe that much more needs to be done to ensure their lives are lived and ended in a truly humane way, but at least the organic standards for livestock are a step in the right direction.

Organic foods are nutritionally rich. Not only does eating organically grown food mean you're ingesting fewer pesticides, it also means you're getting more nutritional benefits from your food! Several studies have shown that organic fruits and vegetables have higher levels of antioxidants than conventionally grown produce.

Organic standards prohibit genetic engineering (GMOs). GMOs are a hot, hot topic, and on page 22 I'll look into what they are and what they mean to our food supply and environment in more detail.

What's important to know here is that the organic standards prohibit the use of genetic modification.

In an ideal world, many of us would eat 100 percent organic food all the time, but the fact is that for most people this isn't possible. Organic food can be expensive and it is still not as readily available as conventional food. With the cost of living already so high, and grocery bills for families feeling astronomical for most of us, what can we do to live a realistically organic lifestyle while staying within our budget? Here are my top tips:

1. Each year the Environmental Working Group puts out a list of what they term the Dirty Dozen and the Clean Fifteen. The Dirty Dozen are fruits and vegetables that are found to have the most pesticide residue, and the Clean Fifteen have the least. So if you can't afford to buy everything organic (and let's be honest, many of us can't), choose organic for at least some of the foods on the Dirty Dozen list and buy conventional for the foods on the Clean Fifteen list. The facing page has a handy chart of the 2016 Dirty Dozen and Clean Fifteen lists published by the Environmental Working Group. Take a snap of it with your phone and pull it out at the grocery store when you're deciding what to buy!

2. Buy produce from small, local farms or farmers' markets, and don't discount the ones that aren't certified organic. Sometimes local farms aren't certified organic (there is a cost to being certified, and it takes quite a long time to meet the standards), but if you speak to the farmer you will learn that the crops are unsprayed and that they are committed to farming practices that mimic organic standards. (Some farms will advertise their produce as no-spray, so keep your eyes open.) And speak to your farmer about any bruised or overripe produce they can offer at a discount. Take these ingredients home for canning, or slice them up and put them in your freezer.

3. In fruit season, get acquainted with U-Pick. Many organic fruit farms offer the opportunity for you to pick the fruit yourself, for a considerable discount—often half the cost you

The Dirty Dozen	The Clean Fifteen
Strawberries	Avocados
Apples	Sweet corn
Nectarines	Pineapples
Peaches	Cabbage
Celery	Sweet peas
Grapes	Onions
Cherries	Asparagus
Spinach	Mangoes
Tomatoes	Papayas
Sweet bell peppers	Kiwi
Cherry tomatoes	Eggplant
Cucumbers	Honeydew melon
	Grapefruit
	Cantaloupe
	Cauliflower

would pay for ready-picked produce. Get the kids, bring your buckets, a lunch, and a big cooler for your pickings and make a day of it. Freeze much of what you pick and eat inexpensive organic fruit all winter long.

4. Eat more organic beans, lentils, grains, and root vegetables. These organic ingredients tend to be less expensive than other organic ingredients, and they can be the basis for all sorts of delicious, nutritious meals.

5. Buy organic staples in bulk at either online specialty stores or big-box stores. Once you start looking, you'll be amazed at the sort of deals you can find.

6. Pay attention to the advertised specials at local natural food stores. They often offer incredible deals on specific organic

ingredients to tempt customers into their stores. Take advantage of this—but just be sure to go in with a list of what you really need and try not to deviate from it, otherwise you won't really be saving anything!

7. Make organic meat and poultry go further by serving it as a side to vegetables and starches, rather than as the main event. Rethinking how we build our plate of food can really decrease the amount of animal protein we eat. If you're buying organic, it will be more expensive, so consider changing your approach to eating meat to one of eating less but eating better.

8. Use meat, poultry, and fish in soups and stews. A family of four will eat less than half as much meat if it is served in a soup or stew that contains broth and other satiating ingredients than if they were each given a steak on their plate. There is no need for more than a few ounces of protein per serving, so make friends with your stockpot and make proteins go further.

What about GMOs?

Oh, GMOs. Probably one of the most talked-about and misunderstood food topics of the moment. I consider myself to be quite knowledgeable about food, but quite frankly, until a couple of years ago, I didn't fully understand GMOs and didn't really appreciate the concerns surrounding them. Now that I've had the opportunity to attend conferences and learn directly from experts in the field, I am concerned. Very concerned indeed. But let's get the definition of genetically modified organisms (GMOs) straight first.

GMOs are organisms that do not occur naturally in the wild and have been altered through genetic engineering with the goal of creating a species that has particular traits. The most common traits created by genetic engineering are:

1. Plants that are resistant to herbicide weed killers.

2. Plants that contain an internal insecticide that kills specific insects that try to feed on the GMO plant itself.

GMO crops have been touted as the answer to the world's hunger problems because, in theory, GMO crops would produce higher yields. So far, this claim has not been substantiated. Biotech industries also promise that genetically modified food could offer increased drought tolerance and enhanced nutrition, among other benefits, but this has yet to be proven.

While it is currently also unproven (although there is evidence to suggest it) that genetically modified foods themselves are harmful to us, only time and more research will tell. Call me crazy, but I feel quite wary of eating a food that has a built-in insecticide that kills the insects that eat it. But this isn't what scares me most about GMOs. I'm more scared by the fact that GMOs are developed to be resistant to toxic herbicides so that they can be sprayed with vast amounts of chemicals that kill the weeds around them but not the GMO crops themselves. A recent study in the US by Charles Benbrook found that between 1996 and 2011, because of herbicide-resistant crop technology, there has been a significant increase in the volume of herbicides used on crops like corn, soy, and cotton. Pretty worrying, if you ask me! So while GMO plants themselves may or may not be safe, the increasing amount of chemicals that are sprayed on them is certainly alarming. We have to ask what these chemicals are doing to our bodies, whether through eating the foods directly or eating the animals that consume them. Not to mention the impact these chemical herbicides have on natural habitats, water systems, farm workers, and the air we breathe. If you take one thing away here, let it be this: It's not just a question of whether GMOs themselves are safe to consume; we also need to be aware of the increasing amount of toxic chemicals that are being sprayed on them.

How Can You Avoid GMOs?

Certain crops are most at risk of being genetically modified. We commonly eat several of these foods directly, or we consume animals that have eaten them. There are also a number of food ingredients that are made from GMO foods and are cleverly disguised with other names. The most reliable way of avoiding them is to choose organic foods or foods that are certified as non-GMO. Unlike in Europe and many other countries, Canada and the US currently have no requirements for food companies to label GMOs, so the only way to know for sure is to look for these standards. However, knowing which foods are most likely to contain GMOs and avoiding these foods is a great place to start, if buying certified organic and GMO-free isn't an option. Here is a handy infographic that lets you know what to look out for. You can snap a photo of this one to keep with you too!

Say No to GMOs
Crops at most risk of being genetically modified

Cotton

Canola

Soy

Sugar Beets

Corn

Papaya

Zucchini and Summer Squash

DID YOU KNOW?

At least 50 percent of the sugar in the US comes from sugar beets, which are highly likely to be GMO sugar beets. Another reason to limit our families' intake of sugar.

DID YOU KNOW?

Animals that eat GMO corn are consuming GMOs and passing them through the food chain. To avoid this, choose grass-fed or organic meat.

DID YOU KNOW?

More than sixty nations, including Germany, the UK, and Australia, require GMO foods to be labeled. It's time for the same thing here!

COMMON INGREDIENTS DERIVED FROM GMO RISK CROPS

Amino acids, aspartame, ascorbic acid, sodium ascorbate, vitamin C, citric acid, sodium citrate, ethanol, flavorings (natural and artificial), high-fructose corn syrup, hydrolyzed vegetable protein, lactic acid, maltodextrin, molasses, monosodium glutamate, sucrose, textured vegetable protein (TVP), xanthan gum, vitamins, yeast products, vegetable oil, canola oil, cottonseed oil, soybean oil, corn oil, corn flour, cornstarch, and cornmeal.

OTHER WAYS TO AVOID GMOs

Buy organic! Organic foods do not contain GMOs. Buy foods that are verified GMO-free. Avoid processed foods, which often contain GMO ingredients.

Top Tips for Keeping Your Family Healthy and Respecting the Planet

I could go on forever about the importance of food quality, but it's probably time to move on and get off my soapbox! If you've stayed with me so far on all of this, I really do thank you for reading. So I'll rein myself in and leave you with my top food tips for keeping your family healthy and respecting the planet!

1. Choose organic when you can, especially for babies and children.

2. Avoid foods containing GMOs and foods that *eat* GMOs.

3. Prepare homemade food from clean, natural ingredients, focusing on ones that are nutritionally dense. (See pages 30–35 for a list of my favorites.)

4. Replace white flour and sugar in baking with more nutrient-dense choices, like whole-grain spelt flour and less refined sweeteners like honey, coconut sugar, or dates (you will notice almost all the treat recipes in this book use these less refined sweeteners rather than classic sugar). And decrease the amount of sweetener in a classic white-sugar-laden recipe by one third.

5. Increase your family's intake of fresh fruits and vegetables. One way to do this is to think of the vegetables as the stars of a snack or meal, and the starches and proteins as the sides.

6. When buying prepared food, look for options that are lower in sodium and sugar. Sodium and sugar can add up very quickly if children are eating processed foods, and it is recommended that they actually don't get very much of them. Children aged 1–3 should aim for approximately 1,000 mg of sodium per day; an appropriate level for children aged 4–8 is 1,200 mg of sodium per day (see www.hc-sc.gc.ca and search "sodium"). Children of all ages should derive no more than 5–10 percent of their overall energy intake from added sugars (see www.who.int and search "sugar"). When you're reading the labels, remember that sugar goes by many names (not all of which end in the infamous "-ose"). (See following page.)

Alternative (Sneaky) Names for Sugar

Agave	Corn syrup	Fructose	Malt syrup
Barley malt	Corn syrup solids	Fruit juice	Maltodextrin
Beet sugar	Date sugar	Fruit juice concentrate	Maltose
Brown rice syrup	Dehydrated cane juice	Fruit juice crystals	Maple syrup
Brown sugar	Dehydrated fruit juice	Galactose	Palm sugar
Buttered syrup	Dextran	Glucose	Palm syrup
Cane juice	Dextrin	Glucose solids	Refiner's syrup
Cane juice crystals	Dextrose	Golden syrup	Sorghum syrup
Cane juice solids	Diatase	High-fructose corn syrup	Sucrose
Caramel	Diatastic malt	Honey	Tapioca syrup
Carob syrup	Ethyl maltol	Lactose	Turbinado
Coconut sugar	Evaporated cane juice		

7. Buy eggs, meat, and dairy from local farms that practice sustainable and more humane farming methods. Let's do what we can to respect the beautiful animals that give their lives to put food on our tables.

8. Regularly incorporate vegetarian protein sources into your family's diet, even if you are meat eaters. Nuts, seeds, and legumes are nutritious and satiating. Cashews are delicious in a stir-fry!

9. Make it your practice to read labels. When you purchase prepared foods, buy ones that contain only real food ingredients. If you can't pronounce it, don't buy it—chances are it is a chemical, not a food. Food should be made with food! And shorter ingredient lists tend to be the better option.

10. Become familiar with common toxic ingredients found in food and aim to steer clear of them as best you can. Visit Healthy Child Healthy World or the Environmental Working Group online for all the information on this you could need. The more consumers demand higher-quality products, the sooner large companies will change and offer better options. If we as parents do this now, imagine the better options that could be available for our children's children and the positive consequences this could have for their future and the planet's.

Find Out More:

WEBSITES:

Environmental Working Group: www.ewg.org

Healthy Child Healthy World: www.healthychild.org

Canadian Food Inspection Agency:
www.inspection.gc.ca (click on Food)

United States Department of Agriculture:
www.usda.gov/wps/portal/usda
(use the A-Z index to find Organic Agriculture)

The Non-GMO Project: www.nongmoproject.org

Just Label It: www.justlabelit.org

David Suzuki Foundation: www.davidsuzuki.org

Charles M. Benbrook's 2012 study, "Impacts of Genetically Engineered Crops on Pesticide Use in the U.S.—The First Sixteen Years," is well worth reading. You can find it online at enveurope.springeropen.com/articles/10.1186/2190-4715-24-24.

BOOKS:

The Dirt Cure (Atria Books, 2016): Written by integrative pediatric neurologist Maya Shetreat-Klein, MD, this meticulously researched book is the best I have ever read on children's health and well-being and how they're connected to and affected by food and the environment. It's an absolute must-read for all health-conscious parents, and especially parents whose children are experiencing health issues including allergies and intolerances. I can't recommend it highly enough!

In Defense of Food (Penguin Books, 2009): While this book by Michael Pollan isn't directly about feeding children, parents who are interested in understanding how to navigate our broken food system and our questionable "Western diet" will find this book a huge help when deciding what to feed their families. Don't be put off by the publication date. This book is still extremely relevant and could have been written yesterday.

The Clean Kitchen and Pantry

Cooking healthy food for your family and retaining some degree of sanity while you do so is much easier if you keep your refrigerator and pantry stocked with a variety of whole-food, nutrient-dense ingredients and avoid buying foods that don't fit this description. Generally speaking, purchasing individual whole-food ingredients over foods that have been processed makes it much easier to ensure your family is eating what is often referred to as "clean" food. This is food that is either just one ingredient—in other words, the food itself—or a prepared food that contains only a simple list of ingredients (and by "simple," I mean no preservatives, artificial flavors, or artificial colors, and low amounts of added sodium or sugar). Ideally, the foods we buy will also be organic, certified non-GMO, or locally grown, and in a perfect world, in season. If all this isn't possible, don't worry—simply reading labels carefully to avoid additives and choosing fresh whole foods have huge value for your family's health and are the key steps to focus on here. If you need to purchase some of these ingredients as non-organic food, use the Dirty Dozen and Clean Fifteen list (page 21) and the list of high-risk GMO crops (infographic, page 24) to help you make the smartest choices. I haven't specified GMO-free or organic in any of the food lists in this book, mainly because I've already made my feelings clear about these.

If I had an empty kitchen and pantry and the goal of filling them with clean, nutritious ingredients, this is the list I would take to the market. Every ingredient required in this cookbook is on the list, plus a few other nutritious favorites that are great extra ingredients to have on hand so you're ready for just about anything. If your family follows a special diet and avoids certain foods, adapt this list to suit your situation.

Clean Food Shopping List

Vegetables

FRESH

Asparagus

Beets

Bell peppers

Broccoli

Butternut squash

Carrots

Celery

Chard

Cucumber: English or field cucumbers when in season

Jicama: Great for dipping, and so good sprinkled with lime juice and sea salt!

Kale

Leeks

Lettuce: red leaf, romaine, butter, iceberg for lettuce cups

Onions: white or yellow, red and spring

Potatoes

Pumpkins

Red cabbage

Rhubarb

Salad greens: spring mix, arugula, pea shoots, lamb's-quarters, etc.

Spinach

Sprouts: Brussels sprouts and leafy sprouts like alfalfa and pea sprouts

Sweet potatoes

Zucchini

FROZEN

Corn

Edamame: Be sure to go organic with these, because conventional edamame (soybeans) are almost certainly GMO, and serve only from time to time rather than every day due to concerns about phytoestrogens, which may cause hormone disruption.

Peas

Rhubarb

Spinach

OTHER

Dried sea vegetables: Very nutrient-rich; can be used in stir-fries or green smoothies or sprinkled on top of salads, for example, as a condiment.

Keep cut-up fresh veggies in the refrigerator to pull out for you and the kids to snack on while you prepare dinner. Keep washed, de-stemmed, cut-up greens like kale and chard handy in the refrigerator or freezer to add to morning smoothies or throw into soups, stews, and stir-fries.

Fruit

FRESH

Buy berries (blueberries, blackberries, raspberries, strawberries) and stone fruits (cherries, nectarines, peaches, plums) in summer, and pomegranates and mandarin oranges near the holidays. Other fruit to buy fresh in season:

Apples

Avocados

Bananas

Grapes

Kiwis

Lemons

Limes

Mangoes

Oranges

Pears

Tomatoes: cherry and regular-size

Watermelon

FROZEN

Blueberries

Cherries

Mangoes

Peaches

Pineapple

Raspberries

Strawberries

DRIED
Ideally, all organic or at least unsweetened and unsulfured.

Apricots

Coconut

Cranberries

Dates

Figs

Goji berries

Mangoes

Raisins

JUICE

Apple, unsweetened

Coconut water

Pomegranate

Frozen fruit will have been picked and frozen at its peak of ripeness and is likely to have higher nutritional value than unseasonal fresh fruit that has probably been kept in a cold warehouse for weeks or even months. Use for smoothies, or thaw and serve with pancakes, or over yogurt.

Meat and Alternatives

MEAT, POULTRY, FISH, AND EGGS:

Beef: stewing, extra-lean ground

Pork: tenderloin

Nitrate-free naturally smoked bacon

Chicken: whole boneless, skinless chicken thighs

Turkey: ground

Wild salmon

Wild white fish like red snapper or halibut

Eggs

 When it comes to meat, eggs, and fish, it pays to be very picky about quality. Meat from factory farms is almost certainly from animals that were not only fed GMO feed and all sorts of medications, but also kept in appalling conditions. Farmed fish are raised with pesticides and other chemicals in very crowded environments and are less nutritious than wild fish. If it is within your budget, try to source wild fish and organic meat, or go for grass-fed, locally raised meat where you can. Remember, to make up for the price, you can try to eat meat less often, serving it in smaller portions alongside lots of veggies, and cooking dishes like soups and stews, which make meat go further. And even if your family isn't on a completely plant-based diet, for your health, the environment, and your budget, consider adding some more plant-based proteins to your diet. Once you get used to eating them as a source of protein, you'll really come to enjoy them.

Legumes

Black beans

Cannellini beans

Chickpeas

Kidney beans

Navy beans

Red and puy lentils

Buy BPA- and sodium-free canned beans or buy them dried.

Nuts and Seeds

Almonds

Cashews

Chia seeds: These little super seeds are very rich in nutrients, and are full of fiber, protein, and omega-3s. They are a key element in several recipes in this book, in particular for gluten-free baking. Buy them whole and then grind them in your food processor if the recipe calls for ground chia seeds.

Flaxseeds: High in fiber and omega-3s, these seeds are called for in several recipes. Buy them whole and grind them yourself if a recipe calls for ground flaxseed.

Hemp hearts: High in protein and omega-3s, these extremely versatile seeds are used in several recipes in this book. You can buy them in natural food stores but also in large supermarkets that have a good natural food section, and usually you can find them for an excellent price at big-box stores.

Pecans

Pumpkin seeds

Sunflower seeds

Walnuts

Natural smooth almond butter

Natural peanut butter, smooth or crunchy

Seed butter: sunflower, pumpkin, or a mix of seeds

Raw and unsalted is the most healthful way to go with nuts and seeds to avoid added oils and excess sodium. Many health experts recommend soaking and dehydrating nuts and seeds to make them more digestible and the nutrients easier to absorb. If you'd like to try this, all you need to do is cover them with water, add a bit of sea salt, and soak them overnight. Rinse thoroughly, then spread out on a baking tray and dry in a very low-temperature oven (approximately 150°F) for 12–24 hours.

Grains

WHOLE GRAINS

Amaranth

Buckwheat groats

Brown long-grain rice or wild rice

Oats: quick, whole rolled, and steel-cut. Quick oats are great for when you need speed and a softer texture in baking. I buy rolled oats to make my oat flour because I find that they blend more easily than steel-cut. Steel-cut are the least processed, but take the longest to cook, so I use them for porridge when I'm not in a rush. Choose gluten-free, sometimes called "pure" oats, if you are concerned about contamination with gluten-containing grains.

Quinoa

A NOTE ON WHEAT: I tend to avoid white wheat flour altogether as it has no nutritional value whatsoever and makes me feel terrible, and I'd rather that white wheat flour didn't become the kids' norm. Even when I'm baking, I try very hard to avoid it and now hardly miss it at all. When I do use a gluten-containing flour, I use organic spelt flour or einkorn flour instead of whole wheat. Many people, including me, find spelt and einkorn easier to digest. Although einkorn can be difficult to find, spelt is now available in almost all grocery stores. The reason so many people seem to be sensitive to wheat is likely due to factors that go way beyond the fact that it contains gluten. Wheat has been hybridized significantly over the past several decades and now contains much more gluten than it did during our grandparents' time. However, many experts feel that the reason wheat intolerance is on the rise is likely due to the increasingly high levels of toxic herbicides that are sprayed on almost all non-organic wheat in North America. So, if you're going to purchase wheat flour or products that contain wheat, like bread, it's really important to go for organic to avoid these herbicides. Or, for wheat-containing foods like crackers and pasta, one option is to buy European varieties, which are less exposed to herbicides.

PASTA

Couscous: whole-grain European, or organic due to the high amount of pesticides used on conventional wheat (see below).

Rice and quinoa pasta (gluten-free)

Spelt pasta

FLOURS

Gluten-containing flours

If you can't find spelt, and you can tolerate wheat flour, organic whole-grain wheat flour can be used as a substitute for any of the recipes calling for spelt flour.

Spelt flour: whole-grain. I look for spelt flour that is very finely ground, which results in lighter baking.

Other ancient whole-grain flours like einkorn

Gluten-free flours

Good-quality all-purpose gluten-free flour blend that contains some whole grains and no xanthan gum. If you would like to make your own using my recipe (page 241), you will need: arrowroot starch, buckwheat flour, brown rice flour, sweet sorghum flour, white rice flour.

Arrowroot flour

Millet flour

Pure oat flour: Oat flour is called for in several recipes, but it's very simple to grind yourself by blending rolled oats in your food processor or blender. Because oats are so soft, you don't even need a fancy high-powered blender to do this. Use "pure" or certified gluten-free oats if you're concerned about contamination with gluten-containing grains.

Quinoa flour

Tapioca flour: good for combining with heavier gluten-free flours and used in my gluten-free pizza dough recipe on page 188

Grain-free flours

Almond flour

Coconut flour

BREAD AND CEREAL PRODUCTS

Breakfast cereals: whole-grain with little or no added sugar

Tortillas: Tortillas, both flour and corn, are one of the worst culprits when it comes to preservatives. Your best bet is to buy from smaller brands and to triple-check the labels for anything that looks suspect. Buy the cleanest, most whole-grain, seedy kind you can find or make your own (see page 240).

Grains (contd.)

Whole-grain breads: To avoid the additives and preservatives that are found in mass-produced bread (ever wonder why some bread can sit so long on a counter and stay soft and mold-free?), buy bread from a bakery, or choose smaller, more artisanal brands, which usually have much cleaner ingredient lists. If you are concerned, as I am, about the huge amounts of herbicides used on wheat, be sure to go for organic or non-wheat bread products.

Consider buying sprouted grains or grain products. Sprouting increases the bio-availability of nutrients in the grains themselves and can make the grains more digestible. There are lots of sprouted grains, flours, and bread products on the market. I particularly like sprouted spelt flour and find it quite easy to find at natural grocery stores. If you can find the time, you can also sprout your own grains. There are many resources online that give excellent instructions on how to sprout grains, and also nuts and legumes, right in your own home.

Milk Products

Organic or grass-fed whole-fat cow or goat milk

Non-dairy milk: almond, cashew, coconut, or hemp. Look for brands that are low in sugar and don't contain carrageenan (a non-digestible stabilizing agent that's linked to inflammation, among other serious issues). Unless otherwise stated, you can substitute non-dairy milk for any recipe in this book that calls for milk.

Unsweetened whole organic cow's milk yogurt, goat or sheep's milk yogurt, Greek yogurt, or unsweetened non-dairy yogurt: Sweetened yogurts have a shocking amount of sugar. If you're looking for a sweetened yogurt, it's much better to control the sweetener by adding it yourself, with a touch of honey, maple syrup, or fruit puree.

Cheese: sharp or aged cheddar, medium cheddar, mozzarella, cream cheese, soft goat cheese, Parmesan cheese, non-dairy cheese

Just as I mentioned for meat products, for milk from cows, goats, or sheep, know that the feed the animals eat becomes the milk we drink. So if they are eating GMO corn and soy, there is essentially GMO corn and soy in your milk. When possible, choose organic or grass-fed milk, or try non-dairy options for an excellent substitution.

Sweeteners

Coconut sugar: Coconut sugar, also called palm sugar, can be substituted very well for brown sugar and even white sugar in recipes and is my baking sweetener of choice. It is made from dehydrated coconut tree sap, and has a lower glycemic index than regular sugar.

Dates: pitted dried, Medjool, Deglet Nour

Honey: raw, unpasteurized, and ideally local

Maple syrup: Go for pure maple syrup, not corn syrup with maple flavor, which is often marketed as maple syrup (read the label—syrups are sneaky!).

Blackstrap molasses

Organic granulated cane sugar: Conventional sugar is most likely to be made from sugar beets, which are almost certainly genetically modified. For those times when only traditional sugar will do, I use organic cane sugar to ensure we're not eating GMOs.

Organic powdered icing sugar: I use this only occasionally when making icing for holiday cookies, or for my Reduced-Sugar Buttery Cream Cheese Frosting (page 237)—you can also simply blend up organic sugar to make your own powdered icing sugar.

All sweeteners are "sugar" and should be consumed modestly, but some sweeteners are less refined, have some nutritional benefits, and are used for healthier treat recipes in this book. Several of these recipes use dates, the most natural sweetener of all.

Fats and Oils

Butter (grass-fed or organic): Some baking is just better with butter, so I keep some on hand for this reason and to use as a condiment for toast, muffins, etc. Almost all the recipes in this book call for unsalted butter, but I like to keep salted on hand too, simply because I love salted butter spread on muffins and bread.

Cold-pressed organic flax oil: I add this excellent source of omega-3s to smoothies and salad dressings. It's not to be used for cooking.

Extra virgin, cold-pressed organic olive oil: This oil is excellent for pouring on cooked vegetables and salads. It has a lower smoke point, so it's best for lower-heat cooking. For some classic Mediterranean foods and recipes, I still use it for cooking at higher heat (although never for frying), simply because I can't wrap my head around using coconut oil for a dish that's classically Italian and just screaming out for olive oil!

Ghee: Essentially clarified butter, it is touted as not only having great flavor, but also some health benefits—especially if it's from grass-fed cows—such as being high in vitamins A and E, and like coconut oil, rich in medium-chain fatty acids, which are currently believed to be helpful for weight management among other benefits.

Toasted sesame oil: To add to Asian dressings and sauces

Virgin, cold-pressed organic coconut oil: This heat-stable oil has anti-inflammatory properties and is incredibly versatile! I use this for most of my baking and for cooking at higher temperatures. I also stir it into grains, add it to smoothies, and spread it on anything the way you would spread butter. At room temperature, coconut oil is solid, so for many of the recipes, you will need to melt it before adding it to the other ingredients.

Children need fat in their diet (as do adults), but most cooking oils and fats are highly refined, processed foods that promote inflammation and are best avoided if possible. So if you have some big plastic bottles of those clear, tasteless oils in your pantry, it's time to let them go. Almost all processed foods contain refined oils (known as vegetable oils), particularly soybean oil, corn oil, canola oil, and safflower oil, so when cooking at home it's important to stay away from these unhealthy sources as much as possible. The oils and fats in the pantry list are the main ones I use and are the only fats called for in the recipes in this book. In my kitchen I also often have cold-pressed nut oils and avocado oil to use on salads and precooked vegetables, but they are nice-to-haves rather than must-haves. Organic or grass-fed ghee is also something you may want to try, especially if you love cooking with butter but have family members who have issues with dairy. Ghee is essentially butter with the milk solids removed, and is excellent for cooking. Many people who are lactose intolerant don't react to ghee. I tend to stick to mostly organic virgin coconut oil simply because not only is it a nutritious choice, it's also easy to find, it's a good substitution for both vegetable oil and butter, and I prefer to use a more environmentally friendly plant-based fat whenever I can. Many recipes in this book call for either virgin coconut oil or ghee—the choice is up to you.

Herbs, Spices, and Other Important Ingredients

FRESH HERBS AND ROOTS

Basil

Chives

Cilantro

Dill

Garlic

Ginger root

Parsley: curly or flat-leaf

Rosemary

Sage

Thyme

Turmeric root

Herbs are very easy to grow at home in just a basic large pot in a sunny spot, so in the summer, grow your own and leave them off the shopping list.

DRIED HERBS AND SPICES

Basil

Bay leaves

Black peppercorns

Chili powder: mild

Cinnamon: ground and sticks

Cloves

Coriander

Cumin: powder and whole seeds

Garam masala

Garlic powder

Ginger

Mustard powder

Nutmeg: ground and whole

Onion powder

Oregano

Paprika: sweet

Sage

Thyme

Turmeric

Choose organic herbs and spices if you can. This way you avoid additives like added flavorings, preservatives, and chemical anti-caking agents and the possibility of irradiation, which is when foods are irradiated to destroy unwanted bacteria and organisms. This process is common for herbs and spices and is deemed safe. It's probably not something to worry too much about, but if it concerns you, buy organic because irradiation is prohibited by the organic standards.

Last, but Certainly Not Least

Pure vanilla extract: The recipes in this book call for extract because it is the easiest to find. If you prefer to use vanilla beans or vanilla bean powder, 1 tsp of extract equals the seeds of 1 vanilla bean, or ½ tsp of vanilla powder.

Natural almond extract

Natural mint extract

Baking powder: ideally aluminum-free and gluten-free

Baking soda

Cream of tartar

Active dry yeast

Nutritional yeast: used to add B vitamins and cheesy flavor to plant-based foods

Grass-fed gelatin powder

Fine-grained sea salt: Whenever a recipe in this book calls for salt, you can assume it is this type.

Balsamic vinegar

Raw apple cider vinegar

Rice vinegar

Canned full-fat coconut milk (from a BPA-free can)

Coconut aminos: Can be used in place of soy sauce or tamari, so is very allergy-friendly.

Tamari: Tamari is like soy sauce but gluten-free and usually with a cleaner ingredient list.

Dijon mustard

Tomato paste

Jarred unsweetened organic tomato pasta sauce

Fruit juice–sweetened jam (apricot, strawberry, etc.)

Ready-made fresh pesto: made with extra virgin olive oil, not vegetable oils

A selection of clean, minimally processed, and ideally organic packaged snack foods (for convenience)

Your favorite specialty superfoods (great for adding to smoothies—see page 124)

Tools and Equipment

STAND-UP BLENDER

Especially if you are whipping up purees for your baby or smoothies for you and the kids, a good-quality blender is paramount. It's also really helpful for whipping together wet ingredients when baking, and I suggest using one quite a bit in this book. I decided to give up lots of little everyday splurges so that I could buy my dream high-powered blender, and for me it was so worth it. If you buy a good blender, you will be able to blend up practically anything. Heck, you can even grind your own flour or make your own nut butters in some of these machines! And it ought to last longer than a less expensive blender. So, if you are going to splurge on a small kitchen appliance, let it be a high-powered blender!

IMMERSION BLENDER

This is a nice-to-have, rather than a must-have. It's great for pureeing things that you want to keep a little chunky, and when you want to puree right in the pan you cooked in, rather than pouring something like soup into a blender. It's also handy for pureeing small batches of baby food and for traveling.

SPECIALTY BABY FOOD BLENDER

I found that I never needed one of these and just used my stand-up blender and immersion blender, but many new parents swear by them.

FOOD PROCESSOR

In my experience you can get away with spending less on this appliance than on a blender. It's such a time saver for cutting and chopping, but it's also great for making dips, and even blending up cupcake batter. Once you have one you won't ever go back!

HAND-HELD OR STAND MIXER

Hand-held mixers are inexpensive and can totally do the job they're made for. A stand mixer is a splurge but will last for years and means your hands are free to do other things while your batter is beating or your cream is whipping.

STAINLESS-STEEL STEAMING BASKET

Makes cooking and draining vegetables easy-peasy. I much prefer an old-school metal steaming basket to an electric steamer, as it steams quicker and is so easy to clean.

SILICONE BAKING MAT

This is a bit of a splurge and is not completely necessary if you have parchment paper, but it's a really nice addition to your kitchen if you like to bake. Nothing sticks to it, and it makes tricky recipes like fruit leather a dream to manage.

STAINLESS-STEEL POTS

Durable as well as free from harmful coating chemicals, stainless-steel pots are a great investment.

CAST IRON SKILLETS

Cast iron pans are less expensive than you would think, will last forever, and are a much safer option than non-stick skillets or skillets that are coated with toxic chemicals that could leach into your food. Plus, they are the best for cooking pancakes, omelets, and frittatas.

BPA-FREE BABY FOOD FREEZER CONTAINERS OR BPA-FREE ICE CUBE TRAYS

Make sure your freshly made organic baby food is stored in a way that is safe for your baby and invest in a few of these specialty freezing options.

METAL RASP

For easy fine grating of lemon zest, nutmeg, hard cheeses, and chocolate.

GLASS OR STAINLESS-STEEL CONTAINERS

These are the safest way to store food in your kitchen and for packing children's lunches. The next time you reach for more plastic containers at the store, think again and make the switch to glass or stainless steel. If you are worried about sending glass to school, wait until they are a bit older, or stick to stainless steel. I send glass containers to school regularly and so far have had no issues!

PARCHMENT PAPER

I go through a lot of parchment paper in my kitchen and suggest using it for several recipes in this book. There is an element of waste, I agree, but it's so much easier than scraping cooked-on food off a baking tray and ensures that your cookies, bars, and other baking come out of the pan looking beautiful (and makes cleanup so much easier). It can also be used as an alternative to plastic wrap to cover leftovers and wrap up snacks like bars and fruit leather.

SLOW COOKER

Not everyone has one or uses them often, so I decided not to include any slow cooker–specific recipes in this book. But they can be incredibly useful for busy families. Of course, if you love your slow cooker, you can use it to make several recipes in the book such as Best Ever Turkey Chili Soup (page 172) or Simple Lentil and Coconut Soup (page 155).

METAL COOKIE CUTTERS

For all those fun-shaped cookies or shaped fried eggs or pancakes.

THIN METAL SPATULA FOR FLIPPING

I don't know where I'd be without this little tool! Use it to transfer delicate cookies to cooking racks and to flip pancakes.

POPSICLE MOLDS

MICROWAVES AND PLASTIC

Microwaves, plastic wrap, and plastic freezer bags aren't my favorites because I'm not convinced they're definitely safe and I'm trying hard to reduce the plastic we use in our family. That said, they are convenient and certainly useful for many recipes in this book. I suggest using alternatives when possible, but don't beat yourself up about using them when you need to.

Meal Planning: Making the Best Use of Your Time in the Kitchen

Maybe you're one of those parents who can wing it in the kitchen, and you don't mind figuring out meals day by day, throwing whatever you happen to find in the refrigerator into the oven or into lunch bags and keeping everyone happy and healthy in the process. To be honest, I go through phases of flying by the seat of my pants when it comes to meals, and there are periods in my life when this method works fine for me. That said, during extremely busy times, meal planning can go a long way in making my life feel less chaotic and helping me feel confident that my family's nutritional needs are being met. If you're at a point where some order in the kitchen could help you feel calmer and more in control, you're trying to keep careful track of your budget, or you're simply someone who thrives on structure and the idea of meal planning brings you a sense of peace and happiness, this section is for you!

So what is meal planning? Essentially, it's a process of mapping out what your family will eat, usually over the course of a week. You can meal plan just for dinners, or for other meals also. The idea is that having an organized plan will help you know what to buy at the supermarket and in the process will help you keep your grocery bill down, reduce your food waste, and make getting meals on the table and lunches out the door just that little bit easier.

You can set out your meal plans in whichever way suits your organizational style. There are plenty of meal planning apps out there you can download, or you could plan right into your phone calendar or make notes on your phone. If you prefer, you can keep it old school and write your meal plan on a wall calendar or in a notebook. Choose whatever works best for you. (See my Sample Weekly Meal Planner on page 45.)

Here is a list of tips to get you started.

Start by looking through your freezer, especially if you've been batch cooking and saving extra portions in the freezer. It's so easy to forget what is in the freezer, but using up what is in there is key to keeping family food costs down, reducing food waste, and meal planning efficiently.

Then look in your refrigerator or pantry. Remember those red lentils you bought 6 months ago? What about that beautiful bunch of rainbow chard in the vegetable drawer? Plan to use up ingredients that might otherwise sit there forever or go to waste.

Next, think about what the family will eat for dinner each night. Leftovers from dinners are very useful for lunches, so it makes sense to think about potential leftovers while you think about the actual dinners.

Some families find it easiest to have a theme one night or several nights per week: Meatless Mondays or Taco Tuesdays, for example. This doesn't mean you have to eat the exact same type of meatless dish or taco every week, but having a theme helps focus your thinking on what to make, and themed nights can be a fun family tradition.

Ask your family what they would like to eat during the week. Taking their requests into account is sure to increase the chances that they'll be happy to eat what is on their plates and in their lunchboxes.

If you have a baby, think about which family meals could work well for the baby as well, adjusting ingredients and how they are served to baby as necessary. Or, think about how baby finger foods could work well as a component of a family meal. For example, the whole family will enjoy mini meatloaves (page 110), and these could be the main component of a family meal. The soup (pages 152–156) and chili (page 172) recipes in the lunch and dinner chapters of this book also puree up beautifully as baby food. Omit the salt if you prefer to feed your baby salt-free food.

Think about batch cooking and freezing portions. By cooking enough for two or three meals, you are making meal planning in the upcoming weeks much easier. Several recipes in this book can be frozen. Just look for the ❄ symbol and check the method for storage instructions.

Keep your refrigerator and pantry stocked with foods your family regularly eats, and add special ingredients to your shopping list each week that will be needed to make your meal plan a reality (see pages 29–35 for tips on stocking your kitchen with healthy foods).

Decide which day of the week works best for you to start meal planning. I prefer to plan Saturday through Friday, because this way I really think about how the meals I make on the weekend can work for what I'd like to serve during the week. You might prefer to plan Monday through Sunday. You know your and your family's schedule. Work around it and plan whichever way works best for you.

Once you've planned out your meals, prep any food you can ahead of time. Prepping ahead of time can seem onerous and like not much of a shortcut, because it still takes time and as busy parents that is something we are all short of, but if you do something pleasurable while you prep, it can make all the difference. While you peel and chop, or bake muffins, try enjoying a glass of wine and some music, watching a few episodes of your favorite show on a tablet set up on the kitchen counter, catching up with a friend on speaker phone, or working together with your other half, chatting about how your week has gone. Get your kids involved as early as you can. They can pack chopped-up veggies in containers, for example. By doing something you enjoy simultaneously, food prep will instantly seem like less of a chore. Once I've done my prepping, I store the food in labeled containers in the refrigerator or freezer to use during the coming week.

Breakfast

Mornings are chaotic in many homes, whether you're trying to get everyone (including yourself) out the door or you're trying to get your day started with some semblance of order (often after a broken night's sleep). And small children are often up at the crack of dawn full of energy, eagerly asking for breakfast while dazed parents fumble for their morning coffee to summon up some energy to get them through the day. Whatever your circumstances, it's so easy to get into the habit of offering basic cereal and toast day in and day out. But with only a small amount of extra effort and a little planning, breakfasts can offer so much more. You can make the mornings a bit easier by making up some options ahead of time. Have fruit and veg cut up and ready to make nutritious smoothies (pages 124–130) (you could do that as part of your weekly meal planning). Muffins and pancakes freeze beautifully, so cook up a big batch when you have time and keep them in the freezer. Try the Roasted Sweet Potato and Blueberry Muffins (page 143) or the Bacon and Apple–Loaded Spelt Pancakes (page 145). For breakfasts on the run, the Peanut Butter Protein Bars are a great choice (page 148) as is the Overnight Strawberry Cocoa Oatmeal (page 141) stored in individual lidded mason jars—kids can just grab these themselves out of the refrigerator and get straight to eating with little involvement from you. Weekend breakfasts are a wonderful time for families to sit down together and connect over a meal. Try the Griddled Oatcakes with Roasted Stone Fruit and Greek Yogurt (page 147), and for an extra-special brunch dessert, the Lemon Coconut Macaroon Nests (page 218) are ideal even for people with strict dietary requirements.

Lunch

At lunchtime, children can be really receptive to food, because they've worked up an appetite from all their morning activities but are typically less tired than they are at that witching hour we like to call dinnertime. So although it's easy to consider lunch a bit of a throwaway meal, a quick bite to get them through the period between breakfast and dinner, it's actually a real opportunity to get some nutritious food in little ones' bellies.

Whether you're eating with your kids at home up on stools by the kitchen counter, or they're eating the packed lunch you've sent with them to day care or school, you'll find the recipes on pages 152–166 have lots of ideas to help you make every lunchtime bite count. You'll notice that some of them are for large batches, which you can cook ahead, freeze, and warm up when you're ready to use them, or you can take them out of the freezer the night before to save time in the morning.

Soups are a wonderful way to include nutritious ingredients in your family's diet, and are an excellent choice for sending to school in a thermos. There's something so satisfying about knowing your kids are happily eating such a warming, nutrient-rich meal while they're out of your sight. Consider cooking up a big batch of soup on a weekend to use for lunches, or even after-school snacks.

And get creative. Even if your kids are older, look at chapter 2, "Finger Foods" (pages 106–121) for lunch options. Some of the breakfast and dinner recipes (pages 134–148 and pages 172–191) can be adapted for lunch, so make the most of all the chapters for extra lunch inspiration. (And don't forget the snack recipes on pages 194–212!)

Dinner

Whether or not you work outside the home, meal planning will be a huge help to you when it comes to preparing healthy, satisfying dinners. The recipes in this book have been created so that parents will love the ingredients and kids will love the taste, and many of these recipes are intended to be enjoyed by the entire family, particularly in the dinner chapter. But if we're honest, we all know that life inevitably gets in the way, and for all sorts of reasons, we can't always eat the same thing at the same time, particularly when our children are very little. As a mom of a 4-year-old and a 6-year-old, I know this firsthand, and while I've certainly had my moments of mom guilt, I've come to terms with the reality of raising a busy family of individuals who occasionally have different needs relating to food. We make it a goal to eat one meal together as many days as we can. It doesn't always have to be dinner— a family breakfast is just as good. Sometimes we eat dinner together, but on other days I'll quickly pull something together that works just for my little ones.

When I'm meal planning, I'll take into account the days I know I'll be making something just for the kids. On those days I'll go for recipes like Go Coconuts for Chia and Almond Chicken Strips (page 180) or a quick Cam's Pesto and Pea Omelet (page 115), which I can whip up in seconds. For when we are able to eat dinner together, I choose whole family recipes like Creamy Chickpea and Spinach Curry (page 189) or One-Pan Roast Chicken and Root Vegetables (page 173), which can be repurposed for meals during the week if there are leftovers.

And as I've mentioned elsewhere, don't be confined by the chapter titles when you're looking for dinner recipes. Many of the recipes throughout the entire book, particularly in chapter 2, "Finger Foods," and chapter 5, "Easy Lunches," are also appropriate for family dinners. The Roasted Sweet Potato Fries (page 106) and Mini Roasted Cauliflower Florets (page 106), suggested as finger foods for little ones, make excellent side dishes for everyone. Not Your Mama's Meatloaf (page 110) is not only perfect for little hands, but also makes an excellent family main course. Even Turkey Pesto Meatballs on Sticks (page 235) from the "Let's Celebrate" chapter can be adapted to be served as a dinner entree. Think outside the chapter titles and make the recipes work for your needs.

Putting It All Together

I've made a sample meal plan to get your creative juices flowing. Note, though, that my kids are no longer babies or toddlers, so this meal plan is suitable for slightly older little ones. The lunches are all suitable for packing up to take to day care or school (or the office!). If you're planning to make up special purees or finger foods for your baby or toddler, and you would like to incorporate this into your plan, you can record what you will be making in the special notes section. Remember, you may be able to make some of the finger food recipes so that they work for the entire family!

I mentioned earlier that it's a good idea to take the time to cut up veggies and keep them in the refrigerator for snacking. These will come into their own on evenings when you fly through the door, hungry and in a rush. You and the kids can snack on the veggies while you cook—making dinnertime meltdowns less likely for the adults and kids alike.

Sample Weekly Meal Planner

SATURDAY	SUNDAY	MONDAY	TUESDAY	WEDNESDAY	THURSDAY	FRIDAY
BREAKFAST	**BREAKFAST**	**BREAKFAST**	**BREAKFAST**	**BREAKFAST**	**BREAKFAST**	**BREAKFAST**
Poppy's Chocolate Green Smoothie (page 130)— will keep kids satisfied while they wait for brunch! (Below.)	Fried eggs on toast (Egg Person Toast, page 139, for the kids)	Overnight Strawberry Cocoa Oatmeal (page 141; prepare overnight oatmeal with the kids)	Powered-Up Cereal Bowl (page 146)	Apple, Carrot, and Almond Butter Wrap (page 134) with Rasp-Peary Dream smoothie (page 128)	Mini Muffin Frittatas (page 136)	Egg Person Toast (page 139) with Berry Beety smoothie (page 130)
BRUNCH/ LUNCH	**LUNCH**	**LUNCH**	**LUNCH**	**LUNCH**	**LUNCH**	**LUNCH**
Griddled Oatcakes with Roasted Stone Fruit and Greek Yogurt (page 147)	Roasted Tomato and Carrot Soup (page 156), Little Spelt Buns (page 242)	Chicken salad with Little Spelt Buns (page 242), raw veggies and hummus	Leftover pasta or meatloaf, raw veggies and hummus	Chickpea Salad Lettuce Wraps (page 164), Roasted Sweet Potato and Blueberry Muffins (in freezer) (page 143)	Leftover pizza, cut-up fruit	Leftover Roasted Tomato and Carrot Soup (page 156) from the freezer, Popeye's Banana Bread (page 196)
DINNER	**DINNER**	**DINNER**	**DINNER**	**DINNER**	**DINNER**	**DINNER**
One-Pan Roast Chicken and Root Vegetables (page 173) and salad	Not Your Mama's Meatloaf (page 110), Roasted Sweet Potato Fries (page 106), veggies and dip	Meatless Monday Pasta with Hemp Hearts (page 185)	Taco Tuesday: Veggie-Loaded Beef Soft Tacos (page 176)	Family-Size Gluten-Free Pizza with leftover taco meat topping (page 188)	Creamy Chickpea and Spinach Curry (page 189), wild rice	Pork Tenderloin with Buttery Apricot Sauce (page 177) and Buttery Cauliflower Mash (page 190), Lemon Coconut Macaroon Nests (page 218)
SPECIAL NOTES	**SPECIAL NOTES**	**SPECIAL NOTES**	**SPECIAL NOTES**	**SPECIAL NOTES**	**SPECIAL NOTES**	**SPECIAL NOTES**
Make chicken stock from carcass Shred and refrigerate extra chicken Make Popeye's Banana Bread (page 196) with kids and freeze in slices for lunches	Freeze extra buns for sliders next week Cut up extra veggies for lunches this week and make hummus (page 166) Bake Roasted Sweet Potato and Blueberry Muffins (page 143) and freeze	Prep veggies for taco meat	Late dinner meeting; just feed kids		Make double batch of curry and freeze half for next week	Friends coming for dinner

Growing Adventurous Eaters

We can cook the most delicious, appealing food in the world, but the fact is we can't make our kids eat it unless they want to—and small children are notoriously wary when it comes to unfamiliar food. Most parents know what it's like to cook a delicious meal, with flavors we know our children would love if only they would give them a chance, only to run up against a flat-out refusal to even try it. This can be incredibly frustrating and deflating, making us feel like it's not even worth bothering.

My children are not perfect eaters by any means (like most kids, they can be wary of trying new foods and get stuck in their thinking that they don't like certain foods), nor am I a picky-eating expert, but certain common-sense strategies have really made a big difference in how my children approach food. Here are some tips and tricks that I've seen work, not only for my children but for other kids too:

1. I'm a big fan of adding vegetables to dishes that wouldn't usually have them to increase my children's nutritional intake, but I don't think it's a good idea to completely hide the fact that the vegetables are there. I know that hiding vegetables in favorite foods has been a popular practice over the last several years, but I really believe it's far better to let your kids *know* that there's spinach in that Popeye's Banana Bread (page 196) or Apple Cinnamon Green Smoothie (page 129) they love so much. Why? Because if they're aware there's spinach in something they really like, it makes it more likely that they'll accept spinach in other forms; they'll come to think of it as a familiar, accepted food that they like. So put vegetables in familiar foods they are likely to eat by all means, but talk those vegetables up, rather than keeping quiet about them.

2. Even though it can feel wasteful, keep giving kids foods they say they don't like, or foods they never want to try. One day

they just might surprise you by tucking in with enthusiasm, but you'll miss this opportunity to expand their tastes if you stick to only giving them foods you know they'll eat. Babies might spit food out and scrunch up their little faces when they try new foods, but don't assume this means they don't like a food and stop giving it to them. It can take many repeated exposures to a food to become accustomed to the taste, so as fruitless as it may seem at times, keep persevering with foods that your baby or child doesn't seem to love. I experienced this pattern repeatedly with my children when they were babies and also more recently in their preschool years. For example, until Cam was three he refused to eat anything that looked remotely like salad even though his sister likes it, and salad is something we eat regularly. But then, quite suddenly, at Christmas dinner, he was drawn in by the pomegranate arils in his bowl of salad, and he unexpectedly ate the entire bowl, greens and all, while going on about how salad is "his favorite." Since then he's been more open to salad, even without the pomegranate on top, and the experience continues to be a good lesson to me to keep putting those vegetables on his plate.

3. Try to include at least a couple of ingredients or prepared foods your kids like, alongside or mixed with unfamiliar or disliked foods you are serving. I find that favorite sauces and dips can work wonders when it comes to trying something new. If your children like tamari on white rice, try putting it on foods they are not as familiar with, like wild rice or quinoa. If your child has a favorite dip, serve it with a new food to increase the likelihood that they will give it a try. Once the new food becomes accepted with said favorite dip, you can gradually serve that food in different ways without the dip as a prop.

4. Cook with your kids. They'll cherish the special time spent with you, will be empowered by being a part of the cooking process, and will be more likely to eat foods they've helped to make. Even very little ones can help pour and stir, and if you teach children about safety and supervise them carefully, you'll be surprised by how early they can learn to peel and chop.

Although baking is very well suited to cooking with children, also cook things together that aren't necessarily considered a treat. Kids are far more likely to try a food if they have had a hand in preparing it, yet we often fall back on making only sweet treats with our kids and miss the opportunity to get them excited about cooking, then eating, more challenging, unfamiliar, or disliked ingredients.

5. Even if just in a very small way, in a window box or plant pot, involve kids in growing their own vegetables and herbs. The excitement of planting a seed and watching it sprout, then the buildup of excitement as a carrot or tomato grows big enough to harvest, is incredibly engaging for children. They will almost certainly be open to trying a bite of what they've grown and will probably come to love many of the vegetables they've helped to nurture.

6. Regularly visit local farms or farmers' markets, making the excursion a fun and exciting family event, showing your children your enthusiasm for picking up some fresh local produce. Not only will this make them excited to try your purchases on the day, it will set them up to appreciate fresh local produce for life, which is a true gift to their health and well-being.

7. When you can (and it doesn't have to be every night if it doesn't work for your family's schedules), eat meals with your children. I find that my kids tend to eat much more when they are sitting with us, chatting about their day and what has been going on in their lives, than when they are sitting at a counter eating on their own while I watch over them. On nights when I've cooked a special dinner just for them (say, for example, on a night my husband and I are planning a dinner out with friends), it helps if I sit down with them at the kitchen counter with a plate of raw veggies for myself, so that it feels like we are still all eating together rather than having me standing there serving them. And your family meal together doesn't have to be dinner. Maybe breakfast is a better time for all to get together. Do what works for you.

8. When you have the energy, make family dinners that little bit extra-special by putting out the nice dishes, lighting candles, and acting like the whole experience is a bit fancy. My kids love when we do this. It doesn't take much time, and strange as it is, there's something about candles lit on the table that makes them more open to new foods!

9. Serve food family-style and have the children serve themselves from larger plates in the center of the table. There's something about dishing the food onto their plates themselves that gives them that sense of control that is so important to little ones.

10. We've all heard this before, but I think it's still worth mentioning. If your children decide they don't like their dinner, whatever you do, stay strong and don't cook them something else instead. It's far better to just clear it away without making a big deal and have them wait until the next meal or snack time. They will survive and they will learn that you aren't a personal short-order cook. The only time I make an exception to this rule is if my kids are under the weather. Then I'll make them a smoothie or something really nourishing that I know they'll want to eat. It's important to be adaptable and not stick too hard to self-imposed rules when circumstances warrant it.

11. Involve your kids in choosing groceries and in meal planning. When they feel like they have some say about the food that goes into their lunches and is on the dinner table, it's more likely that they'll be happy to eat it. (See pages 39–45 for more tips on meal planning.) When they are in the grocery store with you, give them the job of finding certain healthy ingredients, then discuss how they would like to eat them.

12. Avoid children's menus if you can, and just share with your kids off the adult menu. Children's menus tend to be full of unhealthy, unadventurous options, and accustom kids to only eating pizza and chicken nuggets when they're at a restaurant. I admit that I didn't think to do this when my kids were very little, but boy, do I wish I could go back in time and give children's menus a miss altogether.

Cooking with Kids: Strategies for Success

♥ Read over the recipe and set out all the ingredients *before* you invite the kids into the kitchen to get cooking. Being organized ahead of time is key to everything going smoothly. For very small children, have things pre-measured. Older children can get involved in the measuring and improve their math skills in the process!

♥ If you are cooking with two children and you would like them to both be involved in all the steps of the recipe, you can split the ingredients in half, so that they get the chance to each make a half batch, bringing the full recipe together at the end if necessary. For activities like making cookies, give each child a piece of dough to roll out, their own set of cookie cutters, and their own set of icing and decorations. Avoiding arguments is worth the extra setup.

♥ When making sweet treats, kids will understandably want to taste the sweet ingredients, so I find it helps to agree ahead of time on how much they can have. For example, if we're making chocolate chip cookies, I will give them each a dish with a number of chocolate chips we've agreed upon that they can eat while we're baking. This stops them pestering me and makes the whole experience more enjoyable for all of us.

♥ Choose a recipe that doesn't require time at the stove. If you're at the stove for much of the recipe, it's hard to keep an eye on what the kids are up to and they might get bored waiting for you. As a general rule, stovetop cooking isn't safe for young children to help with, so choose a recipe where they can be safely and actively involved for most of the steps.

♥ Take the time to teach your children how to use kitchen equipment safely, then let them go for it, keeping a watchful eye, of course. It's up to you to decide when your child can use a vegetable peeler or a sharp knife because you know them best, but keep in mind that children can do so much more than we often realize. Trusting them to do grown-up tasks in the kitchen can be very empowering for them.

♥ Don't let the inevitable mess get under your skin, and try not to get upset if there are sudden spills. Cooking with kids is messier than cooking alone. This is a fact, and it is best to just accept it and go with the flow. It will take only a few extra minutes to clean up anyway. Get them to help you mop up small messes. Younger kids will often see this as fun rather than a chore. Remember, the whole experience of cooking together is meant to be fun, and it won't be if you get on edge because of the mess.

Starting Your Baby on Solids: What You Need to Know

So you've experienced 9 months of pregnancy, the delivery of your baby, and those blurry first few months of parenthood. Every step of the way will have had its joys and challenges as you began to adjust to the roller coaster that is parenthood. By now your baby will be relatively established with breast-feeding, bottle-feeding, or a combination of both, and fingers crossed you'll all be getting at least a bit more sleep!

But nothing stays the same for long in these first few years, and before you know it, it's time to start thinking about offering your baby solids. As with all areas of parenthood, there is no shortage of advice out there on how to navigate this new world. Family and friends will all have stories about what worked for them and opinions on the right way to do things, and with social media surrounding us these days, you will undoubtedly be feeling bombarded from all sides with an overwhelming amount of information on how you should be feeding your baby.

Now let me just say that if there truly was one right way of doing things, everyone would be doing it. Don't stress yourself out too much by thinking that if you don't get this stage exactly "right" you are going to do some sort of harm to your baby. After all, it's just food, and babies all over the world have been starting their food journeys in different ways for generation after generation. Trust that as long as you use common sense by offering your baby a variety of healthy foods, watching carefully for reactions, and considering safety as you are doing so, all will be well.

There are official recommendations out there, which are a good place to start. But keep in mind, official recommendations change every few years, and there are always new studies being published that provide new information, sometimes quite different from what is in the current recommendations. The fact is that the official recommendations that are in place right now will undoubtedly look very different from recommendations 10 years from now. My best advice is to use the official recommendations as a first point of reference but consider other advice from reputable sources to help you arrive at a philosophy and method that feels right for your family. When I was feeding solids to my babies, I stuck to a few trusted sources that aligned with my innate philosophies rather than reading every baby feeding book or blog that was available to me. Too much information can be overwhelming, and I think that it is important as parents to protect ourselves from exposure to too many sources of information.

You can find the official infant feeding recommendations for Canada and the US here:

- Health Canada (Infant Nutrition 6–24 months): www.hc-sc.gc.ca (search: infant feeding)
- The American Academy of Pediatrics: www.aap.org (search: infant feeding)

There are so many online sources out there that claim to provide expert advice on feeding babies. Ultimately, though, most of these sites do not provide references for where they are getting this information. For well-researched advice on starting solids, baby food recipes, and helpful tips, I always turned to this site when I was starting solids with my little ones. A trusted mom friend told me about it, and it turned out to be a great tip:

- www.wholesomebabyfood.momtastic.com

I respect this website because it backs up its recommendations with links to current studies rather than just sticking to official recommendations or giving advice that could have been pulled out of the air, which is far too common in online sources. I particularly like its section on food allergies. It is very detailed and up to date and is contributed to by experts in the allergy and immunology field. I highly recommend you take a look, particularly if you have allergies in your family.

When Should You Start?

So how do you know if your baby is ready to start solids? Well, generally speaking, babies will be ready to start solids around 6 months, but sometimes as early as 4 months. The best thing you can do is not get too hung up on starting at 6 months exactly, but instead look for signs that your baby is interested in and physically ready to start eating solid foods. It's important to follow your baby's lead, rather than sticking to a fixed starting time that you have decided on. Here are the signs to look for:

1. Your baby will be able to hold her head in a steady upright position. If her head is still bobbing around and her neck doesn't yet seem strong enough to hold it up, wait a bit longer before you begin solids.

2. Your baby is willing to take food in her mouth and doesn't push it back out again with her tongue. This is actually a reflex, and babies begin to lose it around the time that they're ready to begin eating solids.

3. Your baby can sit well upright when supported. This doesn't mean your baby has to sit up fully by herself, but with some propping in her high chair she should be able to sit up pretty straight without flopping around. Being able to do this will make it easier and safer for her to swallow.

4. Your baby is starting to make chewing-like motions with her mouth, moving food from front to back then swallowing. This may take some time to get a hang of, but look for the beginning stages of this movement when you begin solids.

5. Your baby seems hungry, as if breast-feeding or formula-feeding just isn't quite enough anymore.

6. Your baby is showing signs that she's curious about what you are eating. She may just look at you expectantly as you're eating or may even reach out to try to grab some for herself.

Now, you may feel absolutely certain that you want to wait until 6 months before feeding your baby solid food. You may have read that there is no benefit to starting before 6 months or that starting before 6 months may actually have a negative effect on your baby. If your baby is doing well on breast milk or formula, then by all means, wait until 6 months if you can.

However, while I think striving to reach this 6-month point is a worthy goal, I encourage you to be flexible in your thinking and to adapt your plan if it seems your baby might benefit from solid food a bit before the 6-month mark. Let me give you an example from my own experience. With my daughter, Poppy, I had quite a hard time breast-feeding. I just never seemed to have enough milk, and even after feeding on both sides until nothing was left in me, she would often cry and hit my chest with her little fists. It was heartbreaking and very stressful to feel like I didn't have enough milk for my baby, so I decided to supplement with formula. My plan was to give Poppy a couple of ounces of formula as a top-up whenever she still seemed hungry after a full breast-feed. Of course, Poppy had other plans, and never really took to the bottle or the formula, so while I did manage to get a few more calories into her, it was a struggle and my plan wasn't exactly a success. For the first 5 months of Poppy's life she seemed always just a bit unhappy, and was very fussy, especially during the day. Just after 5 months, knowing that I didn't seem to have enough milk and that supplementing with formula wasn't working, I decided to start her on solids. It was earlier than I wanted to start, but I had one unhappy little girl on my hands and my instincts told me that it was because she simply wasn't getting enough milk to satisfy her. She had the readiness signs I mentioned above, so it seemed for many reasons that it was the right thing to do.

Well, let me tell you, starting solids early was the best thing I could have done for her—and for me! As soon as she started eating solid food, she was like a completely different baby; she was relaxed and content and her fussiness disappeared. And I was different too. Suddenly the stress of not being able to provide enough food for her was gone, and I was able to enjoy her and relax more into my new role as a mom. I went from being on edge and feeling guilty and worried all the time to feeling like I had a handle on things and that it all was going to be OK. Taking everything into account, for Poppy and for me, starting solids at 5 months and 1 week was definitely the right move.

What Should You Start With?

So now that you've established that it's time to start solids, what on earth do you feed your baby and how exactly do you go about it? This is where things can get a bit controversial, so hold on tight and try not to panic! While there are many methods out there, currently there are basically two prominent schools of thought on feeding babies:

1. Start with purees or mashed foods, then move on to more textured foods or finger foods when your baby seems ready. With this method, you may offer your baby pureed or mashed foods that you buy or make especially for her, or they may be pureed or mashed table foods that the whole family is eating. Gradually you will make the foods more textured and will also offer soft finger foods that your baby can feed herself.

2. Start with hand-held or finger foods, rather than purees, which your baby feeds to herself. Most likely these will be table foods that everyone else is eating, in easy-to-hold shapes. This method is called Baby-led Weaning (BLW), first introduced by Gill Rapley. You can find plenty of information about it online. If you'd like to learn more, this website is a good place to start: www.rapleyweaning.com.

Now I've got to put my hands up in the air and say that I obviously have a serious conflict of interest here. I do have a baby food company that makes purees after all, so I'm not going to get into a huge discussion about the right course to take because nobody would believe I was being objective anyway! I will make a brief comment, not for the sake of my puree business (really!) but for the safety of babies. Recently, a well-respected pediatrician has expressed concern about the level of research behind the BLW practice, and in particular about the safety and nutritional value of small babies sucking on large pieces of food, which is a suggested feeding method in BLW. If you are using BLW, this is a topic you may want to look into further. (See Tanya Altmann, MD, *What to Feed Your Baby*, HarperCollins, 2016.)

What I will say, as a mom who has gone through this stage with my two little ones and who has watched many friends as they've done the same, is similar to the advice I gave on when to start feeding solids. Try not to get too hung up on which method you use. After all, this is really about what works best for your baby, not your personal philosophy or the advice you're being given by friends, family, and last but certainly not least, the Internet. You might think that you want to start with purees, so you stock your freezer with several batches of delicious, lovingly made organic purees, but then you find that your baby really isn't interested in eating purees and just doesn't seem to like being fed with a spoon. Or, you may be absolutely sure that Baby-led Weaning is the way to go, but then find that your baby doesn't take to it and the method isn't working for you.

Personally, I feel that a combination of the two methods is the best way to go. I don't believe that being very strict about a particular method or theory is the way forward in any situation. I believe we need to be adaptable. Let's face it, babies just haven't been reading the same information as us, and sometimes they just don't jibe with the feeding program we've decided we want for them. For example, with my little guy, Cam, I decided I wanted to introduce more textured food and finger foods earlier than I had for Poppy. So, I tried, I really did, but he had this incredible gag reflex. A good thing, because gagging is actually a helpful response when it comes to choking, but a bad thing because he'd gag so much and so hard that he'd vomit—all the time, and not just a little bit! He would bring up what he'd just tried to eat plus everything in his stomach. I persisted for a while but then became very concerned that he wasn't really getting anything from the food. It quite literally was all ending up on the floor together with the breast milk I was feeding him, and the experience wasn't pleasant for him or for me. I could have backtracked and waited until a little later to introduce solids, but he wouldn't take a bottle (I tried really hard on that too, but he had other plans). I had to go back to work,

so I needed to ensure that he had some sustenance while I was away from him. So thinly pureed food it was until he was about 9 months old, when suddenly textured food and finger foods weren't a problem for him anymore. Here he is at 10 months quite happily eating a quinoa bake similar to the one on page 109.

Now your story will be completely different from mine, but one thing I can tell you for sure is that it won't go exactly as you imagined, so stay open-minded, be flexible, and go with the flow. If you decide that starting with purees is the way you want to do things and it seems to work for your baby, then great! Feel good about it. And if you decide to go straight to hand-held food and it seems to be working for your baby—wonderful! If you decide to combine methods because that is what you need to do for your situation, you should feel really good that you've found a way that works for your baby and for you. The important thing here is to realize that we all do things in different ways and as long as our babies are safe, thriving, and getting a variety of nutritious foods safely starting at around 6 months, we should be patting ourselves and each other on the back and saying "well done." This book lists recipes for purees and mashes before recipes for finger foods, but don't read too much into that order! Just know that whichever foods you decide to offer, you should find some delicious and nutritious recipes that will suit your situation.

What about Allergies?

Food allergies or food intolerances are reactions to a food. They may be merely uncomfortable, but they can also be dangerous, even life threatening, and should be taken very seriously when you're starting your baby on solids. Whether you decide to start solids with purees or mashes, with finger foods, or with a combination of the two, to ensure your baby's safety it is important to follow these two general rules:

1. Introduce one new food at a time to gauge whether or not your baby is accepting the food well and not developing any sort of reaction as a result of eating it.

2. Wait a few days between introducing each new food.

If you introduce several new foods at a time and your baby has a reaction, you won't know what caused it, and backtracking to figure it out will be much more complicated. If you introduce new foods one day after the next, you may never know what is really causing the symptoms because they might not have developed straight after eating a food, but may in fact have taken a couple of days to become apparent. Some doctors (and maybe your mother) may say that waiting 3 or 4 days is a bit excessive, but I know many families who deal with allergies, and figuring out what is causing a reaction can be very difficult and stressful. By introducing one food at a time and waiting for a few days in between each food, at least you will have every chance of finding the food culprit and this decreases the chance of another reaction, which can be incredibly traumatizing for you as a parent and, of course, uncomfortable or dangerous for your baby. Particularly if you have food allergies in your family, you may want to slow the process right down and wait until you are fairly certain that there has been no reaction to a new food.

If you are mostly using commercial baby food, like Love Child Organics, you will notice that there are not many single-food flavors available. This is because it would simply be impossible for food companies to offer single-ingredient purees for every ingredient and, to be honest, many ingredients just aren't all that palatable as a puree all on their own.

The best way to deal with this if you would like to feed your baby store-bought food is to try introducing single ingredients using home-made food first. Once you know they can eat several different fruits and vegetables, you can move on to safely offering commercial purees that contain a variety of ingredients combined together.

Keep in mind, though, that offering foods one at a time doesn't mean that you must offer one food on its own, then have your baby spend 4 days eating only that food then offer another different food all on its own and have 4 days of eating only that food. If you did that, this stage could go on forever and your baby would never get to try some of the yummy puree combinations or delicious table foods that contain multiple ingredients. The easiest way forward is to try something like this: On the first day of eating solid foods, offer your baby a single food, let's say avocado. Your baby can eat that and breast milk or formula for a few days. Once you feel confident there has been no reaction to avocado, you can offer banana. You could offer banana all on its own, or you could mash it with the avocado. They taste great together, and because you know the avocado is safe for your baby because she hasn't had any negative reactions, combining them isn't an issue. A few days later you could add kale, and if you want, rather than serving kale all on its own, you could puree it with banana, avocado, or both since you now know, because your baby didn't have any reactions, that both avocados and bananas are on your baby's safe list. So you just keep adding in new foods, on their own or together with the foods you know are safe, until your baby has a large repertoire of foods you know she can eat.

Food Reactions

So what does a reaction to a food look like and what causes it? When I say "reaction," I mean that your baby could experience one or more of the following as a result of eating a specific food:

Sudden diarrhea or vomiting	Difficulties breathing or respiratory troubles after or during a meal
Skin rashes that come on suddenly	Swelling, particularly of the face, lips, and tongue
Runny nose	Closure or tightening of the throat (obviously this is going to be hard for you to see, but troubled breathing and a change in face or lip color can be signs of this)
Hives	
Irritability or gassiness after eating a new food	

These reactions may suggest a **true allergy** in which there is a response of the immune system that affects numerous organs in the body and can be severe or life threatening, or an **intolerance**, which according to Allergy Canada is generally less serious or severe and often limited to digestive problems. I have to be honest with you: I really think that intolerances should be taken very seriously. I know from my own experience that they can have a serious impact, but I'll save that story for another book. Your baby may outgrow her allergies or intolerances, or it may be something she has to deal with for her entire life.

In terms of the order in which to introduce foods, the current recommendations are that all foods, with the exception of some specific foods that are unsafe for babies for reasons other than allergenic potential (see "Which Foods Should You Offer First and in What Order?" for more on this), can be introduced at approximately 6 months, and that you shouldn't delay introducing foods over worries that introducing them at a young age could cause allergies. In fact, some research suggests that you might be better off introducing allergenic foods early as it may actually help babies to not develop an allergy to the food. (Look for the LEAP study, 2015, online.) If you have food allergies in your family, you will want to discuss this in detail with your family doctor and decide on the best plan of action, and for foods like peanuts, shellfish, and strawberries, which can cause quite intense allergic reactions, you may want to proceed with particular caution. I also suggest you take a look at wholesomebabyfood.momtastic.com and click on Allergies. It's an incredible source of information on all things allergy, including a list of foods ordered by likelihood of allergic reaction. Another of my favorite resources for children's allergies and intolerances is a book I mentioned earlier, *The Dirt Cure* by Dr. Maya Shetreat-Klein (see page 27).

Which Foods Should You Offer First and in What Order?

As noted in the allergy section, almost all foods are safe for your baby as starting foods, so it really is up to you which foods you offer first. Simple fruits and vegetables are often the easiest to prepare and most easily accepted by your baby, so I would suggest them as the best starting point. It is recommended by Health Canada and the American Academy of Pediatrics (see page 54) that iron-rich foods like meat, legumes, and fortified cereal be offered as first foods because your baby's stores of iron deplete after 6 months. There is some debate over whether starting with these foods is absolutely necessary, and to be honest, at this point it is too hard to wade through the noise to figure out the truth of this matter. To simplify things, I recommend you offer nutrient-rich first foods that are easy to digest, have an appealing texture and taste, are easy for you to prepare, and have good nutritional value. For example, avocado, banana, sweet potato, squash, and carrots are all excellent choices. Once you've mastered those you can quite quickly add more iron-rich foods like meat or legumes, and also grains (like infant cereal) or dairy products like yogurt if you like.

And don't worry too much about introducing vegetables before fruit. Some people believe that if babies eat fruit first they'll get used to the sweet taste and turn their nose up at vegetables, but there is little evidence to support this. Breast milk and formula are sweeter than most fruit, and at this stage your baby will still be drinking them regularly, so they could in theory cause the same effect. The important thing is to offer your baby a wide variety of foods that have different types of tastes so that she doesn't get too accustomed to only one type of flavor. That said, you might offer a variety of foods and have your baby decide that for a solid month she'll only eat carrots. It happens, but it's nothing to worry about. Eventually she'll move on to other foods as long as you keep offering a variety of choices.

How Much Food and How Often?

When your baby first starts eating solids, start with one solid meal per day. If that goes well, aim for two to three meals per day, and keep feeding breast milk or formula regularly as you have thus far. Choose a time to offer food when your baby is hungry but not starving and make sure that for the first several months of eating, the meal is also supplemented with breast milk or formula. At this stage your baby's stomach is very small, so start with only a teaspoon to tablespoon or so of food at a time, and work your way up slowly as your baby becomes more accustomed to solid food. If your baby turns her head away, throws food off her tray, and doesn't seem interested, respect that this means she's done for this meal and try again later. It is up to you whether you offer breast milk or formula at the beginning or the end of the meal. You will just have to gauge what seems to work best for your baby. (Are you seeing a pattern here?)

From 6 months, you can also start offering your baby water from a cup. Try not to offer juice, even watered down. Your baby doesn't need it, and it is much better to get her accustomed to the taste of water as a thirst quencher than juice, which has a high natural sugar content and little nutritional value.

At the end of this chapter you will find handy charts to support you as you start offering your baby her first tastes, whether they be through purees and mashes or through finger foods. The charts suggest lists of single foods for you to try and give information about best ways to prepare the foods, what is great about them nutritionally, and, for purees and mashes, what foods they pair well with if you'd like to try combining foods to make your own recipes. They even have a section for you to write notes to help keep track of what you've tried and to make a note of any reactions.

Eventually, by the time your baby is around a year old, you will aim to feed her three meals per day (ideally at the table at the same time you are eating so that she grows accustomed to trying family foods and to the routine of eating as a family) and two snacks, as well as breast milk and formula as a supplement to her daily intake. If you would like more guidance or information on how long to offer breast milk or formula, please visit the Health Canada or American Academy of Pediatrics websites (see page 54).

Extra Tips for Making Baby Feeding Times Go Safely and Smoothly

♥ Make sure baby is sitting supported and upright to reduce the chance of choking, and supervise your baby at all times while she's eating.

♥ Make sure your baby is well rested when beginning solids. Offering a new eater a meal when she really needs a nap probably won't work out as well as you hope.

♥ If serving warm food, always double check the temperature, and be particularly careful to check for hot spots.

♥ Do not save food that has been partially eaten for another time. A puree will pick up bacteria from the spoon going into the baby's mouth and back into the puree; the same will happen to food that has been held and gnawed on. It's best to start with a new serving of food at each meal. (You won't be putting much on baby's plate at this stage, so any waste will be minimal.)

♥ Remember to introduce new foods one at a time, and keep watch for any reactions.

♥ If you are feeding your baby purees, and she's really interested in the spoon, give her her own spoon to hold and let her feed herself with it. It will be messy, but that's OK! (Just think of the photo opps . . .)

♥ If giving finger foods, don't give too much at one time, as it can be overwhelming for the baby. Once your baby has finished what you've put on her tray, you can add more if she still seems hungry.

♥ If you're using bowls and plates, invest in ones that stick to your baby's tray. They're such a sanity saver when it comes to reducing waste and mess!

♥ Bring your baby to the table. When you can, eat with your baby so that she quickly understands that mealtimes are a social affair. The tray will come off of most high chairs, which means you can pull baby all the way up to the table so she's sitting tucked in just like the rest of the family. If appropriate, give her tastes of table foods (making sure she's already tried the ingredients in the foods so that you know she isn't reactive to any ingredients), so that she gets used to eating what everyone else in the family is eating.

♥ Babies enjoy bold flavors, and getting used to "grown-up" tastes early makes transitioning to family food easy. So don't be afraid to add spices and herbs to your baby's food; just be sure to introduce them one at a time, as you would other foods.

♥ If you're worried about mess on the floor, put a mat underneath your baby's chair that you can simply pick up after a meal, brush off, and rinse.

♥ Be patient—and don't lose your sense of humor.

What Foods Shouldn't I Offer My Baby?

Most healthy, unprocessed foods are safe to offer your baby from 6 months onward, but there are a few exceptions. Note that this is a general guide and lays no claims to being an exhaustive list. Please speak to your health practitioner if you have questions about feeding particular foods to your baby (especially if you have allergies in your family) and take a look at the resources I've recommended so far in this section for extra support.

Honey should not be given to babies under 1 year old, due to the risk of infant botulism.

Hard nuts, whole or in pieces, are a choking hazard, as are whole pumpkin or sunflower seeds.

Avoid any round or oval-shaped food that could be a choking hazard (grapes and cherry tomatoes, for example—be sure to cut them lengthwise into quarters).

Hotdogs are a choking hazard. If you choose to feed them to your child, cut them lengthwise into quarters. Hotdogs are a very processed food, however, so are best not served to babies anyway.

Popcorn can be a choking hazard and is best not eaten by very young children.

Avoid nut butters or creamed cheeses on their own—they are sticky and could get lodged in a baby's throat. Spread them thinly on a cracker or toast or stir them into other mashed or pureed ingredients.

Cow's milk should not be offered as a drink to babies under approximately 1 year old. It does not contain the nutrients of breast milk or formula and may be difficult to digest at this stage. Yogurt and cheese are easier to digest and can be offered earlier if you like.

Processed foods that are high in salt, sugar, or preservatives or have artificial dyes should be avoided in the early years. Your baby's body is tiny and so these substances will negatively affect them more than they would a larger child or adult. Try to offer your baby only clean, unprocessed foods.

Making and Storing Baby Food

As special as it is to be lovingly preparing your baby's first bites, it can be time-consuming and the novelty can wear off pretty quickly! The best way to deal with this is to batch cook, which means making several servings at a time. Almost all the recipes in chapter 1, "Purees and Mashes," and chapter 2, "Finger Foods," have been developed to make a large batch that will keep your baby fed for several meals. (And the recipes come with storage information as well!)

To batch cook pureed baby food you will need some special equipment, most importantly a blender of some type (see page 36) and some small storage containers. I find that ice cube trays work wonderfully as storage containers for freezing baby food, but make sure you buy BPA-free trays. You can also purchase special baby food storage containers. There are several nice lidded glass or silicone containers on the market that you can easily order online.

Steps for freezing purees

1. Allow the batch to cool to just warm. Spoon it into ice cube trays or lidded containers. If you're using ice cube trays and you don't plan to transfer the food to another container on the same day, be sure to cover the top, ideally with parchment paper held on tight with an elastic band.

2. Once the puree is frozen, pop it out of the trays or small containers into a larger lidded container or freezer bag.

3. Label and date the batch so that you know what it is and when it was made. Generally speaking, purees will last approximately 3 months in the freezer without becoming freezer-burned, but this does depend somewhat on how well they are sealed. Vacuum-sealed food will last the longest.

4. To serve, allow the cubes of food to thaw in the refrigerator, or defrost them gently on the stovetop or in the microwave.

Steps for freezing finger foods

1. Depending on what you're making, you may freeze finger foods before or after they're cooked. The recipes in this book will suggest which method will work best.

2. To freeze, place the prepared finger foods on a baking tray lined with parchment paper. If you are planning to transfer the foods to a container within a few hours, you don't need to cover them.

3. Freeze until firm, usually a few hours, then transfer to a large lidded container or a freezer bag.

4. Label and date the batch so you know what it is and when it was made. As with purees, finger foods will last approximately 3 months in the freezer, but this is somewhat dependent on how well the food is sealed.

5. Thaw in the refrigerator if you have time, and then reheat gently if you want to serve it warm.

Favorite First Single Foods at a Glance

The charts on pages 68–81 are resources for when you first start feeding your baby solid foods. In the charts you will find:

💜 A list of nutritious single foods to offer your baby, arranged alphabetically by food group for easy reference

💜 Information on how to prepare each food for your baby

💜 A list of foods that combine well with each single food (for the puree chart only)

💜 A list of the most noteworthy nutrients in each food, with extra-potent nutrients identified in bold

💜 A section for you to make any notes you like about each new food you try with your baby

See also pages 20–22 for guidance on which foods you should try to buy organic.

So now, after all this information, I'm hoping you'll feel ready to get started on your solid food journey with your baby. Enjoy this special time!

Favorite First Single Foods at a Glance
purees & mash

Vegetables

Type	Suggested cooking methods	Key nutrients	Combines well with	Notes
Beets	Peel and dice, then steam, boil, or roast	Fiber, **folate**, magnesium, manganese, potassium, vitamin C	Apples, butternut squash, carrots, coconut oil (virgin), onions (cooked), pears, sweet potatoes	Date tried:
Broccoli	Steam	Fiber, **folate**, magnesium, manganese, pantothenic acid, phosphorus, potassium, protein, riboflavin, thiamine, vitamins A, B$_6$, **C**, and E	Apples, beef, carrots, chicken, pears, sweet potatoes	Date tried:
Butternut squash	Peel, dice, and steam Bake in large pieces, then discard skin	Calcium, fiber, folate, **magnesium**, manganese, niacin, potassium, thiamine, **vitamins A, B$_6$**, C, and E	Apples, bananas, beets, carrots, cauliflower, chicken, chickpeas, cinnamon, coconut oil (virgin), cumin, lentils, nut or seed butters, onions (cooked), pears	Date tried:
Carrots	Peel, dice, and steam or boil Peel and roast	Fiber, **vitamins A, E, and K**	Apples, beef, beets, blueberries, broccoli, chicken, chickpeas, cinnamon, coconut oil (virgin), kale, lentils, millet, mint (fresh), onions (cooked), pears, peas, potatoes, quinoa	Date tried:
Cauliflower	Steam Roast	Folate, vitamins C and K	Basil (fresh), butter (grass-fed), butternut squash, carrots, chickpeas, coconut oil (virgin), cumin, lentils, mint (fresh)	Date tried:

Type	Suggested cooking methods	Key nutrients	Combines well with	Notes
Peas	Steam Boil	Fiber, folate, manganese, niacin, protein, thiamine, vitamin K	Butter (grass-fed), carrots, chicken, corn, lamb, mint (fresh), yogurt	Date tried:
Potatoes	Peel, dice, and boil or steam Bake whole	Copper, magnesium, vitamins B_6 and C	Beef, butter (grass-fed), carrots, chicken, coconut oil (virgin), lamb, peas	Date tried:
Sweet potatoes	Peel, dice, and steam Bake whole, then discard skin	Copper, fiber, magnesium, manganese, potassium, protein, thiamine, **vitamins A, B_6, C, and E**	Apples, beef, blueberries, broccoli, chicken, cinnamon, coconut oil (virgin), lamb, nut or seed butters, onions (cooked), pears	Date tried:

Fruit

Type	Suggested cooking methods	Key nutrients	Combines well with	Notes
Apples	Peel, dice, and steam Bake in large pieces, then discard skin	Fiber	Bananas, beef, beets, blueberries, broccoli, butternut squash, chard, chicken, chickpeas, cinnamon, ginger, kale, lentils, mangoes, mint (fresh), nut or seed butters, peaches, pears, prunes, spinach, strawberries, sweet potatoes, yogurt	Date tried:
Avocados	Mash or puree raw	Copper, fiber, **folate**, magnesium, pantothenic acid, protein, vitamins B_6, C, E, and K	Apples, bananas, cilantro, millet, mint (fresh), nut or seed butters, quinoa, tomatoes	Date tried:

(continued . . .)

Fruit, contd.

Type	Suggested cooking methods	Key nutrients	Combines well with	Notes
Bananas	Mash or puree raw Peel and bake whole	Fiber, folate, manganese, magnesium, **potassium**, vitamins B_6 and C	Apples, avocados, blueberries, buckwheat, butternut squash, mint (fresh), nut or seed butters, oats, peaches, pumpkin, quinoa, strawberries, yogurt	Date tried:
Blueberries	Puree or mash raw	Manganese, vitamins C and K	Apples, bananas, buckwheat, millet, nut butters, oats, peaches, pears, quinoa, sweet potatoes	Date tried:
Mangoes	Puree raw	Folate, vitamins A, C, and E	Apples, avocados, bananas, blueberries, chicken, mint (fresh), pears, yogurt	Date tried:
Papaya	Mash or puree raw	Folate, magnesium, vitamins A and **C**	Apples, avocados, bananas, chicken, cilantro, mint (fresh), pears, watermelon	Date tried:
Peaches	Peel and mash or puree raw	Copper, fiber, magnesium, potassium, vitamins A, C, and E	Apples, bananas, buckwheat, carrots, chicken, ginger, millet, mint (fresh), oats, pears, quinoa, strawberries, yogurt	Date tried:
Pears	Peel and mash or puree raw Peel and roast	Copper, fiber, magnesium, vitamins C and K	Apples, bananas, beef, beets, blueberries, broccoli, butternut squash, chard, chicken, chickpeas, cinnamon, ginger, kale, lentils, mangoes, mint (fresh), nut or seed butters, peaches, potatoes, prunes, spinach, strawberries, yogurt	Date tried:

Type	Suggested cooking methods	Key nutrients	Combines well with	Notes
Prunes	Soak in hot water, then drain	Copper, fiber, magnesium, **potassium**, riboflavin, vitamins A, B$_6$, and **K**	Apples, buckwheat, chicken, mangoes, millet, oats, pears, potatoes, quinoa, yogurt	Date tried:

Protein Sources

Type	Suggested cooking methods	Key nutrients	Combines well with	Notes
Beef	Stew	Iron, magnesium, niacin, pantothenic acid, phosphorus, potassium, **protein,** riboflavin, **selenium, vitamin B$_{12}$, zinc**	Apples, barley, basil, carrots, chard, cumin, kale, kidney beans, onions (cooked), pears, potatoes, quinoa, rosemary, sweet potatoes, thyme (fresh)	Date tried:
Chicken	Poach Roast	Magnesium, **niacin,** pantothenic acid, phosphorus, **protein, selenium,** vitamins B$_6$ and B$_{12}$	Apples, apricots, brown rice, butternut squash, carrots, corn, grapes, millet, onions (cooked), peaches, pears, sweet potatoes	Date tried:
Chickpeas	Soak, rinse, and boil (May also use precooked, sodium-free and from BPA-free can)	Copper, **fiber, folate,** iron, **magnesium, manganese,** phosphorus, potassium, **protein,** selenium, thiamine, vitamin B$_6$, zinc	Apples, avocados, bananas, basil, butternut squash, carrots, cilantro, coconut oil (virgin), cumin, kale, mint (fresh), onions (cooked), pears	Date tried:

(continued . . .)

Protein Sources, contd.

Type	Suggested cooking methods	Key nutrients	Combines well with	Notes
Eggs	Scramble or poach hard, then mash or puree	Folate, pantothenic acid, phosphorus, **protein**, riboflavin, **selenium, vitamins B$_{12}$, D, and E, zinc**	Avocados, beets, butternut squash, coconut oil, fresh dill, ghee, green beans, peas	Date tried:
Kidney beans	Soak, rinse, and boil (May also use precooked, sodium-free and from BPA-free can)	Copper, **fiber, folate,** iron, **magnesium,** manganese, phosphorus, **potassium, protein,** thiamine, zinc	Beef, butternut squash, carrots, corn, sweet potatoes, tomatoes	Date tried:
Lamb	Stew	Folate, niacin, pantothenic acid, phosphorus, potassium, **protein,** riboflavin, **selenium, vitamin B$_{12}$,** zinc	Apples, carrots, mint, onions (cooked), peas, potatoes, sweet potatoes	Date tried:
Lentils	Soak, rinse, and boil (May also use precooked, sodium-free and from BPA-free can)	Copper, **fiber, folate,** iron, magnesium, manganese, pantothenic acid, phosphorus, **potassium, protein,** selenium, thiamine, vitamin B$_6$	Apples, basil, beets, butternut squash, carrots, cauliflower, cilantro, cumin, kale, mint (fresh), onions (cooked), pears, sweet potatoes, yogurt (whole milk)	Date tried:
Navy beans	Soak, rinse, and boil (May also use precooked, sodium-free and from BPA-free can)	Copper, **fiber, folate,** iron, **magnesium,** manganese, phosphorus, **potassium, protein,** selenium, thiamine, vitamin B$_6$, zinc	Avocados, butternut squash, carrots, cilantro, coconut oil (virgin), garlic (cooked), mint (fresh), onions (cooked), sweet potatoes, tomatoes	Date tried:

Type	Suggested cooking methods	Key nutrients	Combines well with	Notes
Nuts and peanuts (raw or natural pre-blended nut butters)	Blend smooth, then thin with liquid or combine with other foods so it's not sticky	Copper, fiber, folate, **magnesium**, manganese, phosphorus, potassium, **protein**, **vitamin E**	Apples, bananas, blueberries, butternut squash, carrots, grains (any type), pears, sweet potatoes, yogurt (whole milk)	Date tried:
Organic tofu	Serve raw Bake Sauté	**Calcium**, copper, fiber, folate, **iron**, magnesium, **manganese**, phosphorus, potassium, **protein**, **selenium**, thiamine, zinc	Apples, avocados, bananas, blueberries, carrots, corn, pears	Date tried:
Turkey	Poach Roast	Magnesium, **niacin**, pantothenic acid, phosphorus, potassium, **protein**, riboflavin, **selenium**, vitamins B_6 and B_{12}, zinc	Apples, apricots, butternut squash, carrots, corn, grapes, millet, peaches, pears, peas, potatoes, quinoa, sweet potatoes	Date tried:
Whole-milk yogurt (cow, sheep, goat)	Serve as is	Calcium, magnesium, pantothenic acid, phosphorus, potassium, protein, riboflavin, selenium, **vitamin B_{12}**, zinc	Apples, avocados, bananas, berries (any type), corn, edamame, mangoes, mint, oats, peaches, pears, peas	Date tried:

(continued . . .)

Protein Sources, contd.

Type	Suggested cooking methods	Key nutrients	Combines well with	Notes
Wild salmon	Poach Roast	Copper, folate, magnesium, niacin, omega-3s, pantothenic acid, phosphorus, **potassium, protein,** riboflavin, **selenium,** thiamine, **vitamins B$_6$ and B$_{12}$**	Broccoli, kale, peas, potatoes, spinach, sweet potatoes	Date tried:
Wild white fish (snapper, haddock, halibut)	Poach Roast	Magnesium, niacin, phosphorus, potassium, **protein, selenium,** vitamins B$_6$ and **B$_{12}$**	Avocados, bell peppers, corn, peas, potatoes, sweet potatoes, tomatoes, watermelon	Date tried:

Grains

(For detailed instructions on making homemade baby cereals see page 102.)

Type	Suggested cooking methods	Key nutrients	Combines well with	Notes
Buckwheat	Grind grains to flour Simmer with water	**Copper, fiber,** folate, iron, niacin, **magnesium,** manganese, pantothenic acid, phosphorus, potassium, **protein,** riboflavin, selenium, zinc	Cinnamon, coconut oil (virgin), fruit puree or chopped fruit (any fruit), sweet potatoes, yogurt	Date tried:
Millet	Grind grains to flour Simmer with water	Copper, folate, magnesium, manganese, phosphorus, protein, thiamine, zinc	Cinnamon, coconut oil (virgin), fruit puree or chopped fruit (any fruit), sweet potatoes, yogurt	Date tried:

Type	Suggested cooking methods	Key nutrients	Combines well with	Notes
Quinoa	Grind grains to flour Simmer with water	Copper, fiber, folate, iron, **magnesium,** manganese, phosphorus, protein, thiamine, vitamin E	Cinnamon, coconut oil (virgin), fruit puree or chopped fruit (any fruit), sweet potatoes, yogurt	Date tried:
Rolled or steel-cut oats	Grind grains to flour Simmer with water	Fiber, magnesium, manganese, phosphorus, protein, selenium, zinc	Cinnamon, coconut oil (virgin), fruit puree or chopped fruit (any fruit), sweet potatoes, yogurt	Date tried:

Favorite First Single Foods at a Glance

finger foods

Vegetables

Type	Suggested cooking methods	How to serve	Key nutrients	Notes
Beets	Roast Steam Simmer	Soft-cooked small dice	Fiber, **folate,** magnesium, manganese, potassium, vitamin C	Date tried:
Broccoli	Steam	Soft-cooked small dice	Fiber, **folate,** magnesium, manganese, pantothenic acid, phosphorus, potassium, protein, riboflavin, thiamine, vitamins A, B_6, **C,** and E	Date tried:
Butternut squash	Roast Steam	Soft-cooked small dice	Calcium, fiber, folate, **magnesium,** manganese, niacin, potassium, thiamine, **vitamins A,** B_6, C, and E	Date tried:

(continued . . .)

Vegetables, contd.

Type	Suggested cooking methods	How to serve	Key nutrients	Notes
Carrots	Roast Steam Simmer	Soft-cooked small dice or thin sticks	Fiber, **vitamins A**, E, and K	Date tried:
Cauliflower	Roast Steam	Soft-cooked small dice	Folate, vitamins C and K	Date tried:
Green beans	Steam Simmer	Soft-cooked small dice	Calcium, fiber, folate, iron, magnesium, manganese, potassium, protein, riboflavin, thiamine, vitamins C and **K**	Date tried:
Peas	Steam Simmer	Small, soft-cooked halves or leave whole if peas are very small	Fiber, folate, manganese, niacin, protein, thiamine, vitamin K	Date tried:
Potatoes	Bake Roast Steam Simmer	Soft-cooked small dice or thin sticks	Copper, magnesium, vitamins B_6 and C	Date tried:
Sweet potatoes	Bake Roast Steam Simmer	Soft-cooked small dice or thin sticks	Copper, fiber, magnesium, manganese, potassium, protein, thiamine, **vitamins A,** B_6, C, and E	Date tried:

You can use a crinkle cutter to make shapes that are easier for little fingers to grip.

Fruit

Type	Suggested cooking methods	How to serve	Key nutrients	Notes
Apples	Raw (peeled and grated only) Roast Steam	Small, peeled, soft-cooked dice or thin sticks If raw, grated	Fiber	Date tried:
Avocados	Raw (ripe)	Small, soft dice	Copper, fiber, **folate**, magnesium, pantothenic acid, protein, vitamins B_6, C, E, and K	Date tried:
Bananas	Raw (ripe) Roast	Small, soft dice	Fiber, folate, magnesium, manganese, **potassium**, vitamins B_6 and C	Date tried:
Blueberries	Raw (ripe)	Cut in halves or even quarters if blueberries are large	Manganese, vitamins C and K	Date tried:
Cherries	Raw (ripe)	Pitted and cut in small dice	Copper, fiber, magnesium, vitamin C	Date tried:
Mangoes	Raw (ripe)	Small dice or slices	Folate, vitamins A, C, and E	Date tried:
Papaya	Raw (ripe)	Small dice or slices	Folate, magnesium, vitamins A and **C**	Date tried:
Peaches	Raw (ripe)	Small, peeled, dice or slices	Copper, fiber, magnesium, potassium, vitamins A, C, and E	Date tried:

(continued . . .)

Fruit, contd.

Type	Suggested cooking methods	How to serve	Key nutrients	Notes
Pears	Raw (ripe)	Small, peeled, dice or slices	Copper, fiber, magnesium, vitamins C and K	Date tried:
Plums	Raw	Small, peeled, dice or slices	Vitamins A and C	Date tried:
Prunes	Soak until soft	Pitted and cut in small dice	Copper, fiber, magnesium, **potassium**, riboflavin, vitamins A, B_6, and **K**	Date tried:
Watermelon	Raw	Small dice or thin sticks	Magnesium, vitamin C	Date tried:

If pieces of fruit are too slippery for your baby to pick up, roll them in crushed whole-grain unsweetened cereal.

Protein Sources

Type	Suggested cooking methods	How to serve	Key nutrients	Notes
Beef	Poach Roast Stew (Doneness should be at least medium)	Shredded or very small dice	Iron, magnesium, niacin, pantothenic acid, phosphorus, potassium, **protein**, riboflavin, **selenium**, **vitamin B_{12}**, **zinc**	Date tried:
Cheese (hard)	As is	Grated Small dice or cut in thin sticks	Calcium, phosphorus, protein, selenium, vitamin B_{12}	Date tried:

Type	Suggested cooking methods	How to serve	Key nutrients	Notes
Chicken	Poach Roast (Well-cooked)	Shredded or very small dice	Magnesium, **niacin**, pantothenic acid, phosphorus, **protein, selenium,** vitamins B_6 and B_{12}	Date tried:
Chickpeas	Precooked, sodium-free from a BPA-free can Boiled	Soft-cooked, halved, and slightly smashed	Copper, **fiber, folate,** iron, **magnesium, manganese,** phosphorus, potassium, **protein,** selenium, thiamine, vitamin B_6, zinc	Date tried:
Eggs (white and yolk)	Hard boiled Hard scrambled	Small dice	Folate, pantothenic acid, phosphorus, **protein,** riboflavin, **selenium, vitamins** B_{12}, D, and E, zinc	Date tried:
Kidney beans	Precooked, sodium-free from a BPA-free can Boiled	Small dice and a bit smashed	Copper, **fiber, folate,** iron, **magnesium,** manganese, phosphorus, **potassium, protein,** thiamine, zinc	Date tried:
Lamb	Poach Roast Stew (Doneness should be at least medium)	Shredded or small dice	Folate, niacin, pantothenic acid, phosphorus, potassium, **protein,** riboflavin, **selenium, vitamin** B_{12}, zinc	Date tried:
Lentils	Precooked, sodium-free from a BPA-free can Boiled	Soft-cooked, slightly smashed	Copper, **fiber, folate,** iron, magnesium, manganese, pantothenic acid, phosphorus, **potassium, protein,** selenium, thiamine, vitamin B_6, potassium, zinc	Date tried:

(continued . . .)

Protein Sources, contd.

Type	Suggested cooking methods	How to serve	Key nutrients	Notes
Navy beans	Precooked, sodium-free from a BPA-free can Boiled	Soft-cooked, halved, and slightly smashed	Copper, **fiber, folate,** iron, **magnesium,** manganese, phosphorus, **protein,** selenium, thiamine, vitamin B$_6$, **zinc**	Date tried:
Pork	Poach Roast Stew	Shredded or small dice	Magnesium, niacin, phosphorus, potassium, **protein,** riboflavin, **selenium, thiamine,** vitamins B$_6$ and **B$_{12}$,** zinc	Date tried:
Tofu (soft to firm)	Raw Bake	Small dice Sliced into thin sticks	**Calcium,** copper, fiber, folate, **iron,** magnesium, **manganese,** phosphorus, potassium, **protein, selenium,** thiamine, zinc	Date tried:
Turkey	Poach Roast	Shredded or very small dice	Magnesium, **niacin,** pantothenic acid, phosphorus, potassium, **protein,** riboflavin, **selenium,** vitamins B$_6$ and **B$_{12}$,** zinc	Date tried:
White fish	Poach Roast	Flaked or small dice	Magnesium, niacin, phosphorus, potassium, **protein, selenium,** vitamins B$_6$ and **B$_{12}$**	Date tried:
Wild salmon	Poach Roast	Flaked or small dice	Copper, folate, magnesium, niacin, omega-3s, pantothenic acid, phosphorus, **potassium, protein,** riboflavin, **selenium,** thiamine, **vitamins B$_6$** and **B$_{12}$**	Date tried:

Grains

Type	Suggested cooking methods	How to serve	Key nutrients	Notes
Barley	Steam Boil	Soft-cooked, a bit smashed	Fiber, magnesium, manganese, niacin, selenium	Date tried:
Bread (this isn't quite a "single-ingredient food" so be aware of the list of ingredients and keep as short as possible)	Toast	Small dice or cut into thin sticks (can spread with butter, nut or seed butter, coconut oil, cream cheese, or avocado)	Fiber, folate, magnesium, manganese, niacin, protein, selenium, thiamine	Date tried:
Cereal (unsweetened small or O shaped; this isn't quite a "single-ingredient food" so be aware of the list of ingredients and keep as short as possible)	As is	As is	Fiber, other (fortified cereal will have added nutrients, but this will vary from cereal to cereal), protein	Date tried:
Oats	Boil, then bake in casserole dish (can mix with fruit puree or egg to help hold together)	Small dice or cut into sticks	Fiber, magnesium, manganese, phosphorus, protein, selenium, zinc	Date tried:
Quinoa	Boil Steam	Soft-cooked, as is	Copper, fiber, folate, iron, **magnesium**, manganese, phosphorus, protein, thiamine, vitamin E	Date tried:

Roasted Root Vegetables
and Apples with Quinoa
(page 93)

Cheesy Veggie Mash
(page 89)

purees & mashes

Coconutty Green Vegetables

MAKES: APPROXIMATELY 2 CUPS

PREP TIME: 15 MINUTES

COOK TIME: 7 MINUTES

2½ cups diced unpeeled zucchini

2 cups chopped broccoli florets

1 cup frozen peas, thawed

½ small leek, thinly sliced, white only

1 Tbsp virgin coconut oil

This puree is all about green veg, which might make you wary of cooking it, thinking it won't be popular and will just go to waste. I'm telling you, this puree is delicious, babies love it, and the coconut oil is to thank for that. It somehow brings out the best of the greens while adding this incredible creaminess that makes you want to steal your baby's lunch. And, even better, the coconut fat helps with the absorption of the nutrients from the vegetables and is similar nutritionally to the fat in breast milk. It's a very worthy and appropriate ingredient to add to your baby's diet.

1. Mix all the vegetables together in a large bowl.

2. Put ½ cup of water in a large pot, and place a stainless-steel steaming basket in the bottom. Place the vegetables on top and bring the water to a boil over high heat. Cover, lower the heat, and steam for 5–7 minutes until the vegetables are tender and bright green. Be careful not to overcook or the flavor will be spoiled.

3. Blend with the coconut oil, while the vegetables are still warm, until smooth. This mash can be frozen in ice cube trays or special containers for freezing baby foods. (See page 66.)

Sweet Roasted Carrots, Cauliflower, and Onions

MAKES: APPROXIMATELY 2 CUPS

PREP TIME: 15 MINUTES

COOK TIME: 30 MINUTES

2 large carrots, peeled and diced

1 head cauliflower, roughly chopped

½ small yellow onion

1 Tbsp virgin coconut oil, melted

Who doesn't love roasted vegetables? There really couldn't be a better way to cook them; it basically makes all vegetables taste incredible. I think this is particularly true for cauliflower, though, which really sweetens and mellows with roasting, and which pairs beautifully with sweet carrots and caramelized onion. A touch of coconut oil is nutritious for baby and really improves the overall flavor of this yummy puree.

1. Preheat the oven to 375°F.

2. Lay out the carrots, cauliflower, and onion together on a rimmed baking tray and drizzle the coconut oil over top. Stir until the vegetables are mixed together and fully coated in the oil.

3. Roast in the oven for 30 minutes, stirring and turning the vegetables once, halfway through. Transfer to a blender and blend to the desired consistency. This puree can be frozen in ice cube trays or special containers for freezing baby foods. (See page 66.)

Skip the blending and serve these soft roasted veggies as a finger food to self-feeders. Or sprinkle with a little sea salt and black pepper and serve as a grown-up side dish.

Peas with Greek Yogurt and Mint

MAKES: 1½ CUPS

PREP TIME: 5 MINUTES

COOK TIME: 4 MINUTES

½ cup frozen peas

1 cup Greek yogurt

2 mint leaves

W e often think to mix fruit with yogurt, but blending yogurt with vegetables, like peas, also works really well for babies. This protein-rich puree has a wonderful bright flavor and couldn't be simpler to make. As an alternative, try combining Greek yogurt with another mild soft-cooked blended vegetable and fresh herb or spice that takes your fancy such as butternut squash and thyme, or sweet potato and a pinch of cumin.

1. Place the peas in a pot of boiling water and cook for 4 minutes. Strain and rinse with cold water.

2. Blend with the yogurt and mint to the desired consistency. This puree can be frozen in ice cube trays or special containers for freezing baby foods. (See page 66.)

Classic Sweet Potato, Broccoli, and Apple Puree

MAKES: APPROXIMATELY 2 CUPS

PREP TIME: 10 MINUTES

COOK TIME: 12 MINUTES

2 cups peeled and diced sweet potato

1 large apple (any type), peeled and diced

1 cup coarsely chopped broccoli florets

M y daughter, Poppy, loved this puree when she first started eating solids, and it was our staple for a few months when all she really wanted was sweet potatoes. Sweet potatoes, with their bright-orange flesh, are a true superfood, bursting with vitamin A, and babies tend to love them. The slight bitterness of the broccoli and tartness of the apple make the flavor more complex. I make this using a medium-size lidded pot and my trusty old-school stainless-steel steaming basket. If you use a specialized steaming appliance, you may need to adjust the cooking times. In my experience, electric steamers usually take a bit more time.

1. Put 1¼ cups of water into a medium-size pot. Put the steamer on top of the water and place the sweet potato in the steamer. Bring to a boil, uncovered, then cover and steam over medium heat for 5 minutes. Being careful of escaping steam, remove the lid and add the apple and then the broccoli. Cover and steam for 5 more minutes, or until the broccoli is soft but not overcooked.

2. Put the warm sweet potatoes, broccoli, and apple into a blender and blend to the desired consistency. Use some of the water from the pot to thin the puree if needed. This puree can be frozen in ice cube trays or special containers for freezing baby foods. (See page 66.)

Give a frozen cube of this puree to your baby in a mesh feeding net if they're refusing to eat due to teething pain. Their gums will be soothed, and they'll take in some protein and calories, which will help with fussiness from not eating. Mesh feeding nets can be found in the baby section of well-stocked supermarkets or drugstores.

Minty Apple, Greens, and Quinoa

MAKES: APPROXIMATELY 2 CUPS

PREP TIME: 15 MINUTES

COOK TIME: 15 MINUTES

¼ cup uncooked quinoa

3 large apples, peeled and diced (Galas work well because they are a nice balance of tart and sweet)

½ cup baby spinach, leaves only

½ cup kale, stems discarded

½ ripe avocado

½ banana

1 mint leaf

This is one of my favorite puree recipes of all time and it has been a really popular post on the Love Child Blog. It pretty much ticks all the nutrient boxes you could hope for, and the lone mint leaf really pumps up the flavor. Plus, it's green, and I think it's a good strategy to expose little ones to delicious green food early on so they come to associate green vegetables with pleasant food experiences.

1. Place the quinoa in a pot with ¾ cup water and put the diced apples on top. Bring to a boil over high heat, then turn down to low, cover, and simmer for 14 minutes. Add the spinach and kale to the pot, cover, and simmer for an additional 1 minute.

2. Pour the quinoa, apple, and any leftover water into a blender. Add the avocado, banana, and mint leaf. Blend to the desired consistency, adding water, breast milk, or formula to thin if needed. This puree can be frozen in ice cube trays or special containers for freezing baby foods. (See page 66.) Freeze leftovers straight away so the avocado doesn't brown.

Change things up and turn this into a smoothie for you, or your toddler, by blending it with some almond milk, ice cubes, and a dollop of honey (only serve honey to children over 1 year old—see page 65).

Spread the rest of the avocado on toast for an omega-rich snack for you, or your toddler, or cut it into cubes and freeze to add to smoothies!

Freeze the leftover banana to add to smoothies.

Pears, Mangoes, and Prunes

MAKES: APPROXIMATELY 2 CUPS

PREP TIME: 10 MINUTES

8 pitted dried prunes

2 ripe pears, peeled and diced

2 cups peeled and diced mango (fresh or frozen)

> Freeze the puree into Popsicles to give to bigger little ones who are past the puree stage.

When babies first start eating solids, it's not uncommon for their digestive systems to get a little blocked up. I knew this to be true, but was still so stressed when it happened to Poppy and Cam. As a remedy I would feed them straight pureed prunes, but the prunes were sticky and strongly flavored, so often the babies refused to eat them. I've since learned that like prunes, pears and mangoes are also high-fiber foods that help with constipation. How I wish I'd come up with this recipe combining the three fruits when my children were on purees! Offer this regularly to keep things moving or as an intervention in a constipation emergency. Of course, don't give it at every meal, as it might be too much of a good thing, if you know what I mean.

1. Rehydrate the prunes by placing them in a small heat-safe bowl and covering them with boiling water. Allow them to soak for 10 minutes, then drain.

2. Blend the prunes with the pears and the mango to your preferred consistency.

3. This puree can be frozen in ice cube trays or special containers for freezing baby foods. (See page 66.)

Cheesy Veggie Mash

MAKES: APPROXIMATELY 2½ CUPS

PREP TIME: 15 MINUTES

COOK TIME: 10 MINUTES

2 cups small-dice peeled potatoes (any type)

1 cup small-dice peeled carrots

1 cup frozen peas

1 cup chopped broccoli florets

1 cup grated cheddar cheese (I prefer aged but use whatever strength you prefer)

The cheese makes this the sort of baby food that encourages "one for baby, one for me." Potatoes can become gluey and sticky when over-blended, so mash this by hand. *(Photo on page 82)*

1. In a large, wide pot, place 2 cups of water and set a stainless-steel steamer basket in place, all the way open.

2. Bring the water to a boil over high heat, then place the potatoes and carrots in the steamer. Cover, turn the heat to medium-low, and simmer for 4 minutes.

3. Add the peas and broccoli, cover, and simmer for 4 minutes.

4. Drain the vegetables, then return them to the pot.

5. Sprinkle the cheese over the vegetables ¼ cup at a time, and stir in gently. Mash with a potato masher. Stir again to make sure the cheese is mixed through. Serve warm. This mash can be frozen in ice cube trays or special containers for freezing baby foods. (See page 66.)

Protein-Rich Lentils with Carrots and Pears

MAKES: APPROXIMATELY 2 CUPS

PREP TIME: 10 MINUTES

COOK TIME: 37 MINUTES

⅔ cup green lentils

2 medium carrots, peeled and sliced into thin rounds

2 large ripe pears, peeled, cored, and cut into large chunks

Pinch of ground cinnamon

Rich in iron, protein, and folate, lentils are the best friend of plant-based eaters. They can have a powdery texture and are very dense, making them not entirely baby-friendly though, so I've combined them with carrots and juicy pears to create a velvety texture and sweet flavor that will appeal to new eaters.

1. Spread out the lentils on a tray or plate and check for any little stones, then put the lentils in a sieve and rinse well.

2. Place the lentils in a medium-size pot with 1½ cups of cold water. Bring the water to a boil over high heat. Turn down the heat to medium-low, cover, and simmer for 30 minutes. Add the carrots on top of the lentils, and cover and cook for 5 more minutes.

3. Blend the lentils and carrots with the pears and cinnamon until smooth. Add extra water, breast milk, or formula to thin if needed. Allow to cool before using. This puree can be frozen in ice cube trays or special containers for freezing baby foods. (See page 66.)

Creamy Sweet Potatoes, Blueberries, and Almond Butter

MAKES: APPROXIMATELY 2½ CUPS

PREP TIME: 5 MINUTES

COOK TIME: 1 HOUR

2 small sweet potatoes

1 cup blueberries, fresh or frozen

4 Tbsp smooth raw almond butter

I threw these superfood ingredients together on a whim but with an inkling that I might end up with something amazing, and was rewarded for my craziness. This puree is chock-full of nutrients and is seriously delicious. In fact, I think it tastes a little like milk chocolate, which I realize makes no sense, but it really does! The latest recommendations state that it is fine to give babies foods containing nuts from 6 months, so go ahead and give your baby almonds as long as they are fully ground and you don't have serious allergies in your family. If your family does have a history of allergies, check with your doctor first. (See pages 59–62.)

1. Preheat the oven to 400°F. Place the whole sweet potatoes in a baking dish and prick them a few times with a fork. Bake them for approximately 1 hour until they're oozing and nice and soft.

2. Once the sweet potatoes are cool enough to handle, scoop the flesh into a blender, and blend with the blueberries and almond butter. This puree can be frozen in ice cube trays or special containers for freezing baby foods. (See page 66.)

Roasted Root Vegetables and Apples with Quinoa

MAKES: APPROXIMATELY 2 CUPS

PREP TIME: 15 MINUTES

COOK TIME: 40 MINUTES

Virgin coconut oil, to grease the pan

2 apples, variety of your choice, peeled and chopped into large chunks

1 small sweet potato, peeled and chopped into small dice

1 small beet, peeled and chopped into very thin rounds

Pinch of cinnamon

3 Tbsp cooked quinoa

Juice of ½ orange

This recipe invokes big feelings of nostalgia for me. Not only does it taste like Thanksgiving, but it is also a recipe that I cooked over and over again for Cam when he was a baby. He loved it then, and to this day, beets are still one of his favorite foods. At that time we were also developing new flavors for Love Child Organics, and a version of this is part of our Super Blends range available at supermarkets across the country. Now you can make it at home!

1. Preheat the oven to 400°F. Grease a roasting dish with coconut oil.

2. Spread the apples, sweet potato, and beet in a single layer in the pan and sprinkle lightly with cinnamon. Cover with a lid or sheet of foil, and roast in the oven for 30–40 minutes, until very soft.

3. Allow to cool slightly, then spoon into a blender and puree with the quinoa and a good squeeze of fresh juice from the orange. If you would like your baby to eat a more textured puree, simply leave out the quinoa while you blend, then stir it in whole at the end.

4. Add boiled water, breast milk, or formula to thin the puree to the desired consistency. This puree can be frozen in ice cube trays or special containers for freezing baby foods. (See page 66.)

Turn this recipe into a tasty fall side dish for the whole family. Roast the vegetables and apples as directed, and then serve alongside poultry. No blending required!

♥

Consider cooking extra quinoa to use later for dinner, or freezing extra to use in other recipes such as the Rasp-Peary Dream smoothie (page 128).

Chickpeas with Roasted Bananas and Squash

MAKES: APPROXIMATELY 2 CUPS

PREP TIME: 15 MINUTES

COOK TIME: 30 MINUTES

2 cups peeled and cubed butternut squash

2 bananas, peeled and cut into ½-inch rounds

¼ tsp ground nutmeg

½ cup cooked or canned chickpeas (sodium-free and from a BPA-free can)

Chickpeas are a good plant-based source of protein and iron, and they combine well with other ingredients in baby purees. Bananas and squash may seem like an odd combination, but they're actually delicious together. I've added some nutmeg to give your baby the opportunity to try a new flavor.

1. Preheat the oven to 375°F. Cut two pieces of parchment paper that are just smaller than your baking tray. Lay one of them on the tray.

2. Place the squash and bananas on the parchment. Sprinkle with the nutmeg. Cover with the second piece of parchment. Roll the two pieces of parchment together tightly, all the way around, to create a sealed package. Bake for 30 minutes. Be careful of the hot steam when you open the package.

3. Once the squash and bananas are cool enough to handle, mash or blend them with the chickpeas. You may need to add a little water to thin the puree to the desired consistency. This puree can be frozen in ice cube trays or special containers for freezing baby foods. (See page 66.)

Farm to High Chair Poached Chicken

MAKES: 2 ½ CUPS

PREP TIME: 15 MINUTES

COOK TIME: 20 MINUTES

2 boneless, skinless organic chicken thighs

1 cup peeled and diced butternut squash

1 tsp fresh thyme leaves

2 cups chopped rainbow chard, stems removed

2 ripe pears, peeled, cored, and roughly chopped

You know the Farm to Table movement? Well, to me this recipe represents the baby version: Farm to High Chair. I used to make this exact recipe for Cam with ingredients that I'd picked up at our local farmers' market. This extremely nutrient-rich puree is packed with protein and iron and uses the best of what Mother Nature has to offer.

1. Put ½ cup water in a large sauté pan and bring to a gentle boil over medium heat. Turn it down until it is just simmering, then carefully add the chicken, squash, and thyme. Cover, and cook for 10 minutes.

2. Place the chard on top, cover again, and simmer for an additional 7 minutes.

3. Use a slotted spoon to transfer the warm chicken and vegetables to a blender, reserving the broth. Blend with the pears to your desired consistency. Add the reserved broth to thin the puree. This puree can be frozen in ice cube trays or special containers for freezing baby foods. (See page 66.)

I recommend roasting the bananas and squash in parchment paper so that the bananas don't dry out and the squash doesn't get charred, which would give a burned flavor to the puree.

♥

Freeze any extra chickpeas to use at a later date, or add them to your salad for dinner.

Sweet and Tangy Braised Beef

MAKES: 2½ CUPS

PREP TIME: 15 MINUTES

COOK TIME: 45 MINUTES

2 tsp olive oil

8 oz extra-lean ground beef

2 large apples, peeled and thinly sliced (a sweeter type like Gala works well)

2 cups shredded red cabbage

1 medium beet, peeled and thinly sliced

1 tsp fresh thyme leaves

I know some babies will eat plain pureed meat and poultry, but my babies were never convinced, and it was always a struggle to find protein-based recipes that had a texture and flavor they enjoyed. I was determined to find some fail-proof iron-rich protein purees, and this one became a sure favorite. You can probably tell that many of my baby food recipes are inspired by food I love to eat. Braised apples and cabbage is a best-loved side dish of mine that I often pair with meat or poultry. Here I add beets for extra nutrients and color and cook the meat right with the vegetables to make a one-pot wonder perfect for baby.

1. Over medium heat, heat the oil in a large pot, then add the beef, cooking until browned, approximately 10 minutes.

2. Add the apples, cabbage, beet, and thyme and cook, stirring often, for 5 minutes.

3. Add just enough water so that the ingredients are just barely covered and bring to a boil. Turn the heat to low, cover, and simmer for 30 minutes.

4. Blend to the desired consistency. This puree can be frozen in ice cube trays or special containers for freezing baby foods. (See page 66.)

> Feel free to replace the beef with pork, chicken, or turkey. All work really well in this recipe.

Tropical White Fish, Avocado, and Watermelon Mash

I have to admit, I did a bit of a happy dance when I came up with this fish fiesta of a recipe. Zingy, crunchy, and creamy, and much more of a mash than puree, if there ever was a recipe guaranteed to get your little one interested in eating fish, and OK with texture, this is it. And I bet you'll be stealing bites for yourself too—it's that good. This combination is best very fresh, and this isn't suitable for freezing, so the recipe is for only one serving.

MAKES: 1 SERVING (APPROXIMATELY
⅓–½ CUP)
PREP TIME: 10 MINUTES
COOK TIME: 6 MINUTES

2 oz boneless, skinless white fish
   such as red snapper or halibut

¼ avocado (see page 88 for what
   to do with leftover avocado)

2 oz watermelon flesh, seeds
   removed

1 tsp cilantro

Add some cabbage
slaw, lime, hot sauce,
and a tortilla, call it a
fish taco, and eat this
yourself for dinner.

1. Preheat the oven to 375°F.

2. Cut out a rectangle of parchment paper approximately 6 × 10 inches. Place the fish 2 inches from a short side of the rectangle, then fold the other side of the parchment over top. Roll up the sides tightly to make a sealed package. Place on a rimmed baking tray and bake in the oven for around 6 minutes. You'll know the fish is ready when it's white and flaky but still moist.

3. Carefully open the parchment paper package and allow the fish to cool.

4. Using a large knife, mince the avocado, watermelon, and cilantro.

5. Place the fish in a small bowl and break up gently with a fork. Add the minced ingredients and gently mix together. Mash further if needed. Serve straight away.

Poppy's Salmon Casserole

MAKES: 3-4 CUPS

PREP TIME: 10 MINUTES

COOK TIME: 20 MINUTES

8 oz wild boneless salmon

½ cup uncooked whole wheat couscous (organic if possible due to high levels of pesticides used on conventional wheat, see page 32)

½ Tbsp unsalted butter

1 Tbsp flour of your choice

1½ cups milk

½ cup chopped frozen spinach

¼ tsp garlic powder

¼ tsp onion powder

½ tsp dried mixed green herbs such as basil, oregano, parsley, and tarragon

Sea salt and ground black pepper to taste (optional)

Other grains, such as millet or quinoa, can be substituted for couscous if you prefer to make this wheat-free. Cook them according to their package instructions.

♥

I prefer to buy spinach that is frozen loose in a bag, rather than in cubes so that I can use it right from frozen.

I've been making this for my daughter, Poppy, since she was 9 months old. She is now well out of the baby stage but still loves it (don't worry—it's not a puree!). She also happily eats salmon sandwiches and baked or barbecued salmon fillet. I'm sure it's because from an early age she made positive associations with salmon by eating this casserole.

1. Preheat the oven to 400°F.

2. Rinse the salmon and pat dry. Check it for any bones by running your fingers down the middle, and pull out any that you find.

3. Wrap the salmon (skin side down) in parchment paper or aluminum foil, being sure to seal well. Bake for approximately 15 minutes until cooked through.

4. While the salmon is cooking, make the couscous. Simply pour it into a heat-safe bowl then add 2 cups of just-boiled water. Cover and let stand for at least 10 minutes. Fluff with a fork and let stand 5 minutes, uncovered.

5. While the salmon and couscous are cooking, make the spinach cream sauce. In a pot, melt the butter over medium heat. With a small whisk, blend in the flour and allow it to cook for a couple of minutes. Slowly whisk in the milk. Add the spinach (it's fine if it's still frozen as long as it's chopped up), garlic powder, onion powder, herbs, and sea salt and pepper. Stir well. Simmer gently for approximately 5 minutes, stirring occasionally. Take off the heat.

6. Once the salmon is cool enough to touch, using your hands or a knife, flake the fish into small pieces, discarding the skin. If your baby is just starting out with texture, you may want to use a knife and mince the salmon, but use your discretion. For older children (or for a family meal), leave the salmon pieces a little bigger—you can always mash them up for baby later. Double- and triple-check that there are no bones left in the salmon.

7. Add the salmon to the couscous and gently stir together. Pour the spinach sauce over top and stir until combined.

8. The dish is now ready to serve—no blending or mashing required. The couscous, flaked salmon, and spinach will all be baby-friendly sizes. Serve warm.

9. You can freeze this in cubes just like the purees (see page 66). Once defrosted, you may need to add a little milk to thin it slightly.

Exotic Tofu, Mango, and Coconut Curry

MAKES: 4 CUPS
PREP TIME: 10 MINUTES
COOK TIME: 25 MINUTES

1 small onion, peeled and diced

1 Tbsp virgin coconut oil

1 garlic clove, crushed

½ tsp ground ginger

½ tsp ground cumin

¼ tsp ground cinnamon

1 (13.5 oz) can full-fat coconut milk (from a BPA-free can)

1 cup diced firm organic tofu

½ cup uncooked quinoa

2 cups baby spinach leaves, roughly chopped

1 cup diced fresh or frozen mango (from frozen is fine, just be sure it is thawed before adding to pan)

Traditionally, babies have been given bland food, but this is completely unnecessary. While they might react and make a funny face when first trying a bold new flavor, this is an entirely natural reaction and doesn't mean that they don't like it. Starting early with bold flavors like garlic, cinnamon, and cumin in this plant-based curry recipe gets your baby used to grown-up tastes and makes it more likely that they'll happily eat this way as they get older. This recipe also contains an array of my favorite superfoods—quinoa, mango, and spinach, as well as organic tofu, which is a good vegetarian protein source (just make sure you buy organic).

1. Over medium-high heat, sauté the onion in the coconut oil until translucent and just beginning to brown, approximately 5 minutes.

2. Add the garlic, ginger, cumin, and cinnamon and cook for another minute.

3. Pour in the coconut milk, ½ cup water, tofu, and quinoa, and give it all a good stir.

4. Bring to a boil, then turn the heat to low, cover, and cook for 15 minutes.

5. Stir in the spinach and mango and stir for 1 minute more. (By adding these ingredients at the end like this, their bright color and the fresh taste of the mango will really come through in the puree.)

6. Take off the heat and allow to cool until you can blend it safely. This puree can be frozen in ice cube trays or special containers for freezing baby foods. (See page 66.)

This puree is best if it isn't over-blended, so either pulse it gently in a blender or a food processor fitted with the steel blade, or pull out your immersion blender and give the curry a quick blitz right in the pot. You should still see bits of soft tofu and brightly colored spinach and mango.

♥

This recipe makes quite a large amount, which is great for batch freezing, but you could cut the recipe in half if you don't have freezer space to spare.

Homemade Baby Cereal

Baby cereal is one of those products that people tend to buy rather than make themselves. Instant cereal, especially instant rice cereal, has been fed to infants as a first food for decades. However, homemade cereals are simple to make and are also very cost-effective, so if you're feeding your baby cereals, you might want to give homemade a try.

There are a few things to keep in mind before you set off. First, don't feel that you must serve your baby cereals as a first food. There is no evidence that cereal is a better first food than avocado, banana, or sweet potato, for example.

You will notice that there isn't a recipe for rice cereal here. There are concerns about the arsenic levels in rice and the effect this could have on babies' little bodies. This, and the fact that rice isn't as nutrient dense as many other grains, is why I recommend choosing one of the grains in the chart as an alternative to traditional rice.

The process for making homemade cereal is very simple, and almost any grain can be used. All you really need is a good-quality, high-powered blender or food processor and you will be able to make a cereal just as smooth as any you can buy at the supermarket.

Here's how to get started:

Blend 1 cup of grain in a food processor fitted with the steel blade or a blender until it becomes coarse flour. This makes more than you need, but you can save the rest in a container in the freezer for another day. To make the cereal, simply heat up the recommended amount of water to just boiling, then slowly sprinkle in the flour, whisking constantly to prevent lumps. Turn down the heat and simmer for the suggested time, stirring occasionally.

The suggestions on the facing page each make 1–2 servings, depending on your baby's appetite. Keep any leftovers in the refrigerator for no more than 24–48 hours. You can also batch cook these cereals and freeze them. Simply multiply the recipe as required and make extra to store in the freezer as you would other baby purees (see page 66). You may need to add a little water and give it a good whisk once it's thawed.

> Cereals are a great base for other nutritious ingredients and also add flavor. Mashed bananas, sweet potatoes, blueberries, peaches, avocados, and even virgin coconut oil and grass-fed ghee are all yummy additions, and you can add breast milk or formula if you like, to make the flavor more familiar. A squeeze of Love Child puree is also a very convenient way to add some extra pizzazz to baby cereal.

Grain	Grain flour	Water	Simmering time
Buckwheat groats	2 Tbsp	1¼ cups	5 minutes
Oats (whole rolled)	2 Tbsp	¾ cup	5 minutes
Quinoa	2 Tbsp	1¼ cups	8 minutes

Oats   Quinoa   Buckwheat groats

CHAPTER TWO

finger foods

Roasted Sweet Potato Fries

MAKES: 4 TODDLER-SIZE SERVINGS

PREP TIME: 5 MINUTES

COOK TIME: 30 MINUTES

1 small sweet potato

½ Tbsp virgin coconut oil, melted

Pinch of ground cinnamon
(optional)

> I think coconut oil really complements the sweet potatoes.

We make at least one batch of these per week, and they are always gobbled up. Because they're so soft, they're a perfect finger food for new eaters, but they also can be served as part of a family meal. Sweet potatoes are incredibly rich in vitamin A and a good source of vitamin C, and are very easy to cook, so making these little orange-hued fries a staple in your child's diet is a win-win for everyone.

1. Preheat the oven to 375°F.

2. Peel the sweet potato and slice it into sticks approximately ¼ inch wide and 2 inches long. Don't make them too thin or they'll be too floppy to hold once cooked.

3. Spread out the fries on a baking tray, drizzle them with the coconut oil, and sprinkle them with the cinnamon. Use a spatula to stir the fries and flip them over to coat in the oil.

4. Bake for approximately 30 minutes, turning the fries over once halfway through the cooking time. When done, they should be soft and not overly charred. These keep well in the refrigerator for a few days. Reheat in the oven at 350°F for approximately 5 minutes.

Mini Roasted Cauliflower Florets

MAKES: 2 TODDLER-SIZE SERVINGS

PREP TIME: 5 MINUTES

COOK TIME: 25 MINUTES

1 cup small cauliflower florets

1 tsp virgin coconut oil, melted

½ tsp nutritional yeast (for
non-dairy) or 1 tsp grated
Parmesan cheese (optional)

When cooked, cauliflower has a mild, slightly sweet flavor that is very palatable for little ones. Roasted cauliflower florets are soft but easy to hold, so they're an excellent finger food. Add some nutritional yeast (which is a good source of B vitamins) or a sprinkle of Parmesan cheese for extra flavor.

1. Preheat the oven to 375°F.

2. In a bowl, mix together the cauliflower, oil, and, if using, the nutritional yeast or Parmesan cheese.

3. Spread out in a glass baking dish just large enough to hold everything without crowding and roast, uncovered, for approximately 25 minutes (stirring gently halfway through) until the cauliflower is soft and starting to brown. Leftovers can be stored in the refrigerator for a couple of days and are best reheated in the oven. Around 5 minutes at 350°F should do it.

Lentil Bake Bites

MAKES: 12 TODDLER-SIZE SERVINGS

PREP TIME: 40 MINUTES

COOK TIME: 35 MINUTES

½ cup dry red lentils

1½ Tbsp flax meal

1 Tbsp virgin coconut oil

½ onion, very small dice

1 clove garlic

½ celery stalk, very small dice

½ cup grated carrot

½ cup finely chopped kale, stems discarded

½ tsp dried thyme

½ tsp dried basil

½ cup quick oats ("pure" or certified gluten-free oats if you are avoiding gluten)

¼ cup oat flour

2 tsp nutritional yeast

> This makes an excellent portable lunch for grown-ups too. Just cut it up into bars rather than bite-size pieces.

This vegan savory lentil bake is rich in protein, iron, and B vitamins and is so moreish you'll be stealing some for your lunch. It holds together really well, but is nice and soft for new eaters. *(Photo on inside cover)*

1. Preheat the oven to 375°F and line an 8- × 8-inch baking dish with two pieces of parchment paper crossed on top of each other to form a sort of sling contraption. This will allow you to lift the entire thing out and lay it flat for cutting.

2. Give the lentils a good rinse, picking out any bits of grit, then put them in a pot with 2 cups of water.

3. Bring to a boil over high heat, then turn the heat to medium-low and simmer, uncovered, until soft, approximately 20 minutes.

4. In a large bowl, combine the flax meal with 3 tablespoons of water. Set aside to allow the mixture to thicken.

5. Meanwhile, in a skillet over medium heat, heat the oil, then sauté the onion, garlic, celery, carrot, kale, thyme, and basil for approximately 7 minutes, until the veggies are soft. Pour into a large bowl with the flax and mix to combine.

6. When the lentils are tender, drain them, then puree in a blender or a food processor fitted with the steel blade until smooth.

7. Add the lentils to the veggies, along with the oats, oat flour, and nutritional yeast. The mixture should be quite thick and not at all runny. Add some extra oat flour if necessary.

8. Press the mixture into the pan and smooth it out with a lightly oiled spatula.

9. Bake for 35 minutes. The mixture should be firm to the touch but not overly browned.

10. Allow to cool in the pan for a good 15 minutes before cutting. This will ensure that everything holds together.

11. Serve to your baby in little bite-size squares. Slice leftovers into single-serving-size bars and freeze in an airtight container with parchment or wax paper between the layers. To eat, gently thaw a bar in the oven, then cut into bite-size pieces. Reheat in a 350°F oven for 5–10 minutes, or simply enjoy at room temperature if you're on the go.

Sweet and Savory Quinoa Bakes

MAKES: 36 QUINOA BAKES

PREP TIME: 20 MINUTES

COOK TIME: 15 MINUTES

1 medium-size sweet variety of apple, peeled and grated

1½ cups cooked quinoa

1 cup grated butternut squash

1 cup grated cheddar cheese

¼ small onion, finely minced

2 Tbsp dark raisins, minced

1 egg

¼ tsp ground sage

Quinoa is one of my favorite superfood ingredients. It's gluten-free, gentle on little tummies, and a vegetarian source of complete protein. These soft bites hold together well in little hands, then break up easily in the mouth, so they're perfect for babies who're just getting the hang of eating finger foods. Full of nutritious fall ingredients like apples, butternut squash, and sage, they make a well-balanced lunch or a handy on-the-go snack. They're also perfect as a quick bite for busy moms—so feel free to dig in too!

1. Preheat the oven to 400°F and line a baking tray with parchment paper.

2. Gather the grated apple in your hands and give it a good squeeze over the sink to drain it. Put it in a large bowl along with all the other ingredients.

3. Mix until fully combined.

4. Scoop out tablespoon-size portions of the quinoa mixture and carefully place them on the prepared baking tray in neat little mounds.

5. Bake in the oven for 15 minutes until the bites look golden and the edges are just starting to darken. Serve at room temperature or slightly warm. You can freeze these on a baking tray, then transfer to a freezer bag or airtight container and freeze for up to 3 months. These reheat best if gently warmed in the oven at 350°F for 10–15 minutes. Serve slightly cooled to ensure they hold together well.

Not Your Mama's Meatloaf

MAKES: 24 MINI MEATLOAVES

PREP TIME: 40 MINUTES

COOK TIME: 20 MINUTES

FOR THE MEATLOAVES

2 tsp virgin coconut oil + extra to grease the pan

1 small onion, finely minced

1 garlic clove, crushed

1 lb extra-lean ground beef

1 small sweet potato, peeled and grated

1 egg

½ cup blanched almond meal

1 Tbsp tomato paste

1 Tbsp tamari or coconut aminos

1 Tbsp flaxseeds

1 Tbsp finely minced fresh basil

¼ tsp ground cloves

½ tsp ground cinnamon

½ tsp ground ginger

FOR THE GLAZE

1 Tbsp tomato paste

1 Tbsp tamari

1 tsp pure maple syrup

These individually portioned mini meatloaf "muffins" are easy for self-feeders to hold, and thanks to the power-packed sweet potato, they are soft and break up easily in toothless little mouths. The almond meal and flaxseeds add an extra boost of fiber and other goodness, but you'd never even know they were there. Prepare a batch of these to keep in your freezer and gently warm for an easy meal. And because the recipe is made without bread crumbs or other grain products, these little loaves are perfect for children with a gluten-free or grain-free diet.

1. Preheat the oven to 400°F and grease the cups of a 24-cup mini muffin pan. Be a little heavy-handed to ensure your meatloaves don't stick.

2. For the meatloaves, in a skillet over medium heat, sauté the onion in the coconut oil for approximately 5 minutes, stirring frequently until translucent.

3. Add the garlic and cook for 1 minute more.

4. Transfer to a large mixing bowl. Technically you could skip the step of pre-cooking the onion and garlic, but I think it really improves the flavor and texture, so it's worth the extra few minutes.

5. Add all the other meatloaf ingredients and mix to combine. You may find that using your hands is the most efficient way of doing this. Let stand for 10 minutes to allow the flaxseeds to absorb some moisture.

6. Now you have no real choice but to get messy. Using your hands, put globs of the mixture in the cups of the muffin pan, gently pressing it in to fill the cups. Fill so that the meat just rounds over the top of each cup.

7. For the glaze, in a small bowl, mix together the tomato paste, tamari, and maple syrup.

8. Using a pastry brush, brush the glaze over each meatloaf muffin. Be careful not to get the glaze on the pan itself or else it will burn and really stick.

9. Bake in the oven for approximately 20 minutes, until the meatloaves are cooked through. If you would like to be extra-careful because you're feeding this to a baby, you can use a meat thermometer to check that the internal temperature of the meatloaves is 160°F.

10. Allow to sit for 10 minutes. Run a butter knife around the edge of each meatloaf to loosen it from the pan. Serve warm. Store in the refrigerator for a couple of days, or freeze in an airtight container for up to 3 months. Reheat in a 350°F oven for approximately 15 minutes.

These mini meatloaves aren't just for babies and toddlers. Serve them as part of a family meal, at a child's party, or even as a cute yet hearty canapé at a grown-up party. They will appeal to all ages.

Baked Tofu Sticks

MAKES: 2 TODDLER-SIZE SERVINGS

PREP TIME: 20 MINUTES

COOK TIME: 15 MINUTES

¼ block of medium-firm organic tofu (approximately 4 oz)

1 tsp tamari or coconut aminos

1 tsp virgin coconut oil, melted

½ tsp nutritional yeast

The idea of these is that they are really soft for new eaters, so I use medium-firm tofu. If you're making this for the family and your baby has teeth, you may want to buy firm or extra-firm.

1. Preheat the oven to 400°F and line a rimmed baking tray with parchment paper.

2. Cut up the tofu into little baby pinkie–size sticks and lay them out on the tray.

3. Combine the tamari with the coconut oil and nutritional yeast.

4. Using a pastry brush, coat the tofu with the tamari mixture. Turn the tofu over and brush the other side too.

5. Bake in the oven for 15 minutes. Serve warm. These will keep in an airtight container in the refrigerator for a few days. Reheat in the oven at 350°F for 5 minutes.

Tender Stewed Beef

MAKES: 4 BABY-SIZE SERVINGS

PREP TIME: 15 MINUTES

COOK TIME: 2 HOURS

5 oz stewing beef

1 cup unsweetened apple juice

Moms tell me all the time that it can be hard to get a baby or toddler to eat meat. I suspect this is mainly because the texture is difficult for them. Imagine as an adult trying to eat a chewy piece of meat with no molars! My goal when creating this recipe was for the meat to break apart easily, so that a baby with no teeth could gum it down without any trouble. I'm pleased to tell you that this is exactly what happens! The magic ingredient is the apple juice. Combined with the long length of cooking, it tenderizes the meat, making it just the right texture for new meat eaters.

1. Preheat the oven to 325°F.

2. Chop the beef into ½-inch cubes and put it into an oven-safe pot or casserole dish that has a tight-fitting lid.

3. Pour the apple juice and 1 cup water over the beef. Cover tightly and bake for 2 hours.

4. Remove the beef from the liquid with a slotted spoon to cool.

5. To serve, use a fork to tear the beef into very small pieces and serve to your baby as a finger food. Save a small amount of the cooking liquid for storing any extra beef in the refrigerator. To reheat, gently warm on the stove in the reserved liquid.

Kale Pesto Salmon Sticks

MAKES: 12 SALMON STICKS

PREP TIME: 30 MINUTES

COOK TIME: 6 MINUTES

FOR THE SALMON STICKS

7–8 oz fillet of wild salmon

¾ cup lightly packed very finely minced kale, stems discarded

1 slice of your favorite multigrain sandwich bread

1 egg

1 scant Tbsp virgin coconut oil for frying

FOR THE PESTO

½ cup fresh basil leaves, lightly packed

¼ cup grated Parmesan cheese

⅛ cup pine nuts (or hemp hearts or other nuts like walnuts if you prefer)

1 small clove garlic

1 Tbsp olive oil

In my experience it is a myth that babies prefer bland food, and I really believe it's helpful to get little ones used to big flavors at an early age. The bold taste of pesto is often a favorite with kids and it goes with so much more than pasta. Here it takes salmon to a whole new level. In fact, my husband, John, liked these so much he was happy to eat them for dinner for several days while I perfected the recipe.

1. Preheat the oven to 400°F.

2. Cut a rectangle of parchment paper that is twice as long as, and slightly wider than, the salmon fillet. Place the fillet on one end of the rectangle, fold the other half over, then roll up all the sides to make a sealed package. Put on a baking tray and bake in the oven for 12 minutes.

3. Put the minced kale in a large bowl and set aside.

4. Use a food processer or blender to turn the bread into rough bread crumbs. Add to the kale and mix to combine.

5. Now it's time to make the pesto. Using a food processor fitted with the steel blade or a blender, blend the basil, cheese, pine nuts, garlic, and olive oil. Pause it a few times and use a spatula to scrape the mixture down the sides into the container, then blend until the pine nuts are ground to the consistency of coarse flour. Add the pesto to the kale and bread crumbs. Stir to combine.

6. When the salmon is cooked, remove the fillet from its skin and place it in a bowl. Use a fork to flake it into very small pieces, checking carefully for any small bones. Add the salmon to the kale mixture.

7. Finally, add the egg and stir until very well combined.

8. Use your hands to form the mixture into pinkie-length sticks approximately 1½ inches wide. Place them on a tray or plate.

9. Put the coconut oil in a skillet and heat on medium-high. When the oil is hot, fry the salmon sticks for approximately 3 minutes on each side until brown and crispy. Drain on paper towel before serving. Serve warm. Freeze leftover salmon sticks on a tray, then transfer to a freezer bag or airtight container and freeze for up to 3 months. Reheat gently in the oven at 350°F for 10–15 minutes.

Cam's Pesto and Pea Omelet

MAKES: 1 TODDLER-SIZE SERVING
PREP TIME: 2 MINUTES
COOK TIME: 5 MINUTES

1 egg

1 tsp of your favorite store-bought pesto (or try my Superfood Pesto, page 244)

½ tsp virgin coconut oil, ghee, or butter

2 Tbsp frozen peas

Cam may quite literally have eaten this omelet a hundred times, and I don't see any signs of him giving it up anytime soon—even though he's past the stage of needing finger foods. It's quick to make, so I know I can get it on the table in a high-pressure, hungry-child situation, when we've come in late from a busy morning. Eggs are protein- and iron-rich, so they are an excellent option for kids like Cam who aren't big meat eaters. This also makes a replenishing meal for busy moms, so double the recipe and join your little one for lunch.

1. In a small bowl, using a fork, whisk the egg with the pesto.

2. Add the oil and peas to a small skillet, and cook for approximately 1 minute on medium-high heat until the peas are thawed.

3. Add the egg and let cook for a minute or so to let the bottom firm up. Using a spatula, gently lift the edges, tilting the pan to allow uncooked egg to run to the bottom of the pan and become cooked. Once no more egg runs to the edges, gently lift the omelet and carefully turn it over. If it breaks, don't worry. You'll be cutting it up anyway. Allow to cook for 1 minute longer, then cut into bite-size pieces to serve.

If you can't be bothered with making an omelet just scramble the eggs. We all know they'll taste just the same. Try to leave some big pieces that your child can easily pick up.

Chicken, Apricot, and Fresh Herb Patties

MAKES: 18 PATTIES
PREP TIME: 1 HOUR
COOK TIME: 12 MINUTES

8 dried unsulfured apricots

Small handful cilantro leaves (avoid the stems if you can)

4 boneless skinless chicken thighs (or 10.5 oz ground chicken thighs)

1 tsp chia seeds

¼ cup quick oats ("pure" or certified gluten-free oats if you are avoiding gluten)

¼ tsp ground cumin

I use a food processor to make these flavorful patties, which makes the whole process really simple. There are no eggs or bread crumbs in this recipe, so they're ideal for little ones with food intolerances. Serve all on their own or in a little slider bun (see Little Spelt Buns, page 242).

1. Put the dried apricots in a small bowl and cover them with hot water. Allow to rehydrate for approximately 15 minutes.

2. Drain the apricots, chop them into rough pieces, then put them in the food processor with the cilantro.

3. Put the raw chicken thighs in the food processor, then blend until the chicken looks ground. Add the chia seeds, the quick oats, and the cumin and blend for another 30 seconds or so until everything looks fully combined.

4. Put the mixture in the refrigerator for at least 30 minutes to allow the chia seeds and oats to hydrate and set.

5. When ready to bake the patties, preheat the oven to 400°F and line a baking tray with parchment paper.

6. Using your hands, form 18 small, ¼-inch-thick patties and lay them out on the tray. You'll want to use just under 1 tablespoon of the mixture per patty.

7. Bake for 12 minutes, turning the patties halfway through. When cooked, they will be opaque with patches of darker brown caramelization. Freeze these on a tray, then transfer to a freezer bag or airtight container to freeze for up to 3 months. Warm gently in the oven at 350°F for 10–15 minutes.

If you're not a big cilantro fan, mint or fresh basil also work well in this recipe. Or use a combination of the three!

♥

Older kids might like these with tamari as a dipping sauce.

"Inclusive" Mini Quinoa and Prune Muffins

MAKES: 24 MUFFINS

PREP TIME: 20 MINUTES

COOK TIME: 20 MINUTES

⅓ cup virgin coconut oil, melted, + extra to grease the pan

½ cup pitted prunes

1 cup non-dairy milk

⅓ cup maple syrup

1 tsp pure vanilla extract

1¼ cups quinoa flour

¼ cup arrowroot flour

1 Tbsp ground flaxseed

1½ tsp baking powder

½ tsp baking soda

Allergies and food intolerances can be a big concern for parents (see page 61). These little muffins are not only nutritious and packed full of protein from the quinoa, but also really soft and tasty, and free from the most common allergens. As an added bonus, they contain prunes and flaxseeds for added fiber which will benefit little ones who are having oh-so-common constipation issues. These are perfect to pack for day care or to serve at a party because they really are an "inclusive" muffin that almost anyone can enjoy.

1. Preheat the oven to 350°F. Grease the cups of a mini muffin pan or insert paper liners.

2. Soak the prunes in hot water for 10 minutes, then drain.

3. In a blender, blitz the non-dairy milk, coconut oil, maple syrup, prunes, and vanilla until smooth. If your blender isn't very powerful you may want to cut up the prunes before blending.

4. Combine the quinoa flour, arrowroot flour, flaxseed, baking powder, and baking soda in a large bowl.

5. Pour the mixture from the blender into the bowl and stir to combine. It will start to become fluffy and thick quite quickly.

6. Fill the muffin cups to almost full and bake in the oven for 20 minutes. The muffins will be quite brown but when torn in half will be pillowy soft on the inside. Allow to cool for a few minutes in the pan, then transfer to a cooling rack to cool completely. Freeze in an airtight container with parchment between layers or in a single layer in a freezer bag for up to 3 months.

Spelt Pancakes with Cheese and Broccoli

MAKES: 12 PANCAKES
PREP TIME: 15 MINUTES
COOK TIME: 15 MINUTES

1½ cups spelt flour

1½ tsp baking powder

2 eggs

¾ cup plain Greek yogurt

½ cup milk

1 Tbsp virgin coconut oil, butter, or ghee, melted, plus extra for frying

1 cup grated cheddar cheese

1 cup very finely chopped broccoli florets

Try using the pancakes in place of bread for a little cheese and tomato sandwich.

These fluffy, savory pancakes are made with Greek yogurt and eggs for an added kick of protein. I made these regularly for Poppy when she was a toddler, cutting them into quarters as an easy, portable finger food.

1. In a large bowl, combine the flour and baking powder.

2. In a separate bowl, whisk together the eggs, yogurt, milk, and the tablespoon of oil.

3. Pour the wet ingredients into the dry and stir together until just mixed. Allow to sit for 5 minutes.

4. Add the cheese and broccoli and stir to combine. The batter will be a bit thicker than typical pancake batter.

5. Warm a skillet or griddle over medium heat, and melt a small amount of oil in the pan. I find that medium-high heat will burn these pancakes because of the cheese, so it is better to go for a lower heat and cook a little longer on each side than would be typical with regular pancakes.

6. Once the pan is hot, pour out ¼-cup portions of the batter into the pan. Cook for 4 minutes on the first side, then flip over and cook for 3 minutes on the second side. You will know it's time to flip when bubbles start to break through the surface on the first side.

7. Serve cut into quarters, strips, or bite-size pieces. No sauce or dip required! Freeze these in an airtight container, with parchment between layers, for up to 3 months. Reheat in the toaster, or at 350°F in the oven for 5–10 minutes.

Hard Teething Biscuits

MAKES: 18 BISCUITS

PREP TIME: 20 MINUTES + 24 HOURS
TO HARDEN

COOK TIME: 1 HOUR

2 cups light spelt flour

1 tsp baking powder

1 medium-size ripe banana

2 Tbsp virgin coconut oil, melted

1 tsp pure vanilla extract

Try giving one of these biscuits to your baby slightly cold for extra relief for sore gums. Take a biscuit out of the freezer and let it sit at room temperature until it is comfortable for your baby to hold, but still cold enough to have the desired effect.

When your baby's gums are sore and baby is being fussy, chewing on something hard can provide much-needed relief—and not only for the baby. These biscuits dry out into firm, easy-to-hold breadstick-like biscuits, so they are ideal for babies with few teeth and sore gums. Of course, no biscuit is 100 percent unbreakable, so it is important to always seat your baby upright and supervise her when you're feeding these so you can react quickly if a piece does break off.

I created this recipe with very few ingredients—and no eggs or dairy—so that the biscuits can be given to babies who don't yet have much experience with a variety of foods. Instead of whole wheat flour I have used spelt, but you can substitute whole wheat if you like. And of course, because these are for babies, they have no added sugar, which makes them quite different from most store-bought teething cookies.

1. Preheat the oven to 300°F and line a baking tray with parchment paper.

2. Combine the flour and baking powder in a mixing bowl.

3. In a blender, blend the banana with the coconut oil and vanilla until smooth.

4. Pour the blended banana mixture over the flour and baking powder. Use a spoon to mix until just combined then use your hands to work the mixture into a nice smooth ball of dough. If it is sticky at all at this point, add a little more flour.

5. Squeeze off tablespoon-size balls of dough and roll them in your hands to form sausage shapes 4 inches long and 1 inch wide. Place them on the tray and press down so that they are approximately 1½ inches wide.

6. Bake in the oven for 1 hour, flipping them halfway through.

7. Once cooked, transfer to a cooling rack and let sit in the open air for at least 24 hours. This will allow the biscuits to become really nice and hard. You'll know they're hard enough when you can hit them firmly against the counter without breaking them. These will keep well in an airtight container at room temperature or can be frozen in a freezer bag or airtight container for up to 3 months.

CHAPTER THREE

smoothies

THE VITAMIN VEHICLE

There is no better vehicle than a smoothie for getting vitamins into your kids, and for encouraging them to believe that green foods taste good. In our house, smoothies are part of our daily breakfast routine and I truly believe they are responsible for my kids' belief that kale and spinach are a good idea. When Poppy and Cam are sick and are refusing other food, they always accept smoothies. It gives me peace of mind to know they're getting the nutrients their bodies need to recover, so I worry less about how they haven't eaten a proper dinner in 3 days! Try these simple, superfood-packed recipes for guaranteed smoothie love, or get creative and make up your own, using the handy guide on pages 126–127.

General Tips for Making Smoothies

♥ The smoothie recipes here make approximately 2 cups, enough for 2 children to share, or for one big smoothie for a hungry grown-up. If you're making a smoothie for only one younger child, simply cut the recipe in half. Smoothies will last for a few hours in the refrigerator but aren't something you can blend up ahead of time for the week: they don't store well for long.

♥ For each of these recipes all you need to do is blend the ingredients together. But here's an important tip: put the liquid in the blender before any solid ingredients. This will make pureeing much easier on your blender and less frustrating for you. Pulse the blender to get things started, then blend all the ingredients together for a minute or so on high power until smooth.

Chocolate Sweet Potato Pie (page 128)

♥ Smoothies are best if some of the ingredients are frozen. The frozen ingredients make smoothies perfectly chilled and give them a slightly thicker consistency. I keep bags of frozen chopped fruit, like mangoes, strawberries, blueberries, and bananas, in my freezer all year round, just for smoothies. But if you don't have frozen bananas or frozen blueberries as called for in the recipe, don't worry—just add a few ice cubes with the other ingredients and you'll get a similar result. (And where other recipes in this book call for, say, half an avocado or banana, remember to freeze the rest for smoothies.)

♥ Dairy or non-dairy milk work equally well for any recipe in this chapter that calls for milk. I used almond milk when I tested these with a non-dairy milk, but feel free to use hemp, coconut, or whatever milk you are used to.

♥ Medjool dates are suggested as a sweetener in many of the recipes. If you don't have Medjool dates you can use Deglet Nour or just regular dried dates; however, you may have to add an extra date or two because Medjool dates tend to be much larger and are also very sweet compared to other varieties.

♥ Many of these recipes contain vegetables, but that's not because I think veggies should be hidden from your children! There is no better opportunity to convince your child that veggies taste good than through a smoothie. Have your kids help put the spinach in the blender. When they taste the delicious result, they'll be one step closer to believing that they love vegetables.

♥ You'll notice that only one of these smoothies has "juice" as an ingredient. This is no accident. Juice, particularly mass-produced juice, is high in natural sugars and not much else. A few years ago I started using whole fruits and vegetables and water or non-dairy milk, rather than juice, in my smoothies and I haven't looked back.

♥ If smoothies are a big part of your life, I recommend buying the most high-powered blender you can afford. A powerful blender makes such a difference to the speed of making a smoothie and the final texture. I'd rather have a bunch of other inexpensive kitchen appliances and blow my budget on a good blender. That's how important I think they are!

♥ Many of these smoothie recipes can moonlight as Popsicle recipes! If you have leftover smoothie, pour it into a Popsicle mold and freeze for a refreshing afternoon snack or healthy dessert.

♥ Make smoothies more special by investing in some fun glasses and attractive paper or reusable straws. Straws are a better option for children's teeth than drinking from a sippy cup, and they can make smoothies much more enticing.

♥ As soon as your little one can use a straw or sip from an open cup, they can drink smoothies. Just be sure to offer a variety of other types of food as well so they don't get accustomed to only drinking their meals.

♥ Feel like trying your hand at creating your own smoothie recipes? Use the simple guide on the following page as a jumping-off point. As long as you stick to the suggested measurements and use common sense about which flavorings go together, you can't go far wrong.

The Smooth-o-matic

Take it for a whirl!

Creating your own tasty and nutritious smoothies is easy! Follow these simple instructions and concoct your own family favorites. Kids will enjoy following the steps to come up with their own recipes, so get them involved! These will make approximately 2 cups.

START HERE!

liquid

START WITH 1–1½ CUPS OF LIQUID:

Water

Coconut water

Non-dairy milk (almond, hemp, cashew, coconut)

Organic whole dairy milk

Unsweetened all-natural juice (if you decide to use juice, remember that it is high in natural sugars and dilute it with water by at least half)

fruit

CHOOSE ½–1 CUP CHOPPED FRESH OR FROZEN FRUIT, JUST ONE TYPE OR A FEW IN COMBINATION:

Apples	Peaches
Bananas	Pears
Blueberries	Pineapple
Cherries	Raspberries
Kiwi	Strawberries
Mangoes	Watermelon

healthy fats

HEALTHY FATS ARE SUCH AN IMPORTANT PART OF OUR CHILDREN'S DIET. ALWAYS ADD 1 TABLESPOON OF ONE OF THESE:

Avocado

Cold-pressed flax oil

Virgin coconut oil

Grass-fed ghee

Nut or seed butters

veggies

DON'T FORGET TO ADD VEGGIES! START WITH ⅓ CUP, SHREDDED OR CHOPPED, AND WORK UP TO MORE (2 CUPS OF GREENS ARE COMPLETELY DOABLE!) AS YOUR FAMILY GETS USED TO MORE VEGGIE-RICH SMOOTHIES:

Beets (root and greens)

Broccoli

Butternut squash (cooked)

Carrots

Chard

Cucumber

Kale

Parsley

Pea shoots

Rhubarb

Romaine lettuce

Spinach

Sweet potato (cooked)

extras

TO MAKE YOUR SMOOTHIE EXTRA-SUPER, ADD A SMALL AMOUNT OF ONE OR MORE OF THESE POWER-PACKED INGREDIENTS AND FLAVORINGS:

Acai

Baobab powder

Chia seeds

Chlorella powder

Cinnamon

Flaxseeds

Ginger

Goji berries

Hemp hearts

Lemon or lime juice (fresh)

Mint leaves (fresh)

Moringa powder

Nutmeg

Nuts

Probiotics

Quinoa (cooked)

Spirulina powder

Tofu (organic)

Turmeric

Vanilla

Wheatgrass powder

Whole-milk yogurt

(You may have other favorites in this category. Add what you love!)

sweeteners

IF YOU PREFER A SWEETER SMOOTHIE, ADD A TOUCH OF THESE NATURAL SWEETENERS:

Dates

Honey

Maple syrup

Your other favorite all-natural, unprocessed liquid sweeteners

THROW IN SOME ICE CUBES IF YOU LIKE IT EXTRA-FROSTY! BLEND, POUR INTO A GLASS, AND ENJOY!

On the following pages are some of my family's favorite combinations to get you started.

Rasp-Peary Dream

The flavor of pears and raspberries balance perfectly and the avocado makes this combination extra-creamy. The quinoa kicks up the protein and fiber in your morning smoothie.

1¼ cups almond milk or dairy milk

1 tsp honey or maple syrup (for plant-based)

⅔ cup frozen raspberries

⅓ cup cooked quinoa

1 ripe pear, cored and chopped (no need to peel)

¼ ripe avocado (freeze leftovers, see page 88)

Summer Slushy

This recipe requires a very powerful blender. Once blended, it is very much like a sorbet and is best eaten with a spoon. If your blender is more lightweight, use fresh rather than frozen fruit and add some ice cubes. This will result in a thinner consistency.

½ cup water

1 cup frozen peaches

1 cup frozen blueberries

Chocolate Sweet Potato Pie

Perfect for using up leftover sweet potatoes, this creamy smoothie is rich in vitamins and is a full meal all on its own.

1 cup dairy or non-dairy milk

2 tsp virgin coconut oil

½ small roasted sweet potato (⅓–½ cup mashed)

1 ripe frozen banana

1–2 pitted Medjool dates

1 tsp unsweetened cocoa powder or raw cacao

½-inch piece of fresh turmeric, peeled (optional)

Pinch of freshly grated nutmeg

Pinch of ground cinnamon

PB & J in a Glass

It's so exciting when I have a recipe idea that seems a bit far-fetched but ends up being both a success and a favorite. I ended up absolutely loving this recipe—and I know any PB & J fans will too.

1½ cups dairy or non-dairy milk

1 tsp honey or maple syrup (for plant-based)

Handful of ice

2 Tbsp smooth natural unsweetened peanut butter

1 cup seedless red grapes

¼ cup cooked quinoa

Apple Cinnamon Green Smoothie

My children definitely each have a few favorite smoothies, and this one belongs to Poppy. It tastes much like apple crumble with toasted almond topping. Just yum. A big glass makes for a hearty one-stop breakfast that lasts her through until snack time.

1 cup dairy or non-dairy milk

¼ cup Greek yogurt

1½ Tbsp almond butter

A few ice cubes

1 apple, roughly chopped, unpeeled is fine (choose a sweet variety)

2 pitted Medjool dates

1 cup spinach leaves

Pinch of ground cinnamon

Cu-Kale-Melon Smoothie

Watermelon and cucumber are a match made in heaven and kale gives an extra punch of nutrition. This light and fresh smoothie is perfect on a hot summer's day.

⅔ cup water

Juice of ½ lime

1½ tsp honey or maple syrup (for plant-based)

A few ice cubes

2 cups chopped watermelon

1 cup lightly packed kale leaves, stems discarded

2-inch piece cucumber, roughly chopped (don't worry about discarding skins or seeds)

Purple Greens

OK, thanks to the spinach, this smoothie isn't the prettiest shade of purple, but it tastes delicious and is a perfect on-the-go breakfast option. Yogurt works well in this, so feel free to add some if you like it creamy and are OK with dairy.

1 cup water

¼ cup plain yogurt (omit for dairy-free)

1 tsp honey or maple syrup (for plant-based)

1 banana

1 cup baby spinach

½ cup frozen blueberries

½ cup diced pineapple (can be fresh, frozen, or unsweetened canned pineapple)

¼ ripe avocado (freeze leftovers, see page 88)

Omega Monkey Milkshake

I promise you that everyone in your family will love this smoothie. It tastes just like a milkshake, but is full of healthy fats—perfect for developing brains—and will meet the requirements of even the pickiest eaters.

1½ cups dairy or non-dairy milk

1 Tbsp flax oil

¼ cup almond butter

1 ripe frozen banana

2 pitted Medjool dates

⅛ cup hemp hearts and/or chia seeds

1½ tsp unsweetened cocoa powder or raw cacao

Poppy's Chocolate Green Smoothie

Poppy asks for this smoothie every single morning, and because it's full of power foods like spinach and flax oil, I'm more than happy to make it for her. She's so convinced that spinach is an integral part of the design that she gets upset if we're out and can't include it. Now that is an indication of a really good green smoothie recipe.

1½ cups dairy or non-dairy milk

1 Tbsp flax oil

1 Tbsp almond butter

1 ripe frozen banana

1½ cups spinach

1½ tsp unsweetened cocoa powder or raw cacao

2 pitted Medjool dates

Berry Beety

This smoothie is a gorgeous vibrant pink color and is really bright and refreshing. It's a great way to show children the beauty in beets.

1 cup water

½–1 tsp honey or maple syrup (for plant-based)

¾ cup frozen blueberries

1 small peeled and diced orange (pits removed)

1 very small beet, peeled and grated

Green Freshy

This is a true green smoothie, and there is no way of hiding the vegetables. But it tastes amazing, so if you can convince your child to have even one sip, they'll become a believer.

¾ cup water

¾ cup unsweetened pure apple juice

1 cup lightly packed shredded kale, stems discarded

½ cup chopped broccoli florets

½ cup frozen mango chunks

Cam's Favorite Pink Smoothie

If it were up to my son, Cam, all smoothies would be pink. This pretty classic is his all-time favorite.

1½ cups dairy or non-dairy milk

¼ cup Greek yogurt

½ Tbsp flax oil

1 tsp honey (optional)

1 frozen banana

½ cup strawberries, fresh or frozen

Berry Beety   **Green Freshy**   **Cam's Favorite Pink Smoothie**

CHAPTER FOUR

superhero breakfasts

TO KEEP THEM GOING

(AND GOING!)

Toasted Banana and Avocado Sandwich

SERVES: 1–2 CHILDREN

PREP TIME: 5 MINUTES

2 slices multigrain bread (or gluten-free, if you prefer)

½ small ripe banana (freeze leftovers, see page 88)

¼ soft avocado (freeze leftovers, see page 88)

Drizzle of honey (omit for plant-based)

When my kids were babies, I often blended bananas and avocados to make an easy puree. Now that they're bigger, I still mash banana and avocado together, but now I spread them on toast for a quick and nutritious big-kid breakfast.

1. Toast the bread.

2. Meanwhile, use a fork to mash together the banana and avocado.

3. Spread thickly onto one piece of toast and drizzle with the honey if using.

4. Top with the other slice of toast and cut into quarters. Serve!

> Try this open-faced. My kids like it both ways. It depends on their mood that day!

Apple, Carrot, and Almond Butter Wrap

SERVES: 1–2 CHILDREN

PREP TIME: 10 MINUTES

½ cup peeled, grated apple (choose a sweet variety like Gala)

¼ cup grated carrot

Small pinch of ground cinnamon

½ tsp maple syrup (optional)

1 whole-grain tortilla wrap (gluten-free, if you prefer)

1½ Tbsp almond butter

This is a great way to get some vegetables into your little one first thing in the morning. Cam likes this wrap so much he requests it regularly.

1. Place the apple, carrot, and cinnamon in a small bowl and mix together. Stir in the maple syrup if using.

2. In a large skillet, toast the tortilla on medium-high heat for approximately 1 minute on each side.

3. Spread the almond butter over the warm tortilla and top with the apple and carrot mixture.

4. Roll up and cut in half to serve.

> If your family is avoiding nuts due to allergies, seed butters also taste delicious in this recipe.

Banana Boats

SERVES: 1–2 CHILDREN

PREP TIME: 5 MINUTES (10 IF YOU MAKE THE SAILS)

2 tsp crispy rice cereal

2 tsp almond butter

¼ tsp honey or maple syrup
(for plant-based)

1 banana

1 heaping tsp dark raisins
(optional)

Surprise your kids with these stuffed banana boats for breakfast and you'll earn big smiles even early in the morning. This fun dish is also great as an after-school snack.

1. In a small bowl, mix together the cereal, almond butter, and honey.

2. Peel the banana, then slice lengthwise, but don't slice right down to the bottom. You don't want two separate halves.

3. Using a small spoon, fill the inside of the banana with the almond butter mixture.

4. Place a line of raisins (if using) down the length of the banana, on top of the almond butter mixture.

5. Cut in half to serve and eat by hand.

Mini Muffin Frittatas

MAKES: 12

PREP TIME: 10 MINUTES

COOK TIME: 8–9 MINUTES

Virgin coconut oil or butter, to grease the pan

3 eggs

½ cup total of a mixture of:
Small pieces natural ham or cooked bacon, your family's favorite grated cheese, crumbled feta or goat cheese, finely chopped kale or spinach, grated zucchini, peas (fresh or defrosted frozen peas), quartered cherry tomatoes, fresh herbs like basil or parsley, finely chopped mushrooms, finely chopped broccoli florets

Kids love food that is bite-size and easy to hold. These little frittatas baked in a mini muffin pan cook up in no time and are the perfect base for all sorts of customizable add-ins. *(Photo on inside cover)*

1. Preheat the oven to 400°F and use a heavy hand to grease the cups of a 12-cup mini muffin pan with virgin coconut oil or butter.

2. Whisk the eggs.

3. Stir in your add-ins of choice.

4. Use a spoon to fill the muffin cups with the egg mixture to approximately two-thirds full.

5. Bake in the oven for 8–9 minutes.

6. Run a butter knife around the edges to release the mini frittatas from the pan.

7. Serve warm. No forks or knives required. These lovelies can be enjoyed beyond breakfast. Save any leftovers for up to 2 days in the refrigerator. Reheat gently in the oven for 5 minutes at 350°F.

To make these banana boats into sailboats, make these simple paper sails. Fold one edge of a triangle of paper around a Popsicle stick. Secure the paper with a bit of glue or tape and press the stick into the banana. Ahoy there, matey!

Egg Person Toast

SERVES: 1 CHILD

PREP TIME: 5 MINUTES

COOK TIME: 3 MINUTES

1 egg

½ tsp virgin coconut oil or butter

1 slice of your favorite bread
(gluten-free if you prefer)

½ tsp butter or vegan butter
spread

Did you know you can make eggs look like specific shapes? With the help of your favorite metal cookie cutters, the possibilities are endless. My kids like me to make egg people using gingerbread person cookie cutters. You could make egg hearts on toast for Valentine's Day!

1. Crack the egg into a small measuring cup or container with a pouring spout. If your child prefers over-easy eggs, leave the egg as is. For scrambled, give the egg a quick whisk with a fork.

2. Preheat a skillet on medium-high heat and add ¼ teaspoon of the oil, ensuring that it spreads across the bottom of the skillet.

3. Start toasting the bread.

4. Using a paper towel or your clean fingers, spread a thin layer of oil around the inside edge of a large metal gingerbread person cookie cutter.

5. Put the cookie cutter in the pan to heat up.

6. With an oven mitt on one hand for safety, hold the cookie cutter down firmly in the pan, and then very slowly pour the egg into the cookie cutter.

7. Once it seems like the edges are cooked, release your hold on the cookie cutter and quickly place a pot lid on top of it.

8. Cook for approximately 2 minutes for medium doneness. Butter the toast.

9. Using a thin spatula, carefully lift the cookie cutter and egg out of the pan. Use a butter knife to loosen the egg and place it on the toast to serve.

> Don't go off-recipe and add milk to the egg. It won't set well in the cookie cutter and will just run into a big shapeless mess in the pan, which kind of defeats the purpose.

If your children aren't fans of ricotta, cream cheese or goat cheese make yummy substitutes.

Ricotta, Hemp Seed, and Grape Tartine

SERVES: 1–2 CHILDREN

PREP TIME: 5 MINUTES

1 piece hard pumpernickel or rye bread

1 tsp hemp seeds

2 Tbsp ricotta cheese

6 red grapes, cut into quarters

Dense, firm rye or pumpernickel bread might not seem like an obvious choice for children, but neither of mine batted an eye when I first served it to them (I've come to realize that you really never know what kids are going to like or not like!), and it makes a nutritious change from regular bread. Hemp seeds are high in protein and healthy fats, so they're an excellent addition to your child's diet, and they're relatively soft, so they mix quite discreetly into the ricotta.

1. Toast the bread.

2. Meanwhile, in a small bowl, combine the hemp seeds and the ricotta.

3. Spread the ricotta and hemp on the bread and top with the grapes.

4. Cut into triangles or rectangles to serve.

Overnight Strawberry Cocoa Oatmeal

MAKES: 4

PREP TIME: 15 MINUTES + OVERNIGHT SOAK IN THE REFRIGERATOR

1 cup quick or rolled oats ("pure" or certified gluten-free oats if you are avoiding gluten)

2 Tbsp chia seeds

2 tsp cocoa or raw cacao

2 cups dairy or non-dairy milk

4 tsp honey or maple syrup (for plant-based)

1 cup diced fresh strawberries

The idea with these little pots of wonderfulness is that the children can just open the refrigerator in the morning and help themselves to breakfast with basically no help from you. Of course, you do need to make them the night before, but they're very easy to put together and offer a perfect opportunity to get kids involved in meal prep and to even learn some simple division and measurement skills. These work best in short, wide mason jars with lids. *(Photo on inside cover)*

1. Evenly split the oats, chia seeds, and cocoa between four ¾-cup mason jars.

2. Now pour even amounts of the milk and honey over top, then put the lids on the jars and give them a good shake.

3. Divide the strawberries evenly between each jar, put the lids back on, and place the jars in the refrigerator overnight.

4. These can be eaten straight out of the refrigerator, but if your children are stuck on the idea that oatmeal should be hot, you can heat the jars gently in the microwave to serve. Warming them up will increase the strawberry flavor, which is a yummy benefit. Keep in mind that the oatmeal will have a thicker consistency if heated. These keep for a few days, so prep them on Sunday night and you'll have breakfasts through until mid-week.

Roasted Sweet Potato and Blueberry Muffins

MAKES: 12 MUFFINS

PREP TIME: 15 MINUTES

COOK TIME: 20 MINUTES

Virgin coconut oil, to grease the pan

1 cup rolled oats

1 cup spelt flour

1 tsp baking powder

½ tsp baking soda

¼ tsp sea salt

1 Tbsp milled flaxseed

1 tsp ground cinnamon

1 cup mashed roasted sweet potato (roast this the night before to make it easy)

1 egg

½ cup coconut sugar

¼ cup dairy or non-dairy milk

3 Tbsp virgin coconut oil, melted

¾ cup blueberries (fresh or frozen are fine, and you can add them to the batter straight from frozen)

These muffins are one of the most popular recipes on the Love Child Blog. I have a batch of them in my freezer at all times. Sweet potato and blueberries may not look like an obvious flavor combination, but they're wonderful together, both for health and for flavor.

1. Preheat the oven to 375°F. Lightly grease the cups of a 12-cup muffin pan with coconut oil. I find muffin papers tend to stick to these particular muffins.

2. Place the oats, flour, baking powder, baking soda, and salt in a large bowl with the flaxseed and cinnamon. Stir well to combine.

3. In a separate bowl, place the sweet potato, egg, coconut sugar, milk, and coconut oil. Whisk to combine.

4. Add the wet ingredients to the dry and stir until just mixed. Carefully fold in the blueberries.

5. Fill the muffin cups two-thirds full. Bake for approximately 20 minutes until the muffins are firm to the touch and dark golden. A toothpick inserted in the center of a muffin should come out clean. Allow the muffins to cool for a couple of minutes in the pan, then transfer to a wire rack. Serve warm, maybe spread with a bit of butter. Yum! These muffins will keep for a couple of days on the counter in an airtight container. Freeze leftover muffins in a freezer bag or airtight container for up to 3 months.

> Be sure to choose rolled rather than quick oats so that you get some nice hearty texture in the muffins.

Using this recipe as a base, on busy weekday mornings when I don't have any pancakes saved in the freezer, I leave out the bacon, apples, vanilla, and cinnamon and whip up basic spelt pancakes in a flash. Then I just top them with a few berries and a drizzle of maple syrup.

If you don't have buttermilk, substitute 1 cup of milk mixed with 1 teaspoon of vinegar or lemon juice.

Bacon and Apple-Loaded Spelt Pancakes

SERVES: 4 (10–12 PANCAKES)

PREP TIME: 20 MINUTES

COOK TIME: 15 MINUTES

4 strips thick-cut naturally smoked bacon

1 cup spelt flour

1¼ tsp baking powder

¼ tsp baking soda

¼ tsp sea salt

⅛ tsp ground cinnamon

1 large egg

1 cup buttermilk

1 Tbsp virgin coconut oil or butter, melted + more for frying

½ tsp pure vanilla extract

½ cup ¼-inch cubes apple, peeled or unpeeled (I like the sweetness of Galas in pancakes)

Virgin coconut oil, ghee, or butter for frying

Maple syrup for serving

Yes, there is bacon in these apple pancakes. And it makes them taste reeeeaaaally good. Admittedly, this isn't the healthiest recipe in this book (maybe I should have put this in the celebrations chapter?), but the spelt flour and apple must count for something! This dish makes a nice special breakfast for a holiday or someone's birthday. Or maybe just because you've all made it to Saturday.

1. Preheat the oven to 450°F. Line a rimmed baking tray with parchment paper.

2. Lay the bacon on the tray and place in the oven for 8 minutes, turning halfway through.

3. Meanwhile, in a large bowl, combine the flour, baking powder, baking soda, salt, and cinnamon. Set aside.

4. In a medium-size bowl, combine the egg, buttermilk, melted coconut oil, and vanilla.

5. Pour the buttermilk mixture into the bowl of dry ingredients and stir until just mixed. Allow to sit for 5 minutes.

6. When the bacon is cooked, use a fork or tongs to place it on a plate covered in a couple of paper towels. Pat the bacon to absorb the fat. Cut the bacon into ½-inch square pieces.

7. Add the bacon and the apple to the pancake batter and stir until just combined.

8. Preheat a skillet over medium heat, adding a small amount of oil to prevent sticking.

9. Pour scoops of the batter into the hot pan. Cook for approximately 2½ minutes on each side, until golden brown. You will know it is time to flip the pancakes when bubbles start forming on the surface.

10. Serve warm with maple syrup. Leftovers can be saved for a couple of days in the refrigerator, or up to a month in an airtight container in the freezer and warmed up in the oven for 5–10 minutes at 350°F, or in the toaster.

Powered-Up Cereal Bowl

This isn't exactly a recipe. It's more of a suggestion for how to give your child's favorite cereal more nutritional clout. Most packaged cereal just isn't going to keep kids going for very long—unless you get creative, that is. Think outside of the cereal box.

Take one portion of your child's favorite cereal, the lower in sugar and the cleaner the ingredient list, the better.

Top with 1–2 tablespoons total of one or more of the following:

Raisins or dried cranberries or blueberries

Dried goji berries

Chopped dried dates, figs, mango, apples, or other chopped dried fruit

Hemp hearts

Chia seeds

Flaxseeds

Seeds such as sunflower, pumpkin, or sesame

Chopped nuts, such as almonds, walnuts, or Brazil nuts

Unsweetened shredded coconut

Wheat germ

Chopped cocoa nibs

Fresh berries or fresh diced fruit

Yogurt

Nut or seed butters (try just putting a dollop on the cereal just off to the side and your child can scoop up little bits of it at a time to add to mouthfuls of cereal)

Coconut oil

Flax oil

Add milk or non-dairy milk. Voilà: powered-up cereal.

Griddled Oatcakes with Roasted Stone Fruit and Greek Yogurt

SERVES: 4

PREP TIME: 15 MINUTES (INCLUDING COOKING THE FRUIT)

COOK TIME: 15 MINUTES

2 cups total of sliced plums, peaches, and/or nectarines

1 Tbsp maple syrup (for the fruit)

1½ cups rolled oats ("pure" or gluten-free, if you prefer)

1 Tbsp ground flaxseed

1 tsp baking powder

¼ tsp baking soda

¼ tsp sea salt

1 egg

1 cup milk (I find that dairy milk makes these oatcakes lighter, but you can use non-dairy milk if you prefer)

2 Tbsp virgin coconut oil, melted

1 Tbsp maple syrup (for the oatcake batter)

1 tsp pure vanilla extract

Virgin coconut oil or butter for frying

1 cup Greek yogurt

Extra maple syrup for pouring

This special breakfast is probably not for busy weekdays. But it's perfect for weekend brunch with friends. If you use "pure" or certified gluten-free oats, gluten-free eaters will be able to enjoy these. And it goes without saying that the maple-roasted fruit really kicks things up a notch.

1. Preheat the oven to 400°F.

2. Spread out the sliced fruit on a baking tray. Drizzle with the syrup and roast for 10–15 minutes until soft and starting to brown slightly.

3. To make the pancakes, pulse the oats in a food processor fitted with the steel blade until you have a rough flour.

4. Pour this oat flour into a large bowl and add the flaxseed, baking powder, baking soda, and salt.

5. In a separate bowl, whisk together the egg, milk, coconut oil, maple syrup, and vanilla.

6. Pour the wet ingredients into the dry and stir until just mixed. Allow to sit for 3 minutes to thicken.

7. Heat a skillet over medium heat and coat the pan with a small amount of coconut oil to prevent the cakes from sticking.

8. Pour ladles of the batter into the hot pan. Cook for approximately 2½ minutes on each side. You will know it is time to flip them when small bubbles burst through the top of the pancake and create little holes in the batter. When done, the pancakes will be dark golden and when broken open the inside won't look overly moist.

9. To serve, top the pancakes with a dollop of Greek yogurt, a spoonful of the roasted fruit, and another drizzle of maple syrup.

10. These pancakes are best eaten right after they are made. However, they can be frozen in an airtight container for up to 3 months. They reheat best in the toaster, even straight from frozen.

These pancakes are delish as a quick snack or breakfast on the go, spread with peanut or almond butter.

Peanut Butter Protein Bars

MAKES: 16–24 BARS

PREP TIME: 20 MINUTES PLUS

COOKING TIME FOR THE QUINOA

COOK TIME: 25–30 MINUTES +

1 HOUR TO CHILL

¼ cup virgin coconut oil, plus extra to grease the pan

2½ cups quick (not instant) oats (if you only have rolled oats, pulse them in a food processor a bit to break them down)

½ cup rolled oats

1 cup cooked, cooled quinoa (leftover quinoa is perfect for this recipe)

¼ cup spelt flour

2 Tbsp ground flaxseed

½ tsp sea salt

½ cup natural peanut butter, smooth or chunky

⅔ cup honey or maple syrup (for plant-based)

1 tsp pure vanilla extract

1 heaping cup very finely chopped dates

½ cup raw pumpkin seeds and/or sunflower seeds

Store-bought bars (aside from Love Child Organics' bars, of course!) can rarely be classified as healthy with all those empty ingredients and their high sugar content. Because of this, I've become obsessed with developing my own homemade recipes, but they're surprisingly difficult to get right. I must have made approximately ten versions of this recipe before finally achieving my ideal texture and sweetness, while still being happy with the nutritional value of the ingredients. I think, and hope you'll agree, that after all my tears (yes—I cried after version eight was a mega-fail!), that I've landed on a winner.

1. Preheat the oven to 350°F. Grease an 8- × 11-inch baking pan with coconut oil.

2. In a large bowl, combine the quick oats, rolled oats, cooked quinoa, spelt flour, flaxseed, and salt. Break up any lumps of quinoa as you do this.

3. In a pot, over medium heat, stir together the ¼ cup coconut oil, peanut butter, honey, and vanilla until they are all melted and fully combined, but not bubbling.

4. Add this to the dry ingredients, stirring until they are incorporated completely.

5. Mix in the dates and seeds.

6. Pour the mixture into the prepared pan. Using dampened hands, press down on the mixture until it's evenly spread out and smooth on top.

7. Bake for 25–30 minutes until starting to crisp at the edges and golden brown on top.

8. Allow to cool in the pan on a wire rack until warm, then transfer the pan to the refrigerator to set for an hour.

9. Using a sharp knife, cut into bars. I like to slice three cuts lengthwise then three cuts across so that I have 16 bars that are approximately the size of store-bought bars. Store in an airtight container, with a piece of parchment paper between layers, in the refrigerator for up to 4 days, or in the freezer for up to 3 months.

When slicing into bars, use a large sharp knife first to cut most of the way through, then use a pizza cutter to cut all the way through to the bottom of the pan. This will give you cleaner-looking slices and make it less likely that the bars will crumble.

♥

Try to make these when you're cooking quinoa for another recipe so that you only cook one batch of quinoa.

CHAPTER FIVE

easy lunches

Chunky Chicken Noodle and Superfood Soup

MAKES: 10 CUPS

PREP TIME: 20 MINUTES

COOK TIME: 30 MINUTES

2 Tbsp virgin coconut or extra virgin olive oil, divided

4 boneless, skinless organic chicken thighs, cut into bite-size pieces

1 cup diced white or brown mushrooms

1 medium yellow onion, finely chopped

2 cloves garlic, crushed

1 large carrot, diced small

1 stalk celery, diced small

1 tsp dried thyme

1 tsp dried rosemary

1 tsp dried sage

1 tsp sea salt

1 small sweet potato, scrubbed and diced

1¼ cups chunky pasta such as rotini (gluten-free pasta works very well in this recipe—I like a rice and quinoa blend)

1 cup minced kale, stems discarded

1 cup finely chopped broccoli florets

¼ cup chopped curly or flat-leaf parsley

1½ tsp fresh lemon juice

This flavorful soup comes together quickly and doesn't require pre-made stock. And because I never shy away from a chance to add brightly colored "super-veggies," there are plenty in here to increase the nutritional value of the classic chicken noodle soup.

1. Pour 1 tablespoon of the oil into a large pot over medium heat. When the oil is hot but not smoking, add the chicken.

2. Sauté the chicken, stirring occasionally, until it is browned and just cooked through. Transfer to a dish and set aside.

3. Keeping the pan over medium heat, pour in ¼ cup of water. This will bubble away, loosening the brown bits from the bottom of the pan. Use your spoon to scrape up any brown drippings that are still clinging on and mix them in with the water.

4. Add the remaining 1 tablespoon of oil and then the mushrooms. Cook for approximately 5 minutes, stirring frequently and scraping the bottom of the pan again. This step will add a great deal of flavor, so don't skip it. If the bottom of the pan is browning too much, add a bit of water, 1 tablespoon at a time.

5. Add the onion, garlic, carrot, celery, thyme, rosemary, sage, and salt and stir until well combined. Sauté for 5 minutes over medium heat, stirring frequently. Don't let it burn even the tiniest bit, or your broth won't taste as good.

6. Increase the heat to high. Add the sweet potato and 7¾ cups of water, and bring to a boil.

7. Add the pasta, kale, broccoli, and cooked chicken to the pot. Turn down to a medium boil, and let it bubble away for 10 minutes or so, uncovered, until the pasta is cooked and the sweet potato is soft.

8. Turn off the heat and stir in the parsley and lemon juice. Adjust the seasoning. Freeze leftovers in an airtight container for up to 3 months.

Feel free to substitute vegetables you have on hand for the ones in the recipe. For example, spinach or chard could be substituted for kale, and butternut squash for the sweet potato. I have also made this recipe with rice instead of pasta and it was delicious, so take a chance and experiment to make this chicken noodle soup your own.

Miso Soba Noodle Bowl

SERVES: 2 SMALL CHILDREN
PREP TIME: 10 MINUTES
COOK TIME: 5 MINUTES

2 oz buckwheat soba noodles

1 tsp rice vinegar

1 tsp miso paste (dark or light)

1 tsp tamari or coconut aminos

½ tsp honey (maple syrup or
    coconut sugar for
    plant-based)

½ tsp toasted sesame oil

1 tsp warm water

Pinch of ground ginger

Pinch of garlic powder

1 tsp virgin coconut oil

¼ cup frozen edamame beans,
    thawed

¼ cup diced carrot

¼ cup diced broccoli florets

1 packed tsp minced green onion

Asian flavors tend to be very popular with children in my experience, but many of the ready-made stir-fry sauces contain nasty preservatives that really have no place in little bodies (or big bodies, come to think of it). The sauce in this recipe is much cleaner and tastes just like the real thing.

1. Cook the noodles according to the package instructions. Drain.

2. In a small bowl, combine the rice vinegar, miso, tamari, honey, sesame oil, water, ginger, and garlic powder.

3. In a skillet, heat the coconut oil, then add the edamame, carrot, broccoli, and green onion. Cook for a few minutes, just until the carrot starts to soften.

4. Turn off the heat, add the noodles and the miso sauce to the pan, and stir until fully combined before serving.

Triple the batch and make this a full-size family dinner that you can have on the table in under half an hour.

♥

If buckwheat noodles aren't your thing, substitute any other noodle or try rice.

♥

The sauce can also be used with other stir-fry combinations or as a dip, so make it up ahead and be ready for a quick meal. The sauce can be stored in the refrigerator in an airtight container for at least a month.

Simple Lentil and Coconut Soup (Magic Gold)

MAKES: 8 CUPS
PREP TIME: 10 MINUTES
COOK TIME: 25 MINUTES

1 scant Tbsp cumin seeds

2 Tbsp virgin coconut oil

1 large yellow onion, diced

3 cloves garlic, crushed

2-inch piece of ginger, peeled and grated

1 tsp ground turmeric

1 tsp sea salt

2 cups red lentils

1 (13.5 oz) can full-fat coconut milk (from a BPA-free can)

Zest of ½ lime

Juice of 1 lime, plus more to taste

¼ cup cilantro leaves

If you can convince your kids to try a first bite of this boldly spiced (but not spicy) lentil soup (let's be real here, pureed lentils aren't on many kids' lists of favorite foods), they will eat it and might even admit they like it! (Full disclosure: I initially called this soup Magic Gold at our house to increase the enticement factor, and I think it may have upped my chances of success.) This recipe makes a nice big batch for a family lunch on the weekend, with leftovers for the freezer.

1. Using a mortar and pestle, crush the cumin seeds until you notice their aroma being released.

2. Heat a stock pot over medium heat, then dry-toast the cumin seeds for approximately 1 minute, stirring frequently.

3. Add the oil, onion, garlic, ginger, turmeric, and sea salt. Sauté, stirring occasionally, for 5 minutes or so, until the onion is transparent and tender but not browned.

4. Add the lentils, then 6 cups water and the coconut milk, and stir to combine.

5. Turn up the heat to bring to a boil, then turn the heat to medium-low, and simmer, partly covered, for 20 minutes. Stir occasionally.

6. Take off the heat and add the lime zest, lime juice, cilantro, and if you like, more salt or lime juice.

You can serve the soup as is, or blend it. I find that lentil soup is accepted better by kids if it's blended, so I pull out my trusty immersion blender and give it a brief blast right in the pot so that it is just smooth. Store any leftovers in an airtight container in the freezer for up to 3 months.

Roasted Tomato and Carrot Soup

MAKES: 7 CUPS

PREP TIME: 5 MINUTES

COOK TIME: 45 MINUTES

8 medium tomatoes

2 medium carrots, peeled and chopped into large chunks

2 large cloves garlic, minced

2 Tbsp extra virgin olive oil

Sea salt and ground black pepper

3 cups low-sodium organic chicken or vegetable stock (store-bought is fine, or use my recipe on page 247)

½ cup whipping cream, or canned (BPA-free can!) coconut milk (for non-dairy)

8 fresh basil leaves

1 cup shredded cheddar cheese or dairy-free cheese for serving (optional)

There is just something so homey and soothing about tomato soup on a cold day. Of course, I couldn't just keep it to tomatoes—I needed to add an extra vegetable. The carrots mellow out the sharpness of the tomato while still keeping it tasting very much like tomato soup. But the true magic of this recipe is in the roasting. It brings out the flavors and makes the cooking process really simple. Make this soup dairy-free by substituting coconut milk for cream and using non-dairy cheese as a topping.

1. Preheat the oven to 425°F.

2. Place the whole tomatoes and chopped carrots in a roasting tray.

3. Sprinkle the garlic over top. Pour over the olive oil, and season with salt and pepper. Using a large spoon or your hands, mix the vegetables so that they're covered in the oil.

4. Roast in the oven for 45 minutes.

5. When the tomatoes and carrots are ready, take them out of the oven and carefully scoop or pour them into your blender. Pour in the stock and the cream, and add the basil leaves. Blend at low speed until completely pureed. (The blender will be quite full, and if you blend at high speed it could spray everywhere.) Adjust the seasoning as needed. You'll probably find that you need to add a touch of salt at this point.

6. Serve topped with a small handful of shredded cheddar cheese. Yum! Store extra soup in an airtight container in the freezer for up to 3 months.

In the summer, when tomatoes are in season, any type of tomato will do for this recipe. In winter, I prefer Roma tomatoes (aka, plum tomatoes) as I find them to be the most flavorful when out of season.

Pizza Quesadilla

SERVES: 1–2 SMALL CHILDREN

PREP TIME: 5 MINUTES

COOK TIME: 5 MINUTES

1 Tbsp ready-made pizza sauce

1 whole-grain flour tortilla (see page 32) (gluten-free if preferred)

⅓ cup shredded mozzarella

A sprinkling of your child's favorite pizza toppings, finely chopped

Pizza is obviously a classic favorite with kids, but it can be floppy and hard for little ones to hold, and when it's cut up for them, the toppings often fall off. This version is mess-free and small-hand friendly. It's also extra-easy to make because you use tortillas instead of pizza dough.

1. Spread the tomato sauce over one half of the tortilla.

2. Sprinkle the cheese and toppings over the sauce, then fold the other side on top to make a half circle.

3. In a skillet over medium-high heat, cook the quesadilla until it's lightly toasted and the cheese is fully melted, 2–3 minutes each side.

4. Use a pizza cutter to slice it into wedges. Serve with a side of raw veggies, and you have an easy, healthy, balanced lunch that is destined to be gobbled right up.

I Can't Believe It's Not Cheese Pasta!

MAKES: 2 CHILD-SIZE SERVINGS (1¼ CUPS)

PREP TIME: 10 MINUTES

COOK TIME: 10 MINUTES

3 oz gluten-free macaroni pasta (or regular pasta)

1 Tbsp olive oil

½ cup grated butternut squash

2 Tbsp chopped raw cashews

1 Tbsp finely diced yellow onion

½ cup unsweetened almond milk (or other non-dairy milk)

1 tsp nutritional yeast

Sea salt and black pepper to taste

A non-dairy, much more nutritious version of the classic mac and cheese, with butternut squash, cashews, and nutritional yeast. Does it taste like the original? Well, OK, no, but it's a pretty tasty alternative. If you prefer to use dairy milk and cheese, simply swap out the almond milk for regular whole milk, skip the nutritional yeast, and stir in ¼ cup of shredded sharp cheddar right before blending.

1. Cook the pasta according to the package instructions.

2. Meanwhile, heat the oil, then sauté the butternut squash, cashews, and onion for 3 minutes over medium heat.

3. Add the almond milk, nutritional yeast, salt, and a grinding of black pepper. Bring to a boil, then turn the heat to low and simmer, uncovered, for 5 minutes.

4. When 5 minutes have passed and the squash is soft, blend the sauce in a food processor fitted with the steel blade or a blender until smooth. Be careful, as the sauce is hot and could splatter. Adjust the seasoning.

5. Mix the sauce with the drained pasta to serve.

Sweet Potato and Black Bean Taquitos

MAKES: 12 TAQUITOS

PREP TIME: 30 MINUTES

COOK TIME: 18 MINUTES

TAQUITOS

1 cup grated sweet potato

2 minced green onions

4 Tbsp virgin coconut oil, divided
(2 melted, 2 solid or melted)

2 cups canned or cooked black
beans, rinsed and drained
(sodium-free and from a
BPA-free can)

4 Tbsp ready-made tomato pizza
sauce, pasta sauce, or mild
salsa

½ tsp mild chili powder

½ tsp ground cumin

¼ tsp sea salt

2 eggs

12 small corn tortillas

1 cup shredded Monterey Jack
cheese (optional)

EASY-PEASY YOGURT DIP

1 cup whole-milk yogurt

1 tsp fresh lime juice

¼ tsp ground cumin

A good pinch of salt

These take a little effort and are a tad fiddly. But don't be tempted to flip the page just yet—with a little concentration, they don't actually take too long to come together. (And you could make a batch to keep in the freezer.) Kids love how fun these are to eat, and the flavor combination of the sweet potato, black beans, and spices will make a bean lover out of any bean-suspicious child.

1. Preheat the oven to 450°F.

2. For the taquitos, in a skillet, over medium heat, sauté the sweet potato and green onion in half the coconut oil for 2 minutes, stirring continuously.

3. Add the beans, tomato sauce or salsa, chili powder, cumin, salt, and ⅓ cup water.

4. Cook for around 5 minutes, stirring frequently and mashing the beans as you stir.

5. Whisk the eggs in a small dish. Pour them over top the bean mixture and stir them in well. Cook for 1 minute, until the egg is just cooked. Take off the heat.

6. Wrap the tortillas in foil and put them in the hot oven for a couple of minutes until they are very soft, or warm them without foil in the microwave for 20–30 seconds.

7. To assemble the taquitos, lay the tortillas out on a baking tray. Spread a scoop of filling along one side of each tortilla. If including cheese, sprinkle it over the filling. Brush the other edge of the tortilla with some melted coconut oil. This will help the taquito stick together once it's rolled up.

8. Roll up the tortillas and place them seam side down on the tray.

9. Brush each taquito with melted coconut oil, then bake in the oven for 10 minutes. Turn the taquitos over 5 minutes into cooking to ensure they get crispy on both sides.

10. To make the dip, stir together the yogurt, lime juice, cumin, and salt. Serve the cool dip alongside the warm taquitos. You can make the dip up to a day ahead of time. Just give it a good stir before serving. The taquitos will keep well in the freezer for up to 3 months. If freezing for longer than a few hours, transfer them to an airtight container.

Make these ahead for a children's party (or just to keep on hand, of course). Freeze them on a baking tray once assembled, then bake straight from the freezer at 375°F for 25 minutes.

Chicken, Apple, Spinach, and Cheddar Quesadillas

SERVES: 2 SMALL CHILDREN OR
1 BIG KID

PREP TIME: 10 MINUTES

COOK TIME: 6 MINUTES

⅓ cup shredded cheddar cheese

2 small whole-grain flour tortillas
(gluten-free, if preferred)

¼ cup shredded cooked chicken

1 Tbsp finely chopped baby
spinach leaves

1 tsp hemp hearts for added
nutrition (sounds odd, but
they blend in really well and
they're a great source of
omegas and fiber) (optional)

8 thin slices apple, skin on or off

Quesadillas are the ultimate quick lunchtime staple, and
the possible variations are endless. This savory and
sweet version is one of my favorites. A quick word about
flour tortillas, though. Store-bought ones often contain a long
list of scary preservatives (see page 32). It's worth taking the
time to carefully read the labels and buy cleaner versions
from the refrigerator section of natural food stores. Or make
your own (see Soft Spelt and Flax Tortillas, page 240).

1. Sprinkle half the cheese on one of the tortillas, then top with
the chicken, spinach, the hemp hearts, if using, and slices of
apple. Sprinkle the rest of the cheese on top, then place the
other tortilla on top.

2. In a skillet over medium-high heat, cook for 3 minutes on
each side until the apples are soft.

3. Using a pizza cutter, slice into wedges to serve.

> You can dice the leftover apple and freeze
> it to add to a smoothie.
>
> ♥
>
> Some other yummy quesadilla filling ideas:
> ♥ black beans + cheese + red bell pepper
> ♥ pear + Manchego cheese
> ♥ peanut butter + dried coconut + banana
> ♥ filling from Veggie-Loaded Beef Soft
> Tacos (page 176) + cheese

Individual Baked Vegetable "Lasagnas"

MAKES: 12 "LASAGNAS"

PREP TIME: 30 MINUTES

COOK TIME: 30 MINUTES INCLUDING COOLING TIME

Butter to grease the pan

1 cup uncooked regular or gluten-free pasta (small macaroni or shells work best)

1 cup shredded zucchini

¼ tsp sea salt

1 cup of your favorite ready-made tomato pasta sauce

⅓ cup ricotta cheese

1 Tbsp chia seeds

½ cup navy beans, freshly cooked or canned (sodium-free and from a BPA-free can)

½ cup finely chopped baby spinach leaves

1 Tbsp shredded fresh basil leaves

1½ cups + 1 Tbsp shredded mozzarella cheese, divided

Everyone loves the flavors of lasagna, but with all those fussy layers, it can be time-consuming to make—and in my experience little ones can reject it because it tends to look like a bit of a sloppy mess on the plate. These personal portions of deliciousness taste just like vegetarian lasagna but in a much more kid-friendly package. Yes, chia seeds are an unusual ingredient in lasagna, but as it's one of the ultimate super-foods, I love to include it at any opportunity, and it blends well and helps bind ingredients together in this yummy dish.

1. Preheat the oven to 375°F. Grease the cups of a 12-cup muffin pan with butter.

2. Cook the pasta according to the package instructions, then drain and set aside.

3. Meanwhile, in a small bowl, mix together the zucchini and salt. Set aside for 10 minutes.

4. In a large bowl, combine the tomato sauce, ricotta cheese, and chia seeds. Let sit for 10 minutes.

5. Using clean hands, squeeze the liquid out of the zucchini, then add the zucchini to the tomato sauce mixture. Add the navy beans, spinach, and basil, then 1 cup of the mozzarella and the drained pasta (it's fine if it's still warm). Stir until fully combined.

6. Divide the mixture between the muffin cups, then top with the remaining shredded cheese.

7. Bake in the oven for 20 minutes. Allow to sit for 5–10 minutes before running a knife around the edges and gently easing them from the pan with a spoon.

8. Cook these ahead and store them in the freezer in an airtight container for up to 3 months or in the refrigerator for up to 4 days. Reheat gently from frozen in the oven at 375°F until heated through, approximately 20 minutes.

> Make these in mini muffin pans and serve them as a finger food for toddlers, or as a party food. Adults will love them too.

Chickpea Salad Lettuce Wraps

SERVES: 1–2 CHILDREN

PREP TIME: 10 MINUTES

½ cup cooked or canned chickpeas (sodium-free and from a
BPA-free can), skins removed
if you like

¼ cup grated carrot

1½ Tbsp vegan (or regular)
mayonnaise

1 Tbsp finely diced celery

1 Tbsp finely chopped raw,
unsalted cashews

A good pinch of minced fresh dill

Sea salt and ground black
pepper to taste

¼ tsp fresh lemon juice (or more
to taste)

2 large leaves butter or iceberg
lettuce

My kids both love tuna salad, but I have concerns about mercury levels and sustainability, so I wanted to come up with a safer option I could feel good about. This chickpea salad fits the bill and is a terrific source of vegetarian protein. Because it tastes so much like the tuna salad they're used to, it's really helped convince them that chickpeas are a reasonable thing to be eating! Prefer grains with your chickpea salad? Feel free to use sandwich bread or a wrap in place of the lettuce cups.

1. Put the chickpeas in a medium-size bowl. Use a fork to mash them until they're just broken up. It's better not to use a food processor for this because it destroys too much of the texture.

2. Add the rest of the ingredients, except the lettuce leaves, and mix well to combine.

3. Spoon this filling into the lettuce leaves and roll up to serve.

Stuck in a sandwich filling rut? Here are some of our family favorites:
- ♥ Soft goat cheese and sliced tomato
- ♥ Hummus, avocado, and alfalfa sprouts
- ♥ Shredded chicken mixed with mayonnaise, quartered grapes, shredded carrot, finely diced celery, and a pinch of curry powder
- ♥ Cream cheese or goat cheese and sliced strawberries
- ♥ Cream cheese with alfalfa sprouts and cucumber (I grew up on this one!)
- ♥ Nitrate-free ham, sharp cheddar, and apple (yummy grilled too!)
- ♥ Baby shrimp with mayo, dill, and capers
- ♥ Shredded apples and carrots with almond butter (see page 134)
- ♥ Peanut butter and sliced firm pears
- ♥ Veggie-loaded taco meat sandwich (see Veggie-Loaded Beef Soft Tacos, page 176)
- ♥ Mashed tinned sardines and yellow mustard (kids often like this—really!)

Two Protein- and Omega-Rich Dips
Greek Yogurt Avocado Ranch

MAKES: 1¼ CUPS

PREP TIME: 5 MINUTES

1 cup Greek yogurt

1 ripe avocado

2 Tbsp whole milk

1 Tbsp flax oil

1 tsp fresh lemon juice

½ tsp dried dill

¼ tsp onion powder

¼ tsp garlic powder

¼ tsp sea salt

Serving a side of dip is a tried and true strategy for encouraging children to eat vegetables. But dips can do so much more than provide flavor and disguise unpopular ingredients. These dips are rich in protein, healthy fats, and other nutrients. Make them the central feature of your little one's meal, with crudités, pita chips, or whole-grain crackers for dipping.

1. Place all the ingredients in a blender or a food processor fitted with the steel blade and blend until smooth. Because of the avocado, this dip is best used up quickly.

Roasted Garlic and Squash Hummus

MAKES: 2 CUPS

PREP TIME: 10 MINUTES

COOK TIME: 40 MINUTES

¼ medium butternut squash (cut the squash lengthwise)

1 small head garlic, skin on

2 Tbsp extra virgin olive oil

1 (19 oz) can chickpeas, rinsed and drained (sodium-free and from a BPA-free can)

2 Tbsp fresh lemon juice

2 Tbsp tahini

2 Tbsp water

1 tsp maple syrup

½ tsp sea salt

¼ tsp paprika

If possible, roast up the squash and garlic the night before. Then you can throw the hummus together in just a couple of minutes the next day. Hummus is so child-friendly and a great vehicle for other ingredients like squash. *(Photo on page 168)*

1. Preheat the oven to 425°F.

2. Hollow out the seeds from the squash and set it face up in a roasting pan. Leaving the skin on, put the head of garlic in the hollow of the squash. Drizzle with the olive oil, cover with aluminum foil, then roast for 40 minutes.

3. Once it's cool enough to handle, cut the top off the garlic and squeeze the roasted puree out of the skins into a food processor fitted with the steel blade. Scoop out the squash, leaving the skin behind, and add to the food processor along with all the remaining ingredients. Blend until smooth. Store for 3–4 days in the refrigerator or freeze it for up to 3 months. I like to freeze hummus in small individual-size containers so that I can just pop one in a lunchbox.

Easy Packed Lunches

Ah, good old packed lunches. They sound simple, but never underestimate the stress they cause parents. Believe me, I speak from experience. There is the pressure of packing up something interesting and nutritious that kids will want to eat 5 days per week, the debates between parents and kids about whose job this is anyway, not to mention all those photos on social media showing the most beautiful, nutritious bento box lunchboxes possible . . . It's enough to make any mom feel like going on packed lunch strike (which is something I have actually done, by the way!).

But I've learned by taking a step back and following some simple rules, making packed lunches doesn't need to feel quite so difficult, and they can in fact be pretty simple to throw together. Here are my top tips for making packed lunches more pleasurable than pesky:

♥ Leftovers are your best friend when it comes to packed lunches: Leftover roast or taco meat from last night? They can become fillings for sandwiches or wraps. Only one piece of pizza leftover from dinner? Don't throw it away or let your husband eat it for breakfast; that piece of pizza is perfect for a child's lunch. Enjoyed soup or curry last night? Put a cupful straight into a thermos and send a warming and nutritious pot of goodness to school.

♥ Learn to love a thermos: Not only is the food you put in a thermos likely to be nutritious because it tends to be things like soups and stews, but it's also a really nice treat for your child to have something warm to open up at school, especially in the winter months. Use it for hot food like soup, stew, rice, or pasta, but also for cold food like cottage cheese, yogurt, and fruit or vegetable salads.

♥ Several healthy, balanced snacks make a fun, appealing lunch. Don't feel you always have to pack a main dish, like a sandwich or a thermos of stew for lunch. Containers with lots of different little snacks make a terrific lunch, and this is a really nice change for kids. However, if sandwiches are your kid's fave, check out the ideas on page 164.

♥ Send a smoothie to school and encourage your child to eat it at their early morning break, especially if breakfast that day has been a bit rushed. Blend up a quick smoothie first thing in the morning (see pages 124–130) and pack it in a small mason jar or lidded bottle. Teach your child how to shake it up well before opening and send along a fun straw to make drinking easier.

(continued...)

Turkey Pesto Meatballs (page 235)

Little Spelt Buns (page 242)

Roasted Garlic and Squash Hummus (page 166)

Love you! Have a wonderful day at school. -Mommy xox

💜 Make muffins and bars ahead of time to keep in the refrigerator or freezer and send them to school as a super-powered homemade snack.

💜 Think about balance: Try to send a balanced selection of nutritious vegetables, fruits, proteins, starches, and fats so that your child gets a good injection of nutrients and their blood sugar is kept on an even keel to support all the learning they will be doing.

💜 Include a healthy treat: Help kids get excited about lunch by including a small item they'll really love. With some effort you can actually teach your kids to eat the treat after they eat the rest of their lunch (honestly—I've seen this work!). Just be sure that it's a healthy treat. Teachers hate it when you send candy or junk food to school, not only because it isn't good for learning and attention but also because it can cause issues between the students if one child has candy while the others don't. (I used to be a teacher—I remember!)

💜 Invest in some lunch containers that make packing lunches easier, more environmentally friendly, more fun for your kids, and more inspiring for you. There are lots of reusable bento boxes, containers, and lunch bags in all shapes and sizes available, especially if you look online. And don't forget about containers you already have, such as mason jars and old baby food freezer containers. They work great for packing lunches!

💜 Put a small freezer pack in your child's lunch bag to keep perishables cold and safe.

💜 Certain soft foods just don't pack well: Whole pears, peaches, bananas, and tomatoes are better for lunch at home, unless of course you have nifty containers that will keep them from getting squashed.

💜 Most lunches can be packed the night before to save time during the inevitable morning rush. If you're sending warm food in a thermos as part of a lunch, pack up everything else the night before and have the food for the thermos portioned and ready to go. Just quickly heat it and pour it into a thermos in the morning.

💜 Like the idea of sending a note in your child's lunchbox? Make this easier on yourself by writing up a whole bunch of them ahead of time so that you don't feel pressured to come up with something to say every single morning.

💜 Once kids are old enough, have them pack their own lunches, at least a couple of times per week. Yes, you will need to train them how to do this and set some guidelines, but once they get the hang of it, this little shift in household responsibility will really take the pressure off you, not to mention be empowering for your children. Plus, if they pack it themselves, it's even more likely that they will eat it.

Snack Lunch—A Toddler's Heaven

When my daughter was two she went through a phase where she wasn't interested in eating unless it was called a snack. So we started calling lunchtime "snack lunch" and served small portions of different foods that added up to the equivalent of a well-rounded lunch. Drama over, and she probably ended up eating a better variety of foods than she would have done in a typical lunch.

💜

I love serving a "snack lunch" in a sectioned tray like a muffin pan, or putting little portions in individual muffin papers, or little bowls, set on a tray or plate. Practically anything goes—just try to offer variety and balance, with each food presented in its own little cup.

Cashew Mushroom Sliders
(page 186)

family-friendly dinners

Chard, Squash, and Bacon Frittata
(page 175)

Best Ever Turkey Chili Soup

SERVES: FAMILY OF 4

PREP TIME: 20 MINUTES

COOK TIME: 35 MINUTES

1 Tbsp olive oil

1 lb ground turkey

1 onion, finely chopped

2 cloves garlic, minced

1 bunch kale, finely chopped, stems discarded

1 small sweet potato, scrubbed and diced

¾ cup frozen or fresh corn

1 tsp paprika (I prefer smoked)

½ tsp dried oregano

1 tsp ground cumin

1½ Tbsp mild chili powder

½ tsp sea salt

1 (19 oz) can well-rinsed red kidney beans (sodium-free and from a BPA-free can)

1 (26 oz) can diced tomatoes (sodium-free and from a BPA-free can)

1 Tbsp coconut sugar or brown sugar

Toppings of your choice: shredded cheese, sour cream, yogurt, cilantro, green onions, or chopped red chilis

A version of this was one of the first recipes ever posted on the Love Child Blog, and it's still my favorite chili. The mild spicing and the sweetness of the sweet potato and corn make it a very family-friendly dish, even for very little ones. Plus the hefty helping of kale means that you don't need to bother cooking extra greens—you have your whole supper right here in one pot.

1. In a large pot, heat the olive oil over medium heat and cook the turkey, onion, and garlic for approximately 10 minutes, until the onions are starting to color and the turkey is cooked through.

2. Chop the kale leaves into very small pieces, leaving the stems behind.

3. Add the kale, sweet potato, corn, paprika, oregano, cumin, chili powder, and salt to the pot. Give it a good stir and let it cook for a couple of minutes.

4. Drain the beans, mush them a bit with a fork, and then add them to the pot with 2 cups of water, the tomatoes with their juice, and the sugar.

5. Bring to a boil, then cover and turn down the heat to simmer for 30 minutes.

6. Serve in bowls with your favorite toppings and enjoy! Freeze leftovers in an airtight container for up to 3 months.

> Leave out the salt and make this up as a baby food. Simply puree it to the desired consistency and freeze (see page 66). Your baby will love the bold flavors and be set up as a chili lover for life.

One-Pan Roast Chicken and Root Vegetables

SERVES: FAMILY OF 4

PREP TIME: 20 MINUTES

COOK TIME: 1 HOUR 15 MINUTES

FOR THE VEGETABLES

Virgin coconut oil, to grease the pan

1 sweet potato

4 yellow potatoes, or any other good roasting potato

2 large beets

2 large carrots

1 onion (or a few shallots)

6 cloves garlic, peeled

1 Tbsp virgin coconut oil or ghee, melted

1 Tbsp minced fresh rosemary leaves

1 Tbsp minced fresh thyme leaves

½ tsp sea salt

FOR THE CHICKEN

1 whole roasting chicken (approximately 3 lb)

1 tsp virgin coconut oil or ghee

1 tsp minced fresh rosemary leaves

1 tsp minced fresh thyme leaves

½ tsp sea salt

Ground black pepper to taste

A roast chicken is such a perfect Saturday family supper. It feels worthy of a special meal together but is actually beyond simple to prepare, so you won't spend much of your day in the kitchen. My kids like to get in on peeling the sweet potatoes and carrots, so it's a meal we can make together (if I feel up to that sort of thing!). On Sundays I make chicken stock (see page 247), then use the leftover chicken for quesadillas, sandwiches, or salads during the week. *(Photo on inside cover)*

1. Preheat the oven to 425°F. Thoroughly grease the bottom of a deep roasting pan with coconut oil or ghee.

2. Peel the sweet potato, potatoes, beets, carrots, and onion (or for the potatoes and sweet potato you can scrub them and leave the peels on if you like) and cut them into smallish wedges (around the size of ⅛ of an orange). Spread them out in the roasting pan with the cloves of garlic. Sprinkle the oil or ghee, rosemary, thyme, and salt over top. Use a large spoon or spatula to stir, making sure all the vegetables are coated.

3. Now it's time to address the chicken. Pat it dry and nestle it into the vegetables in the pan, leaving some of the vegetables under the chicken.

4. Rub the chicken with the oil or ghee and sprinkle with rosemary, thyme, salt, and pepper.

5. Place it in the oven, then turn the oven down to 400°F and roast for 1 hour and 15 minutes, turning the vegetables halfway through.

6. Serve the chicken and vegetables with the juices from the pan. This is good with a simple green salad. Dinner is done.

There are many different methods for cooking a roast chicken, so my method might be new to you. This temperature and timing combination always seems to work for me for an average-size bird, especially if I let it rest for a bit after it comes out of the oven. I find that cooking at 425°F all the way through results in vegetables that stick to the bottom and get too charred, but without the little boost at the beginning, 400°F isn't hot enough to crisp up and brown the chicken.

Chard, Squash, and Bacon Frittata

SERVES: FAMILY OF 4

PREP TIME: 15 MINUTES

COOK TIME: 27 MINUTES

6 rashers good-quality additive-free bacon

8 large eggs

⅓ cup plain whole-milk yogurt

⅓ cup freshly grated Parmesan cheese plus 1 Tbsp to sprinkle on top

¼ cup finely chopped chives

¼ cup finely chopped parsley, any type

½ tsp sea salt

Ground black pepper to taste

1 Tbsp olive oil

½ small onion, finely chopped

1 cup very small-dice butternut squash

3 large red or rainbow chard leaves, thick, bottom part of stem removed, leaves finely chopped

If you are low on groceries but have eggs, a few random vegetables, and a bit of cheese or leftover meat, a frittata is a game changer for your "in a pinch" quick supper repertoire. This recipe is a bit more special. It's inspired by a frittata recipe from *Bon Appétit* magazine that I like to make regularly, and it's a great way to use up rainbow chard, which I love to buy but then never seem to get around to cooking. You will need an ovenproof skillet for this, ideally cast iron.

1. Preheat the oven to 350°F.

2. Cut the bacon into small pieces then cook in a large oven-proof skillet. When cooked through, lay the bacon on some paper towel to drain. Remove all bacon fat from the pan, wiping it clean with a paper towel.

3. In a bowl, whisk together the eggs, yogurt, ⅓ cup Parmesan cheese, chives, parsley, salt, and a grinding of pepper.

4. Add the olive oil to the pan and sauté the onion and squash over medium heat until the squash begins to soften, approximately 10 minutes. Add a bit of water to the pan if it becomes too dry.

5. Add the chard, and cook for another couple of minutes until the chard has softened and cooked down. Return the bacon to the pan and combine with the vegetables.

6. Evenly spread out the chard mixture, then pour the eggs into the skillet, ensuring that everything is covered. Let it cook, without stirring, for 2 minutes.

7. Place the skillet in the oven and bake for 13–15 minutes. When done, it should be just cooked through with a little bit of a wobble. Overcooking will make it spongy, which you don't want.

8. Sprinkle with the remaining Parmesan cheese.

9. Cut into wedges and serve alongside a salad and some crusty bread.

Frittatas work best in a cast iron skillet, especially since they go straight from stovetop to oven. If you don't yet have one I promise you it is worth the investment. You will love it! The food won't stick, and cast iron is so much safer than a chemical-coated nonstick pan.

Veggie-Loaded Beef Soft Tacos

SERVES: FAMILY OF 4

PREP TIME: 15 MINUTES

COOK TIME: 25 MINUTES

1 lb lean ground beef

1 Tbsp extra virgin olive oil

1 small onion, diced

2 cloves garlic, roughly chopped

2 packed cups finely chopped veggies of your choice, the more brightly colored the better (spinach, kale, carrots, zucchini, broccoli, butternut squash . . .)

½ tsp sea salt

3 medium tomatoes, diced

1 tsp dried basil

1 tsp ground cumin

1 Tbsp mild chili powder

Ground black pepper to taste

Soft tortillas (gluten-free if preferred)

A variety of your family's favorite taco toppings such as: sour cream or yogurt, avocado, mild salsa, grated cheese. You won't need veggie toppings because there are so many vegetables right in the meat!

Both my kids go crazy for soft tacos, and we make this recipe approximately once per week. I love that the meat is packed full of veggies and that my kids are getting a tasty meal rich in a variety of vitamins and minerals. This recipe makes much more than you will need for a family meal, but that is intentional. Stash the leftovers in the refrigerator and use them for quesadillas, on top of pizza, mixed with rice or pasta, stuffed in a baked potato, or as part of a salad. The kids won't know they're eating the same thing over and over again, and you'll hardly have to think about dinner all week long. My Soft Spelt and Flax Tortillas (page 240) are ideal for this recipe if gluten is not an issue. *(Photo on inside cover)*

1. In a large heavy skillet, over medium heat, brown the beef, breaking it up so that there are no big lumps.

2. Once the meat is cooked, drain off the fat and transfer the beef to a bowl. Set aside.

3. Put the olive oil in the hot pan (no need to wipe it out) and add the onion and garlic. Cook until the onion is translucent and just starting to brown.

4. Add the 2 cups of chopped vegetables and the salt, and cook for another 5 minutes, stirring occasionally.

5. Add the meat, tomatoes, basil, cumin, chili powder, and pepper, and stir to combine everything. Cook for a further 5–10 minutes until the tomatoes are fully cooked down. Check the seasoning and adjust to your liking.

6. To serve, put a couple of spoonfuls of the meat and vegetable mixture in the center of a soft tortilla, add any extra toppings (let the kids choose their favorites), then roll up the taco by folding over the bottom first, then the sides. Freeze extra meat in airtight portioned containers for up to 3 months.

> To keep the filling from dropping out of the bottom of your child's taco as she eats it, wrap the bottom half of the taco in parchment paper. This will keep the taco nice and sturdy for her to hold and will keep any mess to a minimum. This is also a great way to send tacos to school in a lunchbox.

Pork Tenderloin with Buttery Apricot Sauce

SERVES: FAMILY OF 4

PREP TIME: 5 MINUTES + 2 HOURS TO MARINATE

COOK TIME: 35 MINUTES

¼ cup extra virgin olive oil

2 tsp dried sage

2 tsp dried rosemary

3 cloves garlic, crushed

1 tsp sea salt

Ground black pepper to taste

2 pork tenderloins (approximately 1½ lb altogether)

FOR THE SAUCE

1 cup low-sodium organic chicken stock, store-bought or homemade (page 247)

3 Tbsp apricot jam (I like the fruit-juice-sweetened variety)

1 tsp finely chopped fresh sage

1 Tbsp butter

1 Tbsp finely chopped fresh parsley, flat-leaf or curly

Sea salt and ground black pepper to taste

This is the recipe that made Cam quite suddenly decide he likes pork. I love it because it's very simple to throw together, but it's also special enough to serve to guests. It's delicious with classic roast potatoes and greens, or try it with the Quinoa Mushroom Pilaf (page 190) or Buttery Cauliflower Mash (page 190).

1. In a baking dish large enough to hold everything without crowding, combine the olive oil, dried sage, dried rosemary, garlic, salt, and pepper.

2. Lay the pork in the dish and turn it several times so that it is well covered on all sides. Cover and refrigerate for at least a couple of hours or up to 24 hours.

3. When ready to cook, preheat the oven to 425°F.

4. Heat up a large deep skillet over medium-high heat. Place the tenderloins in the skillet one at a time, using tongs to turn them and brown each side. Place the browned tenderloins in a roasting pan (or keep them in the skillet if it's ovenproof), put them in the oven, and cook for 18–20 minutes. If you have a meat thermometer, you can check to see that they are at the ideal internal temperature of 140°F–145°F.

5. Take the meat out of the oven, tent loosely with foil, and let rest for 10 minutes.

6. To make the apricot sauce, place the skillet on the stove over medium heat, and add the chicken stock. Scrape the bottom to loosen all the little bits from browning the pork, and bring to a simmer.

7. Add the apricot jam and fresh sage, and simmer, stirring occasionally, for a further few minutes.

8. Turn off the heat and stir in the butter, parsley, and salt and pepper.

9. Slice the pork into thin slices and serve with the sauce drizzled on top.

Any leftover pork can be used as sandwich meat or as an addition to lunch salads.

My Mom's Shepherd's Pie

SERVES: FAMILY OF 4

PREP TIME: 20 MINUTES

COOK TIME: 40–45 MINUTES

1 Tbsp extra virgin olive oil or ghee, plus extra to grease the dish

4 medium yellow potatoes, peeled and chopped into 2-inch pieces (approximately 1¾ lb)

1 medium sweet potato, peeled and chopped into 2-inch pieces (approximately 12 oz)

1 medium onion, diced small

1 large carrot, grated

1 tsp finely chopped fresh rosemary

1 lb extra-lean ground beef

¾ cup frozen green peas

2 Tbsp flour (regular, spelt, or gluten-free)

1 tsp sea salt

4 Tbsp butter, divided

Substitute ground chicken, turkey, or lamb for the beef if you prefer.

I have eaten this meal many, many times over my lifetime. My mom made it for her family for years, and now I make it for mine—and for any friend who needs a casserole for the freezer. It requires a few different pots and pans for the cooking, but is worth the extra bit of washing up.

1. Preheat the oven to 425°F. Grease an 8- × 8-inch casserole dish.

2. Using two separate pots, bring the potatoes and sweet potato to a boil over high heat, then turn down to medium-low and simmer for 20 minutes.

3. Meanwhile, in a skillet, place the oil and onion. Cook for 3 minutes over medium-high heat.

4. Add the carrot and rosemary and cook for 4 minutes, stirring frequently.

5. Add the beef and cook for 8 minutes, stirring often, until the meat separates and is cooked through.

6. Add the peas, flour, salt, and ¼ cup of water. Mix everything thoroughly, then pour the mixture into the casserole dish.

7. Drain the potatoes and sweet potato. Keeping them in separate pots, mash 2 tablespoons of butter into the potatoes and 1 tablespoon of butter into the sweet potatoes. Add the sweet potatoes to the potatoes, then, using a large spoon, combine them minimally to create a marbled effect in the top layer. Spread this evenly on top of the meat. Dot with the remaining 1 tablespoon of butter and bake, uncovered, for 20–25 minutes. You can make this dish ahead of time and freeze it, covered, right in the casserole dish before you bake it. Reheat by adding 15 minutes to the cooking time. It will keep in the freezer for up to 3 months.

Go Coconuts for Chia and Almond Chicken Strips

SERVES: FAMILY OF 4

PREP TIME: 15 MINUTES

COOK TIME: 12–14 MINUTES

2 large boneless skinless chicken breasts

1¼ cups flaked unsweetened coconut

½ cup whole raw almonds

⅓ cup chia seeds

½ tsp garlic powder

½ tsp sea salt

¼ tsp ground turmeric

2 Tbsp virgin coconut oil, melted

> I love using leftover coating (that hasn't been touched by any raw chicken) as a topping for salads. I always keep some in the freezer just for me!

Most kids love chicken strips, and I suspect parents secretly like it when they get to eat them from time to time too. Although you can now find better, more natural versions, traditional store-bought chicken strips are usually full of trans fats and are absolute sodium bombs. This healthier, grain-free and egg-free version goes the extra nutritional mile, replacing bread crumbs with a superfood coating. We like to eat these with my homemade ketchup or teriyaki sauce as a dip (see pages 245 and 248), but they're also very tasty all on their own.

1. Preheat the oven to 425°F and find a large baking tray. You might need two trays, depending on the size of your tray.

2. Cut the chicken into long strips, then cut in half again so that that they are approximately 2 inches long and 1 inch wide. Lay the chicken in a dish.

3. In a food processor fitted with the steel blade or a powerful blender, blitz the coconut, almonds, chia seeds, garlic powder, salt, and turmeric until the mixture looks like coarse crumbs and there are no big pieces of almond, then pour the mixture onto a plate or wide bowl.

4. Pour the melted coconut oil into a shallow dish. One at a time, dredge each piece of chicken first in the coconut oil, then in the coconut-almond mixture until fully coated, using your fingers to pat coating onto any bare patches. Place each piece on the baking tray.

5. Bake for 8 minutes, then flip the chicken and cook for another 4–6 minutes, until browned and baked through. Freeze leftovers on a baking tray, then transfer to an airtight container or freezer bag and keep for up to 3 months.

Orange Miso Glazed Salmon

SERVES: FAMILY OF 4

PREP TIME: 15 MINUTES

COOK TIME: 13–15 MINUTES

Virgin coconut oil, to grease the pan

1 large wild salmon fillet (half a salmon) or 4 individual fillets

¼ cup unsweetened fresh or bottled orange juice

1 small clove garlic, crushed

½ tsp minced fresh ginger

2 Tbsp miso paste

2 Tbsp extra virgin olive oil, or virgin coconut oil, melted

1 Tbsp tamari or coconut aminos

½ tsp Asian sesame oil

1 Tbsp toasted sesame seeds to serve (optional)

The Asian flavors in this tangy, salty dish bring kids over to team salmon with little convincing. Although in my experience I do find that salmon is an easier sell to kids than many other types of seafood due to its soft yet meaty texture, and mild fish flavor. Serve with simple grains and greens, or try with my Buttery Cauliflower Mash (page 190).

1. Preheat the oven to 400°F. Grease a baking dish with coconut oil and place the salmon on it skin side down.

2. To make the glaze, whisk together all the remaining ingredients, except the sesame seeds, until the miso is fully blended with no lumps.

3. Use a pastry brush or spoon to cover the salmon with the glaze. (If you like, you can add more glaze to the salmon halfway through cooking.)

4. Bake the salmon, uncovered, for 13–15 minutes, depending on its thickness. When it is done it will be opaque but still moist looking, and will flake with a fork.

5. Serve sprinkled with toasted sesame seeds if you like.

If you have time, you can marinate the salmon in the glaze for up to a few hours before cooking to intensify the flavors.

♥

Wild-caught salmon is high in omega-3s and packed with tons of other vitamins and minerals too, so is an excellent addition to your child's diet!

♥

Save the leftovers for sandwiches the next day. Simply mash the salmon with a little mayo, or olive oil and lemon juice, and spread between your favorite bread or use to fill a tortilla or lettuce wrap.

Meatless Monday Pasta with Hemp Hearts

SERVES: FAMILY OF 4

PREP TIME: 15 MINUTES

COOK TIME: 15 MINUTES

10 oz gluten-free penne, rotini, or other similar-size pasta of your choice

2 Tbsp olive oil

2 cloves garlic, crushed

1 cup frozen peas (thawed)

2½ cups broccoli florets cut small

1 Tbsp fresh lemon juice

½ cup fresh basil, finely chopped

⅓ cup hemp hearts, plus more for garnish

1–2 Tbsp nutritional yeast

¼ tsp sea salt

Ground black pepper to taste

Lemon wedges for serving

At first glance, pasta and hemp hearts may seem like an odd combination, but they work together incredibly well. Ideal for those days when you are going meatless (even one dinner a week will make a difference to our precious planet), hemp hearts are an impressive vegetarian protein source. Here they don't just add nutrition; they also contribute texture and a nutty flavor that works so well with lemon, vegetables, and the cheesy flavor of nutritional yeast. You'll notice the recipe calls for 1–2 tablespoons of nutritional yeast. This is because I find people's tastes tend to vary with this flavoring. Start with 1 tablespoon, then add more if you prefer the flavor to come through more strongly.

1. Begin by getting the pasta cooking according to the instructions on the package.

2. In a large skillet over medium heat, heat the oil, then cook the garlic for approximately 2 minutes, stirring frequently.

3. Add the thawed peas and cook for 2 minutes more.

4. Next add the broccoli, cooking until it is bright green and tender, approximately 3 minutes, depending how small you've cut it up.

5. Drain the pasta, withholding approximately ½ cup of the pasta water, then add the pasta and the reserved cooking water to the vegetables. Stir to combine, turn off the heat, and add the lemon juice, basil, hemp hearts, nutritional yeast, salt, and pepper. Stir to mix well, then adjust the seasoning and nutritional yeast to your tastes. Serve topped with an extra sprinkling of hemp hearts and lemon wedges.

This dish is 100 percent plant-based, but you can replace the nutritional yeast with fresh mozzarella or goat cheese if you like.

Cashew Mushroom Sliders

MAKES: 12 SMALL PATTIES

PREP TIME: 1 HOUR INCLUDING CHILLING TIME

COOK TIME: 10 MINUTES

2 tsp ground chia seeds

2 Tbsp tamari

1 Tbsp honey or maple syrup (for plant-based)

1 Tbsp nutritional yeast

1 tsp dried thyme

1 small onion, finely minced

2 cloves garlic, minced

¼ tsp sea salt

2 Tbsp virgin coconut oil, divided

⅔ cup raw cashews

½ lb mushrooms, roughly chopped

⅓ cup flat-leaf parsley

¾ cup dried bread crumbs

Slider buns or small bread rolls (try my Little Spelt Buns on page 242)

Toppings: lettuce, tomato, mayo, etc.

My husband is not a veggie burger guy, but he loves these. The trick is to make sure the patties have texture by not processing the cashews or mushrooms too much. These hold together pretty well, but are best served contained inside a bun, as a mini burger. If you like, you can prepare this recipe up to 24 hours ahead and then cook up the patties right before serving.

1. In a large bowl, mix the chia seeds with 2 tablespoons of water, the tamari, honey, nutritional yeast, and thyme. Set aside to allow to gel for 10 minutes.

2. Sauté the onion and garlic with the salt in 1 tablespoon of the oil over medium heat until translucent, stirring occasionally.

3. While keeping an eye on the onion and garlic, in a food processor fitted with the steel blade, blitz the cashews until just chopped into small pieces. Pour on top of the chia mixture.

4. Put the mushrooms and parsley in the food processor and pulse until finely chopped. Be sure not to process them so much that they become pureed. You want some texture. Add to the bowl on top of the cashews, and add the bread crumbs as well.

5. Spoon the cooked onion and garlic into the bowl with everything else, and stir until well mixed.

6. Cover and place in the refrigerator for at least ½ hour.

7. To make uniform-size patties, use a small ice cream scoop to measure out balls of the cashew-mushroom mixture into your hand, then form each into a small disk shape that will fit your slider buns. You can do this one by one, putting them straight into the pan, or form all twelve patties first, laying them out on a plate ready to be cooked.

8. Heat the remaining 1 tablespoon of oil in a large skillet over medium heat. Cook the patties for approximately 4 minutes on each side, flipping carefully and keeping watch that they don't burn. If the pan becomes too hot, turn the heat down as necessary.

9. Serve in a slider bun with your favorite burger toppings. We enjoy ours best with mayo, lettuce, and tomato, and sometimes, to fancy them up, with pickled red onions or chutney.

Commercial bread crumbs are often full of additives and are usually made with white bread. Make your own by drying out slices of your favorite multigrain bread in a low-temperature oven, then giving them a blitz in a food processor. They store really well in an airtight bag or container in the freezer for up to 6 months.

Family-Size Gluten-Free Pizza

SERVES: FAMILY OF 4
PREP TIME: 15 MINUTES
COOK TIME: 30 MINUTES

2 Tbsp olive oil

2 tsp honey

2 tsp active dry yeast

1¼ cups almond flour

1¼ cups quinoa flour

¾ cup tapioca flour

1 Tbsp ground chia seeds

1 tsp sea salt

1 tsp dried basil

1 tsp garlic powder

1 tsp dried oregano

A selection of your family's favorite pizza toppings, finely chopped

To make this into a fully cooked but naked flatbread, bake it for 20–25 minutes at step 9. Try spreading the warm flatbread with hummus (try my Roasted Garlic and Squash Hummus, page 166), then top with diced avocado and crumbled goat cheese.

The dough for this pizza doesn't have the exact texture of regular pizza dough, but even gluten-lovers will enjoy it!

1. Preheat the oven to 350°F and grease or line a solid-bottomed large pizza pan or stone, or a 12- x 18-inch rimmed baking sheet. (You can also use smaller, personal-size pans if you like.)

2. In a medium-size bowl or measuring jug, whisk together ⅔ cup plus 2 tablespoons very warm but not piping hot water, the olive oil, and the honey.

3. Sprinkle the yeast over top and give it a gentle stir. Allow to sit for at least 5 minutes until the yeast blooms.

4. In a large bowl, combine the almond flour, quinoa flour, tapioca flour, chia, salt, basil, garlic powder, and oregano.

5. Pour the yeast mixture into the flour and stir together until it makes a ball of sticky dough.

6. Dump the dough out onto the baking sheet.

7. Dust your hands with quinoa flour, or other gluten-free flour, then press the dough out onto the pan until it is just under ¼ inch thick. You will need to keep flouring your hands as you do this so that the dough doesn't stick to you.

8. Continue to use your floured hands to smooth out the dough as best you can and to even up the edges. Try to make sure the edges are thicker than the center of the dough so that you get a nice rim of crust. While the dough will naturally get quite dark and crispy around the edges as it bakes (and this is fine—the crispy bits taste delicious), this step will help keep the edges from becoming burned rather than browned.

9. Bake the pizza base in the oven for 15 minutes. When it is done, the center will feel soft but dry to the touch and the edges of the base will be starting to darken.

10. Retrieve the base from the oven and top with your favorite pizza sauce and toppings, then put it straight back in the oven for 15 minutes more. When properly cooked, the dough will be dark golden, crispy around the edges, and soft in the middle with a dark golden bottom; the toppings will be hot and bubbling.

11. Cut into squares or wedges and serve warm. Store leftover pizza in the refrigerator for a day or two.

Creamy Chickpea and Spinach Curry

SERVES: FAMILY OF 4

PREP TIME: 15 MINUTES

COOK TIME: 35 MINUTES

1 small onion, finely chopped

2 cloves garlic, crushed

2 Tbsp virgin coconut oil or ghee

1½ tsp fresh grated ginger

1 tsp sea salt

1 tsp ground coriander

½ tsp ground cumin

¼ tsp ground turmeric

¼ tsp ground cinnamon

1 (19 oz) can chickpeas, rinsed and drained (sodium-free and from a BPA-free can)

2 medium tomatoes, finely chopped

1 (13.5 oz) can organic full-fat coconut milk (from a BPA-free can)

1 Tbsp coconut sugar

1 Tbsp tomato paste

3 cups chopped fresh baby spinach

⅓ cup cilantro

Curries are quite simple to make from scratch once you've stocked your pantry with a few spices, and the bold flavors yet mild spice of this curry are child-friendly. So give jarred curry sauce and the takeout restaurant a miss and try a homemade curry!

1. Sauté the onion and garlic in the coconut oil for 5 minutes in a large skillet or pot over medium heat. Add the ginger, salt, coriander, cumin, turmeric, and cinnamon, and continue cooking, stirring constantly, for another 2 minutes.

2. Add the chickpeas, tomatoes, coconut milk, sugar, tomato paste, and 1 cup of water to the pan. Bring to a boil, then turn down the heat and simmer, covered, for 20 minutes.

3. Add the spinach, turn the heat to medium and cook, uncovered, for another 5 minutes. Sprinkle cilantro over each serving. Serve with rice or naan. Freeze leftovers for up to 3 months.

Cilantro is one of my favorite herbs, but it can be an acquired taste. Feel free to substitute cilantro with mint, or sprinkle some unsweetened dried shredded coconut on top instead of herbs.

Three Easy Sides

Buttery Cauliflower Mash

SERVES: 4 AS A SIDE DISH

PREP TIME: 5 MINUTES

COOK TIME: 7 MINUTES

1 medium head cauliflower

1½ Tbsp unsalted butter

Sea salt and ground black
    pepper to taste

This simple side dish can be served alongside almost anything. Feel free to customize it by adding your favorite ingredients. Cheese (Parmesan, cheddar, cream cheese, etc.), roasted garlic, or finely chopped fresh herbs are all good. *(Photo on inside cover)*

1. Cut the cauliflower into florets, discarding the leaves. Place the florets in a large pot of boiling salted water and boil gently for 7 minutes, until tender.

2. Drain the cauliflower well, then pour it onto a clean dry tea towel and pat as much of the water off as possible.

3. Puree the cauliflower with the butter, salt, and pepper, until just blended. An immersion blender is ideal for this. Serve immediately.

Quinoa Mushroom Pilaf

SERVES: 4 AS A SIDE DISH

PREP TIME: 10 MINUTES

COOK TIME: 23 MINUTES

½ lb white or brown mushrooms,
    finely chopped

1 medium onion, finely chopped

1 Tbsp unsalted butter

1 cup uncooked quinoa

¼ tsp dried sage

½ tsp dried rosemary

½ tsp dried thyme

½ tsp sea salt

2 cups organic low-sodium chicken
    stock, store-bought or home-
    made (see Chicken Vegetable
    Stock, page 247)

1 Tbsp minced flat-leaf or curly
    parsley

When I was young, on special occasions my mom made a baked barley version of this that I just loved. I've updated the recipe by using gluten-free, protein-packed quinoa in place of barley and making it on the stovetop to keep things simple. This is such a comforting yet deceptively nutritious dish.

1. In a medium-size pot, sauté the mushrooms and onion in the butter for approximately 5 minutes over medium heat.

2. Add the quinoa, dried herbs, salt, and chicken stock and bring to a boil.

3. Turn the heat to low, cover the pan, and simmer for 15 minutes, until all the liquid has been absorbed.

4. Remove the lid and cook for another minute or so, stirring gently, to let any extra moisture evaporate.

5. Stir in the parsley before serving.

Broccoli with Zippy Peanut Sauce

SERVES: 4 (MAKES 1 CUP OF SAUCE)
PREP TIME: 5 MINUTES
COOK TIME: 5 MINUTES

1 medium head broccoli

1 large clove garlic, minced

½ cup crunchy natural peanut butter (smooth will work too, the sauce just won't be textured)

2 Tbsp tamari or coconut aminos

1 Tbsp honey or maple syrup (for plant-based)

1 Tbsp rice vinegar

1 tsp toasted sesame oil

½ tsp ground ginger

Juice of 1 lime

Pinch of chili flakes (optional)

Broccoli tends to be a green that kids will accept, but it can get boring for them if it's always served plain. This peanut sauce makes broccoli seem like a completely different food altogether and is also delicious with other vegetables, chicken, or shrimp.

1. Steam the broccoli until bright green and tender.

2. Meanwhile, whisk together all the other ingredients plus ¼ cup warm water until very well combined.

3. Drain the broccoli really well (to get rid of any drips from steaming), then put it back in the pan and toss with half the sauce. Save the rest for a stir-fry or to use as a dip for chicken, prawns, or raw veggies. The sauce keeps well in an airtight container in the refrigerator for a week or two.

If your kids are wary of sauce on their broccoli, leave the sauce on the side and serve it alongside the broccoli for dipping.

♥

I've only given you three side dish recipes because so many of the other recipes in this book can be adapted as sides. Try the Roasted Sweet Potato Fries (page 106) or Mini Roasted Cauliflower Florets (page 106), for example.

CHAPTER SEVEN

healthier
snacks
& treats

Apple Raspberry Fruit Leather

MAKES: 6 LONG STRIPS (6 CHILD-SIZE SERVINGS)

PREP TIME: 15 MINUTES

COOK TIME: 6–7 HOURS

4 cups peeled and diced Golden Delicious or other sweet apple (approximately 5 apples)

½ cup frozen raspberries

> You can eat the fruit leather straight away, but it will be even better if you put it in a container and let it sit for a day or so to soften up first.

I was determined to include a recipe for fruit leather in this book, but let me tell you, this became my recipe nemesis! I tried all different types of fruit, cooking temperatures, and cooking times, and here's what I learned: fruit leather is unpredictable and has a mind of its own. Because the sugar and water content of fruit vary and oven temperatures often aren't consistent, you may find that your fruit leather takes more or less time than mine. My best advice is to follow this recipe as closely as possible, and check the fruit leather every 15 minutes between the 6- and 7-hour mark so it doesn't burn. I found that using a silicone baking sheet (like a Silpat mat) made my results much more consistent than if I used parchment paper. The baking sheet allows the puree to settle much more smoothly on the tray, which allows it to dry out more evenly. If you use parchment, spend some extra time smoothing and jiggling the puree until it's even before you put it in the oven.

1. Preheat the oven to 170°F and line a 12- × 18-inch rimmed baking sheet with a silicone baking sheet or parchment paper.

2. Cook the apples and raspberries with 2 tablespoons of water over medium heat, stirring often, until soft, approximately 10 minutes. I find that covering the pot when you're not stirring works the best because it helps keep the bottom of the pan from drying out.

3. Transfer the fruit to a blender and puree until smooth.

4. Pour the fruit into the pan and spread it out as evenly as possible to just under ¼ inch thick.

5. Bake for 6–7 hours in the middle of the oven. When done, the fruit leather will be just dry to the touch with no pillowy lumps of wet puree left underneath the surface.

6. Once the fruit leather is cool, peel it from the silicone sheet and lay it on the counter. Use clean scissors to cut it into strips.

7. Roll up each strip, and store them flat side down like little columns, in a wide, lidded container. The fruit leather will keep well for at least a month at room temperature. These are perfect for sending to school as part of a bento box and are much healthier than most store-bought versions.

Aloha Muffins

MAKES: 12 MUFFINS

PREP TIME: 15 MINUTES

COOK TIME: 25–30 MINUTES

⅔ cup plus 2 Tbsp coconut flour

½ tsp baking soda

½ tsp cream of tartar

½ tsp sea salt

4 eggs

2 ripe bananas, mashed

⅔ cup honey

½ cup virgin coconut oil, melted

1 Tbsp fresh lemon juice

1 tsp finely grated lemon zest

1 tsp pure vanilla extract

1⅓ cups ¼-inch dice fresh or frozen thawed mango

1½ Tbsp unsweetened finely shredded coconut

These tropical treat–like gluten-free muffins might be mistaken for cupcakes because they're quite decadent, but because they are full of protein, potassium, and fiber and don't need icing, I would argue they've rightly earned their claim to muffin-hood! Made with coconut flour, they are a welcome treat for families who follow a grain-free diet.

1. Preheat the oven to 350°F. Line a 12-cup muffin pan with paper muffin cups. These muffins are delicate, so it is important to use paper cups rather than just greasing the muffin pan.

2. Sift the coconut flour into a large bowl and stir in the baking soda, cream of tartar, and salt.

3. In a blender or a food processor fitted with the steel blade, whizz together the eggs, bananas, honey, coconut oil, lemon juice and zest, and vanilla.

4. Pour the wet ingredients into the dry and stir to combine. Stir in the mango.

5. Spoon the batter into the muffin cups, filling them almost to the top, then sprinkle coconut over top of each muffin.

6. Bake for approximately 25–30 minutes. When done, the muffins will be golden and a toothpick inserted in the center of one will come out clean. Gently remove the muffins from the pan and allow them to cool completely on a rack. They will feel very soft and delicate as you are doing this, but they will firm up once cool. These are best eaten on the day they are made, but can be frozen in an airtight container for up to 3 months.

> Coconut flour makes these muffins a bit fragile. It just doesn't allow muffins to hold together as well as muffins made from gluten-containing flour, so they need more egg than traditional muffins. To make sure the muffins don't fall apart when eaten, allow them to cool completely before taking off the muffin papers and enjoying.

Popeye's Banana Bread

MAKES: 1 LOAF

PREP TIME: 15 MINUTES

COOK TIME: 1 HOUR

¼ cup virgin coconut oil, melted, + extra to grease the pan

2 cups all-purpose gluten-free flour (see All-Purpose Gluten-Free Flour Blend, page 241)

2 Tbsp flaxseeds

1½ tsp baking powder

½ tsp baking soda

½ tsp sea salt

3 large ripe bananas

2 eggs

½ cup liquid honey

1 tsp ground chia seeds

2 tsp pure vanilla extract

1 packed cup chopped baby spinach leaves, stems removed

⅔ cup chopped pecans or walnuts

½ cup chocolate chips (optional)

Spinach in banana bread isn't exactly traditional, but it gives this treat a boost of green muscle and is hardly noticeable in the finished product. It might be tempting to keep the spinach on the low down, but I recommend pointing out (with convincing enthusiasm) that this banana bread has spinach in it! Even better, have your kids help you make it to encourage the idea that greens are a good thing and nothing to be wary of.

1. Preheat the oven to 350°F. Grease a deep 9- × 5-inch loaf pan with coconut oil and then dust it with gluten-free flour. Even better, use a silicone loaf pan, which doesn't need any preparation and won't stick.

2. Place the flour, flaxseeds, baking powder, baking soda, and salt in a large bowl and mix to combine.

3. In a food processor fitted with the steel blade, combine the bananas, eggs, honey, coconut oil, chia, and vanilla until completely smooth.

4. Add the spinach and pulse gently until it is in very small pieces but not completely blended in. You don't want to turn the mixture green by blending it too much.

5. Pour the wet ingredients into the dry, mix until just combined, and then stir in the nut pieces and chocolate chips (if using).

6. Pour into the loaf pan and bake for approximately 1 hour. A toothpick inserted in the center of the loaf should come out clean, and the top should be dark golden.

7. Allow to cool slightly before removing from the pan and cooling on a wire rack. Slice off pieces as needed and serve plain or spread with butter or coconut oil. To store, wrap whatever is left unsliced in parchment paper or foil. This will keep well for a few days on the counter, or you can wrap slices individually and freeze them in an airtight container for up to 3 months.

If you prefer, this recipe can be made with spelt flour (or organic whole wheat flour). Simply replace the 2 cups of all-purpose gluten-free flour with 2 cups of spelt or whole wheat flour.

Gluten-Free Oatmeal Chocolate Chip Cookies

MAKES: 24 COOKIES

PREP TIME: 20 MINUTES

COOK TIME: 8–10 MINUTES

1 cup all-purpose gluten-free flour (see page 241)

½ cup pure or certified gluten-free rolled oats

2 Tbsp flax meal

¼ tsp baking soda

¼ tsp sea salt

¼ cup unsalted soft butter

⅓ cup coconut sugar

1 egg

¼ cup honey

1 tsp pure vanilla extract

¼ tsp apple cider vinegar

½ cup semi-sweet mini chocolate chips

This book wouldn't be complete without a go-to chocolate chip cookie recipe. These cookies have a traditional texture and taste but are gluten-free, are lighter on sugar and butter than regular cookies, and have some flax for extra fiber.

1. Preheat the oven to 350°F. Line a baking tray with parchment paper.

2. In a large bowl, mix together the flour, oats, flax meal, baking soda, and salt and set aside.

3. In a separate large bowl, using an electric mixer or a stand mixer, beat the butter until creamy.

4. Add the sugar and beat for 2 minutes more, then add the egg, honey, and vanilla and beat for another 2 minutes.

5. Sprinkle in the apple cider vinegar and beat for another 10 seconds.

6. Add the flour and mix on low speed until well combined.

7. Lastly, mix in the chocolate chips, again on low.

8. Drop teaspoon-size dollops of batter onto the tray, approximately 2 inches apart.

9. Wet a small spoon and use it to flatten the unbaked cookies into flat disks approximately ½ inch thick.

10. Bake for 8–10 minutes. When ready, the centers will still be slightly soft to the touch and the edges will be dark golden.

11. Cool on the tray for 5 minutes, then transfer to a wire rack to cool.

12. Store in a cookie jar for up to 2 weeks (not that these will possibly last that long!) or freeze them in an airtight container for up to 3 months.

Pizza Love Buns

MAKES: 12 BUNS

**PREP TIME: 1 HOUR 50 MINUTES,
INCLUDING RISING TIME**

COOK TIME: 13–15 MINUTES

1 unbaked recipe Little Spelt
  Buns (page 242), excluding
  the whisked egg for the egg
  wash and the sesame seeds

⅔ cup ready-made jarred tomato
  pasta sauce

2 Tbsp extra virgin olive oil

½ cup finely grated cheddar
  cheese (use whatever
  strength your kids like)

½ cup finely grated Parmesan
  cheese

½ tsp dried basil

½ tsp dried oregano

> My kitchen is always
> stocked with a jar of
> good-quality, no-
> sugar-added organic
> pasta sauce. It keeps
> well and can be used
> as a quick option for
> many different meals
> when I don't have
> time to make my own
> sauce.

These yummy heart-shaped snack buns are amazing
served warm and gooey straight out of the oven and are
also really good at room temperature in a lunchbox.

1. Line a baking tray with parchment paper.

2. Follow the Little Spelt Buns recipe on page 242 to step 7.

3. Punch down the dough, and then divide it into twelve balls.
Leave them on the counter, covered by a dry tea towel.

4. One at a time, use your hands to roll out each ball of dough
into a long log shape, approximately 12 inches long. Form the
log of dough into the outline of a heart shape (so that there is
an empty heart-shaped space in the middle), pinching the ends
together to close the heart.

5. Carefully place the hearts on the lined baking tray, 2 inches
apart, and cover with a dry tea towel while you are making the
rest of the hearts. You may need to make these in two batches.
If you put them onto two trays and bake them all at once, put
each tray on a different shelf in the oven, with one sitting
toward the left of the oven and the other to the right, and
rotate them halfway through baking.

6. Use a butter knife to make Xs all along the dough on each
heart. These indentations won't really show once the buns are
cooked but will help lots of pizza sauce to stick to the dough.
Cover the hearts back up again with a dry tea towel and leave to
rise for 20 minutes.

7. Preheat the oven to 375°F. Whisk together the tomato sauce
with the olive oil.

8. In a separate small bowl, combine the cheddar, Parmesan,
basil, and oregano. Use a pastry brush to generously cover the
top of each heart with the sauce, then sprinkle each of them all
over with the cheese mixture.

9. Bake for 13–15 minutes. When done, they will be nicely puffed
up and browned on the bottom, and the tomato sauce and
cheese will be all bubbly and melty.

10. Cool for a few minutes on the tray then transfer to a rack.
Serve warm or at room temperature. Eat within 24 hours or
freeze in an airtight container for up to 3 months.

Mini Pumpkin Chocolate Chip Muffins

MAKES: 24 MUFFINS

PREP TIME: 10 MINUTES

COOK TIME: 18 MINUTES

3 Tbsp virgin coconut oil, melted, + extra to grease the pan

1¾ cups spelt flour

1½ tsp baking powder

½ tsp baking soda

¾ tsp ground cinnamon

¼ tsp sea salt

Pinch of ground nutmeg

1 egg

1 cup pumpkin puree

½ cup maple syrup

⅓ cup mini semi-sweet chocolate chips

If you want to make a muffin more appealing for a small child, make it mini! These are perfect for sending to school. Sweetened with maple syrup and pumped up with nutrient-rich pumpkin, these minis are the epitome of a healthier treat.

1. Preheat the oven to 350°F. Grease the cups of a mini muffin pan with coconut oil or line them with mini muffin papers (petits fours papers).

2. Place the flour, baking powder, baking soda, cinnamon, salt, and nutmeg in a large bowl and mix to combine.

3. In a separate bowl, whisk together the egg, pumpkin puree, maple syrup, and coconut oil until frothy.

4. Pour the wet ingredients into the dry and mix until just combined. Stir in the chocolate chips.

5. Fill the muffin cups almost to the top and bake in the oven for 18–20 minutes, until a toothpick inserted in the center comes out clean. Let them cool on a wire rack. Serve them warm or at room temperature. These will keep well for a couple of days in an airtight container, or you can freeze them in an airtight container or freezer bag for up to 3 months.

Cheesy Little Crackers

MAKES: APPROXIMATELY 6 DOZEN
CRACKERS

PREP TIME: 20 MINUTES INCLUDING
CHILLING TIME

COOK TIME: 10 MINUTES

¾ cup spelt flour

⅓ cup oat flour

2 Tbsp hemp hearts

½ cup grated sharp cheddar
    cheese

3 Tbsp unsalted butter

¼ tsp sea salt

Mini cheese crackers are very, very popular with small children, but many store-bought varieties contain vegetable oils that promote inflammation and are highly likely to be GMO. They also contain autolyzed yeast, which sounds OK but is actually a flavor enhancer not dissimilar to MSG. This recipe contains hemp hearts for a little boost of protein and omega-3s, and whole-grain spelt flour. Much better than the alternative and way less junk-like.

1. Pulse all the ingredients in a food processor fitted with the steel blade until the mixture becomes dough-like.

2. Tip the mixture into a bowl and use your hands to fully bring the dough together. Form it into a disk shape, wrap it in parchment paper, and refrigerate for 15 minutes.

3. Preheat the oven to 350°F. Line a large baking tray with parchment paper.

4. Sprinkle the countertop with spelt flour and also rub some on a rolling pin to prevent the dough from sticking. Roll out the dough to ⅛ inch thick.

5. Now use mini cookie cutters to cut out your crackers into little shapes, or you can simply cut them into small bite-size squares using a knife, pizza cutter, or pastry wheel if you have one.

6. Carefully lay the crackers out on the tray, ¼ inch apart.

7. Bake for 10 minutes until just golden.

8. Allow to cool right on the tray. These are best eaten straight away, but will keep for a few days in a very airtight container. I like to put them in a paper bag and fold it down all the way to get as much air out as possible, then put the bag inside a lidded glass container. It doesn't look that pretty, but it keeps the crackers crisp for longer than if they were just loose inside the container.

Chewy No-Bake Goji Chip Bars

MAKES: 12–18 BARS

PREP TIME: 20 MINUTES + 2 HOURS TO CHILL

½ cup chopped dried pitted dates (the very dark, very dried type, not Medjool or Deglet Nour)

¼ cup dried goji berries

Virgin coconut oil, to grease the pan

½ cup smooth almond butter

1 tsp pure vanilla extract

1¼ cups rolled oats ("pure" or certified gluten-free oats if you are avoiding gluten)

¼ cup flaxseeds

⅓ cup semi-sweet mini chocolate chips

¼ cup finely chopped raw almonds

A true superfood, bright red goji berries are full of antioxidants and are an excellent addition to your child's diet. These bars contain a few chocolate chips but no other sweeteners besides dried fruit. Combined with the oats, almonds, and flaxseeds, they'll keep kids going through their many activities without a sugar crash.

1. Soak the dates and goji berries for 10 minutes in hot boiled water.

2. Lightly grease an 8- × 8-inch cake pan with coconut oil.

3. Drain the dates and gojis and puree with the almond butter and vanilla in a food processor fitted with the steel blade until they make a thick paste. You will probably have to stop several times and scrape down the sides of the processor bowl.

4. Add 1 cup of the oats and the flaxseeds to the food processor and blend again, until the oats are fully broken down and pureed. If the dough forms into a lump while blending, stop the food processor and break it up with a spatula and pulse until pureed. You will notice that some of the flaxseeds will still be whole no matter how much you puree. That's fine.

5. Tip the mixture into a large bowl, and add the rest of the oats, the chocolate chips, and the chopped almonds. Using damp fingers, squish and squash everything together until fully combined.

6. Using your hands again, press the mixture into the prepared pan. Smooth down and even out the top using damp hands or the back of a damp spoon. If there are chocolate chips left in the bowl that have come loose from the dough, pour them on top and press them in with your hands. Chill, covered, in the refrigerator for at least 2 hours.

7. Cut into bars and wrap them individually with parchment paper. These can be stored in an airtight container in the refrigerator for up to a week, or in the freezer for a few months.

Maple Kettle Corn with Hemp Hearts

MAKES: APPROXIMATELY 6 CUPS

PREP TIME: 15 MINUTES (INCLUDING MAKING THE POPCORN)

COOK TIME: 5 MINUTES

1 tsp + 1 Tbsp virgin coconut oil

⅓ cup organic popcorn kernels

2 Tbsp maple syrup

1 Tbsp hemp hearts

Sea salt to taste

If you make your popcorn in an air popping machine, join the recipe at step 5.

♥

Popcorn can be a choking hazard for very young children. Wait until they are past the preschool years before serving them this treat.

At our local Sunday farmers' market in Whistler, British Columbia, the kettle corn is legendary. Crispy, sweet, and salty, and with a tantalizing smell that wafts through the crowds, it's almost impossible not to bring home a bag. This popcorn is inspired by Sundays at the market, but with a maple and hemp heart twist.

1. Preheat the oven to 350°F. Line a 12- × 18-inch rimmed baking sheet with parchment paper.

2. Add the 1 teaspoon coconut oil to a large pot with a lid and heat it over medium-high heat.

3. Add the popcorn, cover, and listen closely for the popcorn to begin popping.

4. To avoid burning the popcorn, you will need to shake the pot every 15 seconds or so while the corn is popping. To do this, put on your trusty oven mitts and, holding the pot lid tightly shut, lift up the pot and give it a good shake. Continue to set the pot on the heat for 15 seconds then lift it and shake again until the popping almost stops. Take off the heat and let sit for 1 minute before lifting the lid.

5. Using a small pan on the stove or the microwave, warm the 1 tablespoon of coconut oil and the maple syrup together until runny. Whisk the mixture with a fork, then drizzle half of it over the popcorn.

6. Sprinkle the popcorn with half the hemp hearts and some sea salt, then stir, bringing the dry popcorn from the bottom up to the top.

7. Drizzle the remaining coconut oil and maple syrup mixture over top, then add the remaining hemp hearts and a bit more salt.

8. Turn the popcorn out onto the prepared baking sheet and spread it out in one layer.

9. Bake for 3 minutes, give it a stir, and then bake for 1–2 minutes more, being careful not to char the hemp hearts.

10. Ideally, eat this straight away, but you can also store it in an airtight container for a couple of days.

Four Frozen Pops

MAKES: 6-8 POPS, DEPENDING ON TYPE OF POPSICLE MOLD

Nothing says summer like a frozen pop on a stick. You can pretty much blend up any combination of fruit, juice, and yogurt with a bit of natural sweetener, freeze it in a Popsicle mold, and be confident that you'll make something delicious. These recipes have been vetted by my little ones and are tried and true favorites. I love that they are getting some nutrition in what they see as a really special treat, and also that we are avoiding artificial colors and copious amounts of sugar, common in store-bought Popsicles.

The Nutty Chocolate Banana Pops, the Minted Blueberry Watermelon Pops, and the Banana Peach Cream Pops are all made in the same way. The Creamy Strawberry Rhubarb Pops require an extra step (see facing page).

Nutty Chocolate Banana Pops

PREP TIME: 5 MINUTES + TIME TO FREEZE

2 ripe bananas

1 cup full-fat milk, or coconut milk from BPA-free can (for plant-based)

2 Tbsp unsweetened cocoa (or cacao)

2 Tbsp maple syrup

2 Tbsp smooth almond butter

Good pinch of grated nutmeg (optional)

Minted Blueberry Watermelon Pops

PREP TIME: 5 MINUTES + TIME TO FREEZE

2 cups watermelon

½ cup blueberries

¼ large avocado (freeze leftovers, see page 88)

1½ Tbsp honey

Juice of 1 lime

1 large mint leaf

Banana Peach Cream Pops

PREP TIME: 5 MINUTES + TIME TO FREEZE *(Photo on facing page)*

2 cups sliced, peeled peaches

1 ripe banana

½ cup full-fat coconut milk (from a BPA-free can)

2 Tbsp honey

1. Blend all the ingredients together in a blender or a food processor fitted with the steel blade.

2. Pour into Popsicle molds, place the sticks in carefully, and freeze for at least a few hours.

3. To release the pops from the mold, run them under hot water for a minute or so. They should come out with a little tug.

Creamy Strawberry Rhubarb Pops

PREP TIME: 10 MINUTES + TIME TO FREEZE

1½ cups diced strawberries

½ cup diced rhubarb

1 cup unsweetened apple juice

1½ Tbsp honey

½ tsp pure vanilla extract

½ cup plain whole-milk yogurt

1. Simmer the strawberries, rhubarb, apple juice, and honey in a pot over medium heat until the fruit is soft. Remove from the heat and allow to cool.

2. Blend the fruit mixture with the vanilla and yogurt and freeze in Popsicle molds for at least a few hours.

3. To release the pops from the mold, run them under hot water for a minute or so. They should come out with a little tug.

Frozen Chocolate Peanut Butter Banana Bark

MAKES: 8- × 8-INCH PAN OF BARK

PREP TIME: 10 MINUTES

¾ cup canned navy beans, rinsed and drained (sodium-free and from a BPA-free can)

⅓ cup maple syrup

¼ cup raw cacao (Dutch-processed cocoa is fine to substitute but won't have as many health benefits as raw cacao)

¼ cup natural unsalted smooth peanut butter

¼ cup almond milk

2 Tbsp virgin coconut oil, melted

Pinch of sea salt

1 small ripe banana

1 Tbsp semi-sweet chocolate chips (dairy-free)

1 tsp almond milk

I once had the opportunity to try some chocolate hummus at a trade show for natural foods. It was so popular that the staff at the booth didn't have time to thaw it properly before handing it out to customers, and my sample was still frozen. It was so delicious this way that I thought they should have been marketing it as ice cream, and I was inspired to create this frozen chocolate bark. Beans may seem weird in a sweet recipe, but you don't taste the mild flavor of these navy beans, and their extra-soft texture works perfectly here. Plus, along with the peanut butter, they pump up the protein of this yummy super-powered frozen treat.

1. Line an 8- × 8-inch baking pan with parchment paper, letting the paper hang over the sides a little.

2. In a food processor fitted with the steel blade, puree the beans, maple syrup, cacao, peanut butter, almond milk, coconut oil, and salt until very smooth.

3. Pour it into the prepared pan. Smooth out the top of the bark as best you can.

4. Slice the banana into thin rounds, then cut each round into quarters. Place them all over the top of the bark.

5. Gently melt the chocolate chips with the almond milk and stir together until well combined.

6. Drizzle the chocolate over the bark.

7. Freeze, uncovered, for at least 3 hours. Cover it if you're planning to leave it in the freezer for longer.

8. To serve, take the bark out of the freezer and set the pan on the counter for 10 minutes or so to soften slightly. Use a knife to break it into large chunks or cut it into bite-size pieces. Store the cut-up bark in the freezer in an airtight container or freezer bag for up to 1 month—any longer and it tends to get freezer-burned.

> If serving in larger bark-like pieces, wrap the bottom of each piece in parchment or wax paper so that it is easier to hold and doesn't melt all over warm little hands.

A Healthier Jelly

SERVES: 4

PREP TIME: 5 MINUTES + 3 HOURS TO CHILL

Virgin coconut oil, to grease the mold

1¾ cups pure fruit juice, divided (we like orange/mango or an apple/grape mix but see the note on the facing page)

1 Tbsp grass-fed gelatin powder

⅓ cup just-boiled water

Berries for serving (sliced strawberries, raspberries, blueberries)

Traditional jelly desserts have little nutritional value and are full of sugar and artificial colors, which do nothing for children's ability to learn or manage their emotions or behavior. But jelly is a really fun treat for kids, and if you make it with real food ingredients rather than a package, there is no reason you shouldn't serve it. Grass-fed gelatin is becoming very popular and is said to have several health-promoting properties.

1. Very lightly grease four small (they should hold ½–⅔ cup of jelly) glass or ceramic bowls with coconut oil.

2. Put ¼ cup of the juice into a medium heat-safe bowl. Slowly add the gelatin, whisking it briskly into a smooth paste.

3. Next, whisk in the hot water until there are no lumps and the gelatin is dissolved. Add the rest of the juice and whisk.

4. Pour the jelly into the serving bowls, cover, then place in the refrigerator for at least 3 hours.

5. To serve, run hot water over the bottom of a bowl to heat the dish. Uncover it, and use a butter knife to carefully turn out the jelly onto a small serving plate. Serve with some fresh berries on the side.

Pickled Beet Sticks

MAKES: ½ CUP

PREP TIME: 5 MINUTES

COOK TIME: 15 MINUTES +

30 MINUTES TO CHILL

2 beets, peeled and cut into thin sticks

¼ cup apple cider vinegar

½ tsp honey

¼ tsp pickling spice (optional)

Good pinch of sea salt

So I will admit that only one of my children will eat these, but he doesn't just eat them, he devours them like they are a plate of his favorite cookies! If you have a child who likes beets or pickles, give these a try. Serve as a snack, cold from the refrigerator, or even as a quick side dish with something like an omelet. These do stain though, so be careful that your child isn't wearing his favorite party shirt when he eats them.

1. Put the beet sticks in a lidded pot with 1 cup water and the apple cider vinegar, honey, pickling spice, and salt.

2. Bring to a boil over high heat, then cover and simmer on low for 15 minutes.

3. Drain, then ideally chill for at least ½ hour. These will keep refrigerated in an airtight container for approximately 1 week.

Practically any juice except pineapple juice will work for the jelly. The enzymes in pineapple will prevent it from setting.

♥

To shake things up a bit, you can also put sliced fruit right in the jelly before placing it in the refrigerator to chill. Avoid pineapple, kiwi, papaya, and figs, though, if you want your jelly to set properly.

♥

For simplicity, you can bypass tipping the jelly out onto a plate and eat it straight from the bowls.

Frozen Fruit on a Stick

MAKES: 4 SKEWERS

PREP TIME: 15 MINUTES + 3 HOURS
TO FREEZE

4 (12-inch) bamboo skewers

32 bite-size pieces of assorted
  fruit (8 for each skewer)

These are perfect for serving on warm days at snack time or as a kids' dessert at a summer barbecue, and are proof that if you put food onto a stick, you will capture children's attention. Make it frozen and call it a treat, and they'll think they've really hit the jackpot. It goes without saying that it's a good idea to have a conversation with kids about safety with skewers, and it's probably best to save these for children who are past toddler age.

1. Skewer eight or so assorted pieces of fruit onto each skewer, then freeze on a tray or in a freezer bag for at least 3 hours.

2. Let thaw for 5–10 minutes before serving.

> Try halved grapes and strawberries, slices of banana, chunks of mango or watermelon, raspberries, or blueberries.

Sugar-Free Hot Chocolate

MAKES: 1 CUP

COOK TIME: 3 MINUTES

1 cup dairy or non-dairy milk

1 large pitted Medjool date, or
  2 regular dates

½ tsp Dutch-processed cocoa (or
  you can use cacao)

This frothy treat is sweetened with a single Medjool date (often called nature's candy due to its intense natural sweetness) and is a healthful alternative to conventional hot chocolate, which is full of GMO sugar and other nasties. You can substitute ½–1 teaspoon of honey, coconut sugar, or maple syrup for the date if you prefer.

1. In a small pan, heat the milk over medium heat to the desired temperature, making sure that it doesn't boil. Kids have less tolerance for hot food and drinks than adults and they spill often, so aim for warm rather than hot.

2. Pour the milk into a blender, add the date and cocoa, and blend until the date is liquefied. Serve warm in a child-friendly mug. The milk will be so frothy from being whizzed in the blender that your child won't miss marshmallows one bit.

Chocolate Velvet
Cupcakes
(page 228)

Pomegranate Punch
(page 232)

Baked Grilled
Cheese Sandwiches
(page 231)

Turkey Pesto
Meatballs
(page 235)

CHAPTER EIGHT

let's celebrate

Dressed-Up Fruit Cocktail
(page 232)

Raspberry Lemonade Valentine's Cookies

MAKES: APPROXIMATELY 6 DOZEN (3-INCH) HEART-SHAPED COOKIES

PREP TIME: 1 HOUR 45 MINUTES FOR THE RASPBERRY SUGAR + 1 HOUR FOR THE COOKIES INCLUDING CHILLING TIME

COOK TIME: 7–8 MINUTES

¼ cup frozen raspberries

½ cup organic granulated sugar

Ingredients for Basic Gluten-Free Cookie Dough (page 224), substituting 1½ tsp fresh lemon juice + 1 tsp grated lemon zest, packed, for the vanilla and mint extract

Many people consider making heart-shaped cookies with their children for Valentine's Day to be a rite of passage. These ones don't require icing, just a simple sprinkling of raspberry sugar to make them look pink and pretty, perfect for little helping hands. It's best to make the raspberry sugar ahead of time—although it's easy to make, it takes some time to dry out in the oven.

1. Warm the raspberries on the stove or in the microwave until they are hot and look like the juice is coming out of them.

2. Place a fine strainer over a bowl and pour the berries and juice into it. Use the back of a spoon to push through as much juice as possible, leaving the seeds and fiber of the berries in the strainer and a thick-looking juice in the bowl. Place the bowl of juice in the freezer for 5–10 minutes to cool completely.

3. Preheat the oven to 200°F. Line a rimmed baking tray with parchment paper.

4. Mix together the sugar and raspberry juice. Spread it out on the baking tray, breaking up clumps of sugar as much as possible.

5. Bake for approximately 1½ hours, breaking up the sugar a bit more with a spoon or knife every ½ hour.

6. Allow to cool completely, then pulse in a food processor fitted with the steel blade until it is approximately the texture of berry sugar. This recipe makes more than you will need for the cookies, but you can save the extra for decorating other cookies or desserts. It keeps well in an airtight container for at least 1 month in a cool place.

7. Make the cookie dough according to the recipe on page 224, with the substitutions noted in the ingredient list.

8. Roll out the cookie dough as per the recipe and use a 3-inch heart-shaped cookie cutter to cut out the cookies.

9. Sprinkle with the raspberry sugar. Bake for 7–8 minutes. When done, they will turn a darker golden around the edges. Allow to cool for a couple of minutes on the baking tray, then transfer to a rack to cool completely. Store in an airtight container for up to 1 week.

Make It Together Chocolate Bark for Gifts

MAKES: ENOUGH FOR 1-2 GIFTS

PREP TIME: 15 MINUTES + 2 HOURS TO CHILL

8 oz good-quality dark or milk chocolate

⅔ cup toppings of your choice (seeds, chopped nuts, pretzels, dried fruit, candied ginger or orange peel, shredded coconut, etc.)

> For a delicious and attractive swirled effect, melt dark and milk chocolate separately, then use a spatula to gently swirl them together.

If you enjoy cooking with your kids and like giving home-made gifts, this recipe is perfect for you. Chocolate bark will be very well received by anyone who loves chocolate, especially if you customize the add-ins to suit personal tastes. I make this with the kids for Father's Day gifts, but it would be perfect for other gifting occasions too.

1. When you're cooking with your child, it will go more smoothly if you have all the ingredients set out and ready to go. Make sure you've lined a tray with parchment paper.

2. Have your child break up the chocolate and place it in a large microwave-safe bowl. Microwave the chocolate for 30 seconds, then stir, repeating several times until the chocolate is fully melted. While I'm not super-keen on microwaves, I think they work best for this task if you want your child to be involved. Double boilers work very well for melting chocolate but aren't safe to use if you are cooking with a little one.

3. Pour the chocolate out onto the tray, using a spatula to scrape the sides of the bowl, then together, spread out the chocolate until it is approximately ¼ inch thick. It won't cover the whole tray and it doesn't need to be spread into a perfect shape because you're going to break it into pieces anyway.

4. Now it's time to sprinkle the chocolate with goodies. We like to sprinkle between one and three different toppings on each half of the chocolate to create two different kinds of bark. Our favorite combinations are pistachios, dried apricots, and sea salt, and chopped cashews with minced goji berries.

5. Once the toppings are on, place the tray in the refrigerator for a couple of hours to allow the chocolate to harden completely.

6. To finish the bark, get the kids to help break it into pieces, then wrap it up nicely in tissue and place it in a gift bag or box.

Lemon Coconut Macaroon Nests

MAKES: 8 NESTS

PREP TIME: 20 MINUTES + TIME TO CHILL AND COOL

COOK TIME: 12–15 MINUTES

1 (13.5 oz) can full-fat coconut milk (from a BPA-free can)

2 large egg whites

⅓ cup + 2 Tbsp liquid honey, divided

1 tsp pure vanilla extract

Pinch of sea salt

2½ cups finely shredded unsweetened coconut

1 Tbsp fresh lemon juice

Zest of 1 small unwaxed lemon

1 cup fresh blueberries

Children and adults alike love these macaroon nests, free of dairy, gluten, nuts, and refined sugar and topped with blueberry "eggs," which makes them perfect served as dessert at a special Easter family brunch. Have your kids help you assemble them—they'll be so proud to contribute to the special feast when their family and friends oooh and aaah over what they've helped to make. (Note that you need to chill the coconut milk the night before you make these.)

1. The night before, place the can of coconut milk in the refrigerator.

2. Preheat the oven to 350°F. Line a baking tray with parchment paper or a baking sheet.

3. In a large bowl, whisk together the egg whites, ⅓ cup honey, vanilla, and salt for 1–2 minutes until frothy on top. This can easily be done by hand with a whisk.

4. Add the coconut and stir to combine.

5. Spoon the macaroon mixture onto the baking tray into eight mounds, a few inches apart. Use damp fingers to form the mounds into nest shapes by flattening them out, smoothing out the edges, then creating a well in the center of each, ensuring that there is still a good layer of coconut at the bottom of each well.

6. Place the nests in the oven and bake for 12–15 minutes. When they're done, the bottom and edges will be dark golden brown and the centers will be just slightly sticky.

7. Allow them to cool on the baking tray. Place a bowl and beaters in the refrigerator to chill for at least 15 minutes. (You can use a stand mixer or a bowl and a hand-held mixer.)

8. To make the lemon coconut cream, remove the bowl and beaters from the refrigerator.

9. Scoop out the firm coconut cream from the can (it should be separated from the coconut water) and put it into the chilled bowl. Discard the coconut water or save it for another use.

10. Whip the coconut cream until very fluffy.

11. Add the 2 Tbsp honey and whip again until fully combined.

12. Keeping the beater on high, slowly add the lemon juice, a small trickle at a time.

13. Sprinkle in the lemon zest and beat for another 10 seconds or so.

14. Place the macaroon nests on individual dessert plates or together on a platter and fill each one with a dollop of the lemon coconut cream. Place blueberries on top of the coconut cream in each macaroon, so that they become the eggs in these pretty and festive nests. The macaroons can be made up to 24 hours ahead of time so that all you have to do before serving is make the lemon cream and top with blueberries.

Ghoulish Crispy Rice Pops

MAKES: 12 POPS

PREP TIME: 30 MINUTES + 15
MINUTES TO CHILL

3½ cups brown puffed rice cereal

½ cup nut-free seed butter

¼ cup honey

⅓ cup coconut sugar

1 Tbsp virgin coconut oil

1 tsp pure vanilla extract

Pinch of sea salt

12 Popsicle sticks

⅓ cup semi-sweet chocolate
    chips

Small clear cello bags and
    Halloween-themed ribbon
    (optional)

These spooky-looking Halloween treats are 100 percent inspired by my mom. I grew up on a small island where everyone knew each other and it was perfectly acceptable to hand out homemade treats to trick-or-treaters on Halloween. It was my mom's tradition to make marshmallow crispy rice treats on sticks decorated with happy faces made out of Smarties. She would wrap them up in plastic wrap and give them out to all the trick-or-treaters who came to our door. Luckily we only ever had about ten kids come by each Halloween, so it wasn't as much work as it sounds! I always looked forward to the tradition of making them with her every year.

Now that I'm all grown up I've created my own healthier version that I make with my kids, revamped with nut-free seed butter, brown rice crisp cereal, and unrefined sweeteners. I like to use chocolate to draw scary-looking monster faces on each pop, then wrap them up individually in clear cello bags tied with a tag and a black ribbon. If you like, you can substitute almond butter or peanut butter for the seed butter, or to make them a true ghoulish green color, you can use pure pumpkin seed or pistachio butter, which have a distinctive green tinge.

1. Line two baking trays with parchment paper.

2. Put the cereal into a large bowl.

3. Place the seed butter, honey, sugar, coconut oil, vanilla, and salt in a pot over medium heat. Stir continuously until it starts to bubble.

4. Pour this mixture over the cereal and use a large wooden spoon or spatula to stir until the cereal is completely coated.

5. Allow to cool slightly, then, with damp hands, form twelve evenly sized balls. Lay each of them on the trays, spaced well apart.

If you live in a close-knit community and plan to hand these out to trick-or-treaters, you can make parents feel more comfortable with a homemade treat by sticking a label on the bag that says it was made by you and includes your house number and street, your email address, and a list of ingredients. Usually I hand out store-bought treats to kids whose families I don't know, and reserve these goodies for any of Poppy's and Cam's little friends who come to the door.

6. Holding a ball still with your hand, gently press a Popsicle stick into the side of the ball, right in the center. Use your hands to push the ball down into a disk around the inserted end of the stick, so that you now have what looks like a lollipop. Repeat with the rest of the puffed rice balls.

7. To decorate them, put the chocolate into a small microwave-safe bowl. Melt it on high for 20 seconds then take it out and give it a stir to encourage it to melt. Repeat two or three times until the chocolate is fully melted.

8. If you have a small pastry piping bag, spoon the chocolate into a bag with a fine tip. If you don't have a pastry bag, spoon the chocolate into a plastic sandwich bag. Carefully snip the corner of the bag to create a tiny hole for the chocolate to squeeze through.

9. Working carefully, squeeze the bag and draw a chocolate monster face on each rice pop. I like to do big round eyes and a jagged mouth.

10. Transfer the tray to the refrigerator for 15 minutes to allow the chocolate to harden and the treats to really firm up.

11. If you're giving these out as a Halloween gift, place each pop in a cello bag and tie closed with a piece of ribbon. You can make these ahead of time and freeze them for up to 1 month in an airtight container.

HAPPY HALLOWEEN

Spelt Gingerbread Cookies

MAKES: 24 MEDIUM-SIZE COOKIES

PREP TIME: 1½ HOURS, INCLUDING CHILLING TIME

COOK TIME: 8-10 MINUTES

1 Tbsp ground chia seeds

2¼ cups spelt flour

1½ tsp ground ginger

1½ tsp ground cinnamon

¼ tsp ground cloves

¼ tsp ground nutmeg

¼ tsp fine sea salt

½ tsp baking soda

¼ tsp baking powder

⅓ cup virgin coconut oil, melted

¼ cup molasses

½ cup coconut sugar, packed

Gingerbread cookies are perfect for spelt flour because they're dark-colored and hearty by nature. These crispy gingerbread cookies have just the right amount of warm spices and sweetness. And they happen to be egg- and dairy-free!

1. In a small bowl, combine the chia with 3 tablespoons of water and set aside to gel.

2. Put the spelt flour, ginger, cinnamon, cloves, nutmeg, salt, baking soda, and baking powder into a bowl and stir to combine.

3. Using a stand mixer fitted with the beater attachment or a hand mixer, mix together the coconut oil, molasses, and chia. Mix on high for a minute or two then add the coconut sugar and mix again on high until the sugar is very well blended in.

4. Add the flour mixture, ½ cup at a time, mixing on low.

5. Use your hands to bring the dough together into a smooth ball, then split it in half, forming each half into a disk. Wrap each disk in parchment or plastic wrap and place in the refrigerator for an hour.

6. Preheat the oven to 350°F. Line two baking trays with parchment paper.

7. On a floured counter and using a floured rolling pin, roll out the dough to ¼ inch thick. Cut out cookies with gingerbread person or other holiday cookie cutters and lay them on the trays 1 inch apart.

8. At this stage, if you would like to make these into tree decorations, use a straw to poke a hole in the top of each cookie. Once they're baked and cooled, you can loop string or ribbon through the hole so that you can hang them on the tree.

9. You can bake two trays at once by placing one on the middle rack and the other just above it on another rack, but remember to rotate the racks halfway through baking.

10. Bake for approximately 8 minutes. The cookies should feel slightly soft. They will crisp up as they cool and can easily be overcooked.

11. Cool on a rack so that they don't crisp up too much from the hot tray, and decorate as desired. Store in a cookie jar for about 1 month, or in an airtight container in the freezer for up to 3 months.

Chocolate-Dipped Minty Star Cookies

MAKES: APPROXIMATELY 100
(1½-INCH) STAR COOKIES

PREP TIME: 1 HOUR INCLUDING
CHILLING TIME

COOK TIME: 7–8 MINUTES

BASIC GLUTEN-FREE COOKIE DOUGH

¼ cup unsalted butter (at room temperature)

⅓ cup sugar (remember that regular white sugar is likely to be GMO, so try to use organic if you can)

1 egg

1 tsp ground flaxseed

1 tsp pure vanilla extract

¼ tsp natural mint extract (see note on facing page)

1½ cups all-purpose gluten-free flour (see page 241)

½ tsp baking powder

¼ tsp sea salt

COOKIE DECORATION

½ cup semi-sweet chocolate chips

½ tsp virgin coconut oil

2–3 drops natural mint extract

These pretty and festive stars are the perfect little winter holiday cookie, and they're fun to make with your kids. The basic cookie dough is ideal for any holiday cookie—pumpkins, stars, angels, hearts, or bunnies; you are only limited by your cookie cutter collection! And with very little sugar, a buttery crunch, and no gluten, you'll be pulling out this recipe over and over again.

1. Using a stand mixer or a hand-held mixer, cream the butter and sugar on medium-high speed until very creamy.

2. Add the egg, flaxseed, vanilla, and mint extract and mix for 2 minutes more.

3. In a medium-size bowl or measuring jug, mix together the flour, baking powder, and salt.

4. With the mixer running on low speed, add the flour mixture ½ cup at a time. Mix until a rough ball of dough forms.

5. Use your hands to scoop out the dough and bring it together into a smooth ball. Flatten it into a 1-inch-thick disk, wrap in parchment or wax paper, and refrigerate for at least 45 minutes. The dough will seem soft, but will firm up to rolling consistency in the refrigerator. If you are short of time, you can cheat and put it in the freezer for 10–15 minutes. If you leave it to chill for longer than this and it becomes too firm to roll, just leave it out on the counter until it has warmed up enough to be pliable.

6. Preheat the oven to 350°F. Line a baking tray (or two) with parchment paper or silicone baking sheets.

7. Roll out the dough to between ⅛ and ¼ inch thick, and then use a small (mine is 1½ inches) star-shaped cookie cutter to cut out cookies from the dough. Use a thin metal spatula to gently lift the cookies up and lay them close together on the baking trays (they won't spread very much).

8. Bake for approximately 8 minutes (until the cookies are just turning golden around the edges) then transfer immediately to a wire rack to cool.

9. Melt the chocolate and coconut oil in a double boiler or in the microwave. If you microwave it, just heat it for 30 seconds at a time, stirring in between so that it doesn't burn. Once the chocolate is melted, stir in the mint extract.

10. To decorate, pick up a cookie with your fingers and simply dip half of it in the chocolate. Tap it lightly to get the drips off, and then lay it on parchment on a tray. Place the dipped cookies in the refrigerator to allow the chocolate to harden up. These keep well in a cookie jar or tin for at least a couple of weeks, but are also very freezable (even after being dipped in chocolate). Freeze on a tray, then store in an airtight container or freezer bag for up to 3 months.

Send these for the school Christmas party, give them as gifts, or set out a plateful when you have holiday guests.

♥

If you're not making these at Christmas, you can omit the mint flavoring in the cookies.

First Birthday Smash Cake

MAKES: 1 DOUBLE-LAYER (6-INCH)
ROUND CAKE

PREP TIME: 2 HOURS INCLUDING
COOLING AND DECORATING TIME

COOK TIME: 30 MINUTES

¼ cup virgin coconut oil, melted,
+ extra to grease the pans

2 cups light spelt flour

2 tsp baking powder

½ tsp baking soda

½ tsp ground cinnamon

¼ tsp sea salt

1 ripe pear, peeled and roughly
chopped

¾ cup peeled, roughly diced
carrot

⅓ cup non-dairy milk (regular
milk is fine as a substitution)

½ cup coconut sugar

2 eggs

1½ tsp pure vanilla extract

1 recipe Fluffy Coconut Cream
Frosting (page 236)

Finish off with natu-
rally colored sprinkles,
berries, edible flowers,
and/or a special first
birthday cake topper.
Then get your camera
ready for some ador-
able (and very messy)
shots of your 1-year-old
on their special day.

If you haven't heard of first birthday smash cakes yet, let me explain. On a first birthday, a baby is given her very own cake and while she plays with it and eats it, making an adorable mess of herself, photos are taken to capture the moment. Bakery-made smash cakes tend to contain a lot of sugar and artificial colors, which you might prefer to avoid. Just in case your baby decides to really dig in, this recipe is more nutritious than regular cake, with pears and carrots, whole-grain flour, no dairy, and only a moderate amount of coconut sugar. Frost it with Fluffy Coconut Cream Frosting (page 236).

1. The day before the big day, place a can of coconut milk in the refrigerator (this is for the frosting).

2. To make the cake, preheat the oven to 350°F. Grease two 6-inch springform pans with coconut oil and line the bottoms with parchment paper cut to fit.

3. In a large bowl, sift together the flour, baking powder, baking soda, cinnamon, and salt.

4. Using your food processor, puree the pear and carrot with the non-dairy milk, coconut sugar, eggs, melted coconut oil, and vanilla.

5. Pour the wet ingredients into the dry and mix together until the dry ingredients are completely incorporated. Avoid overmixing.

6. Divide the batter evenly between the two cake pans, then bake in the middle of the oven for 30 minutes. A toothpick inserted in the center of a cake should come out clean when it is done. Allow to cool in the pans on a cooling rack for 10 minutes, then carefully remove the cakes from the pans, allowing them to cool completely on a wire rack before decorating.

7. Take the coconut milk out of the refrigerator and use it to make the frosting.

8. Place one layer of the cake on a serving plate. If the top is very rounded, even it out by cutting off a thin horizontal slice to make it flatter.

9. Spread a thin layer of frosting on this bottom layer, then top with the other cake.

10. Carefully spread the remaining frosting on the top and sides of the cake, adding some pretty piping around the edge if you like.

Chocolate Velvet Cupcakes

MAKES: 12 CUPCAKES

PREP TIME: 45 MINUTES

COOK TIME: 28–30 MINUTES

¾ cup uncooked quinoa

¾ cup peeled, small-dice beets

3 large eggs

1¼ cups coconut sugar

½ cup virgin coconut oil, melted

1½ tsp ground chia seeds

1 tsp pure vanilla extract

¼ tsp pure almond extract

⅔ cup brown rice flour

½ cup unsweetened cocoa
  powder

1½ tsp baking powder

½ tsp baking soda

¼ tsp sea salt

1 recipe Reduced-Sugar Buttery
  Cream Cheese Frosting
  (page 237) (omit for dairy-
  free, or use Fluffy Coconut
  Cream Frosting, page 236)

Perfect for a birthday party or for Valentine's Day, these moist and light gluten-free cupcakes taste so much like traditional chocolate cupcakes made with white wheat flour that no one will notice the difference. And with a healthy helping of beets and quinoa in these cupcakes, you could make the case that they are nutritious enough to serve for breakfast! You will need a food processor to make this recipe.

1. Preheat the oven to 350°F. Line the cups of a muffin pan with paper liners.

2. Put the quinoa and the beets into a medium-size lidded pot. Pour 1¾ cups of water over the beets and quinoa. Bring to a boil, then cover and simmer on low for 17 minutes. This is longer than one would normally cook quinoa, but we want it to be extra-soft so it purees to a completely smooth texture. Drain any excess water, then spread the quinoa and beets out on a large plate so that they cool quickly.

3. In a food processor fitted with the steel blade, blend the eggs, coconut sugar, coconut oil, chia, vanilla, and almond extract.

4. Once the beets and quinoa are warm but not hot, add them to the mixture and puree very well, until completely smooth.

5. Add the brown rice flour, cocoa, baking powder, baking soda, and salt and blend again, for 2–3 minutes until very well blended. Use a spatula to scrape down the sides, then blend again until you're sure the dry ingredients are very well mixed in. Because there is no gluten in the batter, don't worry about overmixing. The batter will be thicker than traditional cupcake batter.

6. Spoon the batter into the cupcake papers, filling them almost to the top and smoothing out the surface as best you can.

7. Bake for 28–30 minutes in the middle of the oven. When they're done, the cupcakes will feel firm and bounce back if you press on the tops with your finger.

8. Once cool enough to handle, take the cupcakes out of the pan and allow them to cool completely on a wire rack before frosting with Reduced-Sugar Buttery Cream Cheese Frosting (or Fluffy Coconut Cream Frosting, if you prefer). Freeze in an airtight container for up to 1 month, frosted or unfrosted. I like to make them ahead, freeze them, then thaw and frost them as needed.

To make a sheet cake rather than cupcakes, pour the batter into a greased and parchment-lined 8- × 11-inch pan and bake for 40 minutes.

Brontosaurus's Lunch (a.k.a. Veggies in Dip)

SERVES: 6

PREP TIME: 1 HOUR

2 medium carrots, peeled

½ English cucumber, skin on

2 stalks celery

1 bell pepper (red, yellow, or orange)

2 cups Greek Yogurt Avocado Ranch dip (page 166) or Roasted Garlic and Squash Hummus (page 166) (for plant-based or dairy-free) (or dip of your choice)

6 paper cups (regular children's drinking cup size)

6 Popsicle sticks

Colored paper or card stock

Non-toxic glue

Scissors

Like the Dressed-Up Fruit Cocktail (page 232), this is another recipe that uses a simple trick to get kids interested in foods they might otherwise bypass at a birthday party. Veggies and dip in a personal cup with our favorite plant-eating dinosaur getting in on the action will encourage even the most green-wary child to at least try a bite or two. You can, of course, swap out the brontosaurus for a monkey, pirate, pony, or any other themed cut-out.

1. Cut all the veggies up so that you have six pieces of each, all 4–5 inches long and ½ inch wide.

2. From this point, it's all about assembling. Simply spoon ⅓ cup of the dip into each paper cup, then stand up the veggies in the dip.

3. To make the decorative dinos, trace the image below onto white paper or tracing paper and then cut it out to make a template. Use the template to cut out dinos from your paper or card stock of choice. You will need to make twice as many dinos as you have children attending the party.

4. Lay a dinosaur flat on a table, spread it with some glue, then lay approximately 2 inches of the end of a Popsicle stick on the bottom of the dino's belly. Lay another dinosaur on top, being careful to match up the edges. You should now have a double-sided dinosaur on a stick. If you like, you can use felt-tip pens to add eyes or markings, or to write names right on the dinos. Pop the dinos in the cup, so that it looks like they are about to nibble on the veggies.

Baked Grilled Cheese Sandwiches

MAKES: 24 QUARTER SANDWICHES

PREP TIME: 15 MINUTES

COOK TIME: 9 MINUTES

12 pieces multigrain bread (or gluten-free, if you prefer)

2 Tbsp butter

1½ cups grated cheddar cheese (medium cheddar is a good bet if you're trying to keep everyone happy)

Variations:

♥ Mix ⅓ cup shredded kale together with the shredded cheese. Fill the sandwiches with the kale and cheese mix and bake as normal.

♥ For a pizza grilled cheese, spread the inside of each slice of bread with your favorite pizza sauce, then assemble with the cheese and bake as above.

♥ Add thinly sliced apples, tomato slices, or natural ham slices on top of the cheese before topping with the other slice of bread.

Grilled cheese sandwiches are very popular with kids, but there's just no way at a birthday party, with everything going on, you'd have the time to grill them to order. These baked grilled cheese sandwiches are prepped ahead of time then simply baked in the oven for an almost identical result—but with much less time and effort. If you want to make them a bit healthier or more interesting, you can try some of the variations suggested below. But do so at your own risk. Today may not be the day to get too hung up on making sure everyone gets their greens. The goal here should be that the kids get some acceptably healthy food into their tummies to keep their moods up and give everyone the best chance of having a good time. You can prep these the day before the party if you like, so that on the day, all you need to do is pop them in the oven. *(Photo on inside cover)*

1. Butter one side of all twelve pieces of bread. Set six of the pieces butter side down on a large baking tray.

2. Sprinkle ¼ cup of cheese on each slice of bread then top with another slice, butter side up. At this point, these can be covered, set on a baking tray, and placed in the refrigerator for up to 24 hours.

3. When you're ready to bake them, heat the oven to 400°F. Bake for 5 minutes, then flip the sandwiches over and bake for another 4 minutes.

4. Allow to cool slightly, then slice into quarters and serve.

Dressed-Up Fruit Cocktail

SERVES: 6

PREP TIME: 15 MINUTES

3 cups colorful mixed cut-up fruit and berries

6 pretty cups or bowls

6 paper umbrellas

6 small forks or spoons (optional— they can just use the cocktail sticks to eat the fruit)

Put in a little effort to make everyday foods look more appealing, and you'll be amazed at how excited kids get about eating them. This is simply fruit salad, displayed in pretty little bowls or cups with cocktail umbrellas. And I promise you, at a birthday party these will be just as popular as any cupcake. Just keep an eye out to make sure the children are playing with them as little umbrellas rather than using them to poke each other!

1. Divide the fruit evenly between the paper cups.

2. Poke the cocktail umbrellas jauntily into a piece of fruit so that they stand up nicely, and serve with little forks or spoons. Easy, right?

Pomegranate Punch

MAKES: APPROXIMATELY 7 CUPS, SO SHOULD SERVE 10-12 CHILDREN

PREP TIME: 15 MINUTES

COOK TIME: NONE, BUT YOU WILL NEED A FEW HOURS TO FREEZE THE ICE CUBES

½ cup blueberries (fresh or frozen)

⅓ cup pomegranate arils

4 cups unsweetened apple juice

2 cups sparkling water

1 cup unsweetened pomegranate juice

1 small orange, sliced into thin rounds

A fancy drink at a party makes everything a bit more special. This punch is attractive, is very simple to make, and calls for sparkling water instead of soda pop for the fizz. While I was developing this recipe and had an overabundance of it hanging around, my husband took to drinking it with gin (apparently it makes quite a good cocktail), but as this book is a family affair, I suggest you serve this punch in its pure form at a children's party. What you do with the leftovers is entirely up to you. *(Photo on page 214)*

1. At least several hours before the party, divide the blueberries and pomegranate arils between the molds of an ice cube tray and cover them with water. Freeze. If you have fancy-shaped ice cube trays, they'd be perfect for this.

2. Just before the party begins, take the ice cubes out of the tray and place them in a serving jug or a punch bowl.

3. Pour over the apple juice, sparkling water, and pomegranate juice, then float the orange slices on top.

> Water is best for kids, but when you do serve juice, choose unsweetened, and organic if possible. Make it a habit to dilute it with water or sparkling water—it will still taste delicious and will cut the sugar in half.

A good combo for this is ½ cup strawberries, ½ cup blueberries, ½ cup mango, ½ cup pineapple, ½ cup watermelon, and ½ cup grapes, but the potential variations are pretty endless. One birthday party, I simply served little cups of cottage cheese with cocktail umbrellas and pretty spoons and everyone loved them. Dressed-up Greek yogurt with a drizzle of honey and some fresh berries would also be very popular with little ones at a party. Grown-ups will also enjoy these.

Turkey Pesto Meatballs on Sticks

MAKES: 24 MEATBALLS
PREP TIME: 10 MINUTES
COOK TIME: 30 MINUTES

FOR THE MEATBALLS

Virgin coconut oil, to grease the rack

1 lb ground turkey thighs

1 egg

¼ cup almond meal

¼ cup homemade pesto (see Superfood Pesto, page 244) or store-bought pesto

¼ cup finely grated Parmesan cheese

¼–½ tsp sea salt (depending on how salty your pesto is)

FOR THE DIP

1 cup whole-milk yogurt

¼ cup pesto

Squeeze of lemon juice

Sea salt to taste

Cocktail or short lollipop sticks

I remember a friend once telling me that in an act of desperation to get her kids to try something new, she put a taco on a stick. How on earth she managed that I still can't quite work out, but the thought of her trying always makes me laugh. It is true, though, that food on a stick is always popular with kids, and here the sticks make these meatballs a fun party food proposition. Plus, as birthday parties often involve more sugar than a regular day, these are a much-needed, potentially sanity-saving protein-rich choice to help keep blood sugar levels stable and the party on an even keel. These grain-free meatballs are baked in the oven rather than fried like traditional meatballs, because the last thing you need at a kids' party is to be frying meatballs on the stovetop.

1. Preheat the oven to 375°F. Grease a metal roasting rack with coconut oil and set it over a roasting pan.

2. Combine all the meatball ingredients together in a large bowl. Use a wooden spoon or your hands to bring them together.

3. Roll tablespoon-size amounts of the turkey mixture into balls and set them on the rack over the spaces so that the drippings will fall through.

4. Bake the meatballs in the oven for 30 minutes, until just starting to turn golden on top.

5. To make the dip, simply whisk together all the ingredients in a medium-size bowl.

6. To serve, stick cocktail sticks or lollipop sticks into the meatballs and serve on a platter alongside the dip.

To prep for the party ahead of time, you can freeze these meatballs on a tray before cooking them. At party time, place them in a 375°F oven and add 5 minutes to the cooking time. These are also ideal as a finger food, as part of a family meal, or to put in lunchboxes.

Fluffy Coconut Cream Frosting

MAKES: APPROXIMATELY 1 CUP

PREP TIME: 5 MINUTES

1 (13.5 oz) can full-fat coconut milk (from a BPA-free can)

1 Tbsp maple syrup

1 tsp pure vanilla extract

Pinch of ground cinnamon (optional)

> I find that for whatever reason, some brands of coconut milk don't separate well. Try a few different brands and find one that seems reliable.

This dairy-free, refined sugar–free frosting may just change your life. It is unbelievably simple to whip up and is ideal if you are concerned about allergies or trying to avoid sugar. You won't believe how delicious it is! Use this recipe for frosting a baby's First Birthday Smash Cake (page 227) or topping practically any dessert either as "frosting" or as a dairy-free whipped creamy topping. (Note that you have to chill the coconut milk the day before you plan to make this.)

1. The day before you plan to make this, place the can of coconut milk in the refrigerator.

2. Fifteen minutes before beginning, place the bowl and beaters you will be using in the freezer to chill. A stand mixer or a large bowl and a hand-held mixer will both work just fine.

3. Using a spoon, scoop out the firm coconut cream, which will be at the top of the can and separated from the coconut water at the bottom. Put the cream in the chilled bowl and discard the water (or save it for another use).

4. Beat the coconut cream on high until light and fluffy.

5. Add the maple syrup, vanilla, and cinnamon and beat for another minute or so. I find that natural food coloring made from beets works beautifully here if I am looking for a pink icing. (See pages 250–251.)

Reduced-Sugar Buttery Cream Cheese Frosting

MAKES: 2 CUPS

PREP TIME: 10 MINUTES

1 cup organic icing sugar, sifted

8 oz (1 package) cold firm cream cheese, cut into small pieces

½ cup cold unsalted butter, cut into small pieces

1½ tsp pure vanilla extract

1 tsp coconut flour (the more finely ground the better)

Many recipes for cream cheese frosting call for up to 5 cups of icing sugar, but it is completely unnecessary to use so much. This recipe is one of the few in this book that call for sugar, but it still uses much less than traditional recipes, which often are way too sweet. The thing is, once in a while, we all want to make a frosting that looks and tastes like we haven't compromised to make it healthier. This is the recipe for those days, and with far less sugar, you won't feel one bit of guilt. Well, unless you end up eating three cupcakes yourself, which is certainly a possibility once you get a taste of this frosting. Use this to top Chocolate Velvet Cupcakes (page 228) or any cake that calls for cream cheese frosting. For healthier food colorings to tint this frosting, see pages 250–251.

1. In a stand mixer fitted with the beater attachment or with a hand-held beater, beat the cream cheese on high speed until very creamy and fluffy.

2. Slowly, with the mixer running on medium speed, add the butter, a piece at a time, beating until it is fully blended with the cream cheese and is light and fluffy-looking. Add the vanilla and beat for another minute.

3. With the beater still on medium speed, slowly add the sugar 1 tablespoon at a time until fully mixed and very fluffy.

4. Add the coconut flour and beat for another minute or so.

5. Spread this onto cakes or cupcakes or use it for piping. Because of the coconut flour, it has great structure and pipes really well. Store frosted cupcakes or cake in the refrigerator, but serve them on the day that the icing is made. The icing will firm up when chilled, so take the cupcakes out of the refrigerator ½ hour before serving.

make it yourself, make it better

Soft Spelt and Flax Tortillas

MAKES: 12 TORTILLAS

PREP TIME: 15 MINUTES

COOK TIME: 12 MINUTES

3 cups spelt flour

1 Tbsp flaxseeds

1 tsp sea salt

½ tsp baking powder

¼ cup extra virgin olive oil

¾ cup warm water (don't worry about an exact temperature)

Almost all commercial tortillas, unless made by a specialty natural food company, contain a ridiculously long list of additives. These are presumably included to keep them from spoiling or drying out, but at what cost to our families' health? Homemade tortillas are very easy to make, and these ones are very soft and pliable for a whole-grain spelt tortilla.

1. In a large bowl, mix together the flour, flaxseeds, salt, and baking powder.

2. Drizzle the oil over the flour, then use your fingers to cut it in all the way until it looks like rough bread crumbs.

3. Pour almost all the water into the bowl, reserving about a tablespoon, then, using your hands, bring the dough together into a ball. The dough shouldn't be wet or sticky. Add the rest of the water if you need to, or a bit more flour if the dough is sticky. All whole-grain flours are slightly different, so you may find you need a bit more or less than the recipe calls for.

4. Knead the dough on the counter until very smooth, 2–3 minutes.

5. Roll out the dough into a log, and use a serrated knife to cut it into twelve even portions. Roll them into balls, place them on a clean tray, and cover them with a damp paper towel or tea towel so that they don't dry out.

6. Heat a skillet over medium heat. I highly recommend a seasoned cast iron skillet for this. If you don't have one and are using a pan that tends to stick, make sure you grease your pan lightly with coconut oil in between cooking each tortilla.

7. Working with one ball of dough at a time, roll out a very thin tortilla. I find that rolling it out on parchment paper makes it much easier to pick up the tortilla to transfer it to the skillet. I also find that rubbing flour on the rolling pin keeps the dough from sticking but leaves less extra flour on the tortilla than if you were to sprinkle it right on the ball of dough. You may find it hard at first to make nicely shaped circles, but it gets easier. I flatten the ball of dough with my hand first, pressing it into a circle, then finish it off with a rolling pin, making it as thin as I can. If you have a tortilla press you can, of course, use that and forgo all the rolling.

8. Lifting up the parchment paper, carefully transfer the tortilla to the skillet and cook it for between 30 seconds and 1 minute, just until the dough begins to bubble. Flip it over and cook for another 20–30 seconds. Do your best not to overcook them, or the tortillas won't be as pliable.

9. Place the cooked tortilla in a deep pan, like a casserole dish, and cover the pan with a large damp tea towel. This will steam the tortilla and help keep it soft.

10. Roll out and cook the rest of the tortillas, each time placing them in the baking dish under the tea towel until all the tortillas are cooked. Eat straight away as the tortillas for Veggie-Loaded Beef Soft Tacos (page 176), or use for quesadillas (page 157 and page 160), as flatbread, or as an easy and nutritious pizza base. Store wrapped in a tea towel, then sealed in a container in the refrigerator for up to 4 days. Or, freeze them for up to 3 months in an airtight container or freezer bag with parchment paper between each tortilla. These are best reheated by wrapping them in foil and warming gently in the oven at 350°F for 5–10 minutes.

All-Purpose Gluten-Free Flour Blend

MAKES: 6 CUPS

PREP TIME: 5 MINUTES

2 cups white rice flour

1½ cups brown rice flour

1¼ cups arrowroot flour

¾ cup buckwheat flour

½ cup sorghum flour

Blending your own gluten-free flour blend is simple and totally worth it from a budget perspective. Plus, by making your own, you can include more nutritious flours like the sorghum and buckwheat in this recipe. While I am not a gluten-free expert by any means, I have done my research and experimented a lot myself, and a truly all-purpose gluten-free flour blend seems to need a balance of approximately 40 percent whole-grain flours and 60 percent lighter flours to ensure that it bakes up well in delicate recipes. This is why I've included more white flours here than I would typically use. If you go off recipe and exchange any of the whiter flours for more whole-grain ones you might end up with a flour that isn't quite as versatile.

1. Combine all the flours together in a bowl, stirring well so that they are fully mixed. Store in a container in a cool dry cupboard or in the freezer for 6–9 months.

This blend doesn't contain any gums that are often included in gluten-free flour blends because there's mounting evidence that they're hard for some people to digest. Try using ½ teaspoon of ground chia seeds or ground flaxseed per 1 cup of flour as a replacement in any gluten-free recipe that calls for xanthan gum. All the gluten-free baking in this book calls for ground chia seeds or ground flaxseed rather than gums.

Little Spelt Buns

MAKES: 18

PREP TIME: 1 HOUR 45 MINUTES,
INCLUDING RISING TIME

COOK TIME: 15 MINUTES

¼ cup butter, melted

1 egg separated + 1 egg whisked
for brushing on buns

1 cup warm water

1½ Tbsp honey

2 tsp active dry yeast

3½ cups + 1 Tbsp organic spelt
flour

1¼ tsp sea salt

1½ Tbsp sesame seeds

Children love foods that are little. Make these 100 percent whole-grain spelt buns and you can offer them little slider burgers (see Cashew Mushroom Sliders, page 186), little "bunwiches," or just little rolls alongside soup. And because they are homemade, they have no white wheat flour, much less sweetener, and none of the preservatives found so often in commercial rolls.

1. Whisk the melted butter with the egg yolk.

2. Add the warm water, honey, and egg white and whisk again until well combined.

3. Sprinkle the yeast over top, give it a gentle stir, then allow to sit for 10 minutes or until the yeast has bloomed.

4. Mix together the spelt flour and salt in a large bowl.

5. Pour the liquid ingredients over the flour and stir until it forms a dough.

6. Use your hands to bring the dough together into a ball, then turn the dough out onto a floured surface and knead for 3 minutes. Add a bit more flour if you need to.

7. Oil a large bowl, then place the dough in the bowl, covered by a tea towel. Allow to rise for 45 minutes. The dough should just about double in size.

8. Line a baking tray with parchment paper.

9. Punch down the dough, then form it into a log shape.

10. Tear or cut off one piece of dough at a time, forming it into a disk.

11. Place the disk in your hands with your thumbs sitting on top. Use your thumbs to stretch the dough over your fingers, bringing it under and pinching it together at the bottom, creating a nice dome-shaped bun. Place the bun on the baking tray and continue with this process until you have eighteen dome-shaped buns on the tray, spaced 1½ inches apart.

12. Cover the buns with a tea towel and allow them to rise for 30 minutes.

13. Preheat the oven to 375°F.

14. Brush the buns with the whisked egg, then sprinkle with the sesame seeds.

15. Bake for 15 minutes. The buns will be nicely rounded, dark golden, and shiny when done.

16. These will keep in an airtight container on the counter for a couple of days, or you can freeze them in an airtight container for up to 3 months.

Superfood Pesto

MAKES: APPROXIMATELY ¾ CUP

PREP TIME: 10 MINUTES

2 cloves garlic

2 cups basil leaves, loosely packed

1 cup loosely packed curly kale, stems discarded

1 cup loosely packed flat parsley leaves

½ cup hemp hearts

¼ cup grated Parmesan cheese (omit for plant-based and dairy-free)

4 tsp fresh lemon juice

Good pinch of sea salt

⅓ cup extra virgin olive oil

Pesto is one of those foods we're used to buying because it's readily available and making it doesn't seem worth the effort. But pesto is such an opportunity to include really nutritious ingredients in something your family loves, and it takes no time at all to throw together. Plus, a homemade version is likely to be made with much higher-quality oil than store-bought varieties, which often use canola or soybean oil rather than pure extra virgin olive oil. This version contains protein- and omega-3-rich hemp hearts as a substitute for pine nuts, which are expensive and tend to go rancid easily. And I've added kale and parsley, two of my favorite superfoods, for extra goodness and to help balance out the peppery taste of the basil for little ones.

1. Put the garlic, basil, kale, parsley, hemp hearts, Parmesan (if using), lemon juice, and salt in the bowl of a food processor fitted with the steel blade and pulse it several times until the greens are minced. I prefer to leave just a bit of texture so that it isn't a completely smooth puree.

2. With the food processor running, slowly pour in the olive oil, blending until combined. Stop and scrape down the sides with a spatula as needed.

3. Store in a mason jar in the refrigerator for up to 1 week, or freeze in individual portions in sealed containers for up to 3 months and thaw as needed.

Use this as a marinade for meat, poultry, prawns, or tofu, stirred into pasta or grains, or to fancy up scrambled eggs. Try it in Cam's Pesto and Pea Omelet (page 115) or the Turkey Pesto Meatballs on Sticks (page 235).

A Cleaner Ketchup

MAKES: 1 CUP

PREP TIME: 10 MINUTES

COOK TIME: 1 HOUR

2 Tbsp olive oil

1 large onion, diced

2 large cloves garlic, crushed

2 stalks celery, diced

2-inch piece ginger, peeled and minced

2 lb ripe tomatoes (any type), skin on, roughly chopped

2 tsp sea salt

1 tsp whole black peppercorns

1 tsp mild paprika

½ tsp dried mustard

½ tsp ground allspice

⅓ cup honey or maple syrup (for plant-based)

3 Tbsp white vinegar

½ Tbsp arrowroot powder

Most kids would shovel ketchup into their mouths with a spoon if they could. But traditional big-brand ketchup contains lots of GMO high-fructose corn syrup, which isn't ideal. Even so (and quite understandably), making your own homemade ketchup may not be high on your priority list. However, if you do want to have a go, this much cleaner version is delicious and tastes very close to the real thing.

1. Warm the oil in a large pot over medium heat, and sauté the onion, garlic, celery, and ginger for 5 minutes.

2. Add the tomatoes, salt, peppercorns, all the spices, and ½ cup of water. Bring to a boil, then turn the heat to medium-low and simmer, uncovered, for approximately 20 minutes, until the mixture reduces by half. Approximately 10 minutes in, give it a good mash with a potato masher to release the juice from the tomatoes.

3. Carefully strain through a fine-mesh sieve, using the back of a spoon to push through as much of the liquid as possible. Discard the remaining solids.

4. Rinse out the pot, then place the strained mixture back into it. Whisk in the honey, vinegar, and arrowroot, and bring to a boil over medium-high heat. Turn the heat to medium-low, and simmer for approximately 30 minutes until the sauce thickens and becomes a dark reddish-brown color.

5. Pour into a jar or bottle and store in the refrigerator for a couple of weeks. The ketchup will thicken more once it cools.

> It is possible to sterilize bottles for storing this ketchup and essentially use a canning process so that it can be kept in the cupboard for months. You'll find plenty of instructions online for how to do this if you would like to make your ketchup last longer.

Creamy Dreamy Almond Milk

MAKES: 3¾ CUPS

PREP TIME: 15 MINUTES + 8–12 HOURS TO SOAK

1 cup raw almonds

½ tsp sea salt + a pinch, divided

2 pitted Medjool dates (or 3–4 smaller pitted dates like Deglet Nours)

½ tsp pure vanilla extract

Before I started making my own almond milk, I assumed it was a really difficult process and just not worth the effort. But one go at it and I was completely converted! I promise you, making it yourself is extremely easy, and the flavor and clean ingredient deck just can't be beat. You will need a nut milk bag or fruit straining bag (the kind used for jam) to make this recipe. You could use cheesecloth, but that will likely be a messier affair. All of these products can be found online or at your local specialty cookware shop.

(Photo on inside cover)

1. In a bowl or jar, cover the almonds with water. Add the ½ teaspoon salt and leave to soak overnight.

2. Drain and rinse the almonds well, then puree them in a powerful blender with 3¾ cups of water, the dates, vanilla, and pinch of salt.

3. Place the bag in a 4-cup measuring jug with the mouth of the bag face up and open, or, ideally, stretched over the sides of the jug. Pour the pureed almond mixture into the bag, a third at a time. Tighten the top of the bag and use your hands to squeeze the milk through the cloth into the jug, leaving the almond pulp in the bag. Remove the pulp from the bag, then pour in more of the liquid, repeating the squeezing process until the almond milk has been strained through the bag.

4. Keep in the refrigerator in a sealable bottle for up to 4 days. Shake well before serving.

Wondering what to do with the almond pulp? Make granola! Mix it with some rolled oats (in a ratio of about 1 part almond pulp to 5 parts oats), some maple syrup, and some melted coconut oil to coat, then a sprinkling of cinnamon and sea salt. Spread it out on a lined baking tray and toast in a 375°F oven until golden brown, stirring often.

Chicken Vegetable Stock

MAKES: 5-6 CUPS

PREP TIME: 10 MINUTES

COOK TIME: 1½-2 HOURS + AT

LEAST 4 HOURS TO CHILL

2 large cloves garlic

2 small-medium carrots

2 medium yellow onions

2 medium celery stalks

1 organic chicken carcass, meat removed

8 black peppercorns

½ tsp sea salt

Leftover sweet potato, carrot, or onion peelings from making One-Pan Roast Chicken and Root Vegetables (page 173) (optional)

M any chicken stock recipes require two chicken carcasses, but it can be difficult to find the freezer space or patience to save up the bones you need. My solution is to use only one carcass and to add extra vegetables to bump up the flavor as well as the nutritional value, creating, if you like, a sort of chicken/vegetable stock crossbreed. This stock doesn't use herbs or other aromatics besides onions and garlic, so it has a neutral flavor that is perfect for adding to all types of dishes. If you prefer, you can include herbs like thyme, sage, rosemary, or bay leaves, or even more intense and exotic aromatics like ginger or turmeric root. If I'm not feeling too wiped out, I like to set this stock simmering on Saturday night after a family dinner of roast chicken (page 173).

1. Peel the garlic, scrub and chop the carrots, and chop up the onions and celery.

2. Place them all in a large pot or stock pot with the chicken carcass, peppercorns, salt, and extra peelings if you have any.

3. Pour 7 cups of water into the pot. The water should just cover everything. If you've added extra peelings, increase the water by 1 cup and add an extra pinch of salt.

4. Bring to a boil over medium-high heat, then cover, turn the heat to low, and simmer for 1½-2 hours, depending on how much time you have. Two hours will give a slightly deeper flavor, but 1½ hours is fine if you're short on time.

5. Remove from the heat and strain through a medium-fine sieve.

6. Allow the stock to cool for 20 minutes or so, then cover and place in the refrigerator overnight or for at least 4 hours.

7. Skim off and discard the fat, then freeze the stock in 1-cup portions for up to 3 months. Use in any recipe that calls for chicken stock.

Bone broth has become very popular recently as a gut-healing, anti-inflammatory food remedy. To make bone broth, add an extra cup of water, a few more chicken bones if you have them (it is bone broth after all!), and simmer, covered, on very low heat for 12-24 hours, until the chicken bones crumble easily when squeezed between your fingers. Follow the straining and freezing instructions for making stock.

Natalie's Classic French Vinaigrette

MAKES: ⅔ CUP
PREP TIME: 5 MINUTES

½ cup extra virgin olive oil

2 Tbsp balsamic vinegar

2 Tbsp fresh lemon juice

1 generous Tbsp Dijon mustard

1 medium clove crushed garlic

¼ tsp sea salt

Ground black pepper to taste

My good friend Natalie has served this dressing to her kids as a dip practically since they started eating vegetables, and to this day, those kids happily eat more vegetables than any kids I know. My theory is that it's all because of this tasty dressing, and Natalie wouldn't disagree. And without all the stabilizing gums, sugar, and inflammatory vegetable oils that are often found in commercial salad dressings, this classic favorite is much healthier for adults and kids alike.

1. Whisk together all the ingredients in a medium-size bowl until well blended. Store in an airtight bottle or jar in the refrigerator for up to approximately 2 weeks. Shake or stir well before serving.

Teriyaki Sauce

MAKES: APPROXIMATELY ⅔ CUP
PREP TIME: 5 MINUTES
COOK TIME: 5 MINUTES

1½ tsp arrowroot flour

½ cup gluten-free tamari

2½ Tbsp honey

1 Tbsp rice vinegar

1 small garlic clove, minced

½ tsp freshly grated ginger

Teriyaki sauce is delicious, but the ingredients list is a who's who of chemical ingredients like benzoates and high-fructose corn syrup. Making it yourself with clean ingredients takes no time at all, and if your family loves Asian flavors, they'll be all over this. Use it to baste almost any protein or vegetable before grilling, use it as a stir-fry sauce, or try stirring it into regular or vegan mayo for a decadent dip.

1. Put the arrowroot flour in a pot with 2 tablespoons of water and whisk them together.

2. Add the rest of the ingredients and warm over medium heat for a few minutes, whisking continuously, until the sauce just begins to thicken, coating the spoon.

3. Store this in a mason jar in the refrigerator for up to 1 month. When the sauce comes out of the refrigerator, it may be a bit too thick and jelly-like. Gently warm the portion you plan to use and it will loosen up nicely.

Natural Food Coloring

A few years ago I clued in to the fact that food coloring is nasty stuff, and I haven't looked back since. Like far too many processed products, food coloring is made from ingredients that can't be considered real food (petroleum, anyone?!). And evidence is mounting that they may cause a scary assortment of side effects, such as hyperactivity in children and even cancer.

To me, a brightly colored treat just isn't worth the risk, so I use natural food colors in my icing. Natural food stores usually carry at least one brand of ready-made natural coloring, but they are very expensive and hard to find where I live, so recently I've been making my own using brightly colored fruits and vegetables.

Homemade natural colors are not as vibrant as artificial ones—they're definitely more "earthy" looking—but there is beauty in that, and my kids don't seem to notice the difference at all. And even better, they don't notice any odd flavor coming through. To them, it's just yummy colored icing.

Because most of these colors are a bit less concentrated, I recommend making your icing thicker than normal so that it doesn't become too thin once you add the color. Add just a little coloring to your icing at a time, so that you can carefully gauge the color, thickness, and taste. Too much color, and you'll have a soupy mess that tastes like cooked vegetables.

I like to make up these colors the day that I am going to use them, because the smell of the vegetables can increase over time.

When I want to decorate cookies with colored icing using these techniques, I use a very simple mix of organic icing sugar and a bit of water, and that is the icing recipe that these colors have been tested with. Feel free to experiment with your own favorite icing, but know that these formulations may react differently if there are other ingredients in the icing, like lemon juice or fat. That said, the red/pink, yellow, and orange colors have also been tested with cream cheese frosting, and the color held up really well. The blue coloring definitely holds up best with icing made of only icing sugar and water.

Red/Pink: Chop a quarter of a beet into very small pieces. Put the beet in a small pot and just cover it with water. Simmer gently for approximately 3 minutes. Pour the beet and water into a fine sieve or some sheets of cheesecloth with a bowl underneath and press out as much moisture as possible into the bowl. Presto—red food coloring. Add to the icing ¼ teaspoon at a time until you get the hue and consistency you need.

Yellow: This is the easiest. Just add a pinch or two of ground dried turmeric to your icing.

Orange: Add ¼ teaspoon of red color at a time as described above for red/pink icing, plus a pinch of turmeric.

Light Purple: Chop up a quarter of a purple cabbage, put it in a pot, and cover it with water (approximately 1½ cups). Boil over medium heat for at least 10 minutes. The water should be a deep purple. Use a slotted spoon to fish out the cabbage, and discard it. Put the purple water in a bowl. Allow to cool completely. Add this to your icing ½ teaspoon at a time. You will have plenty extra, but it's necessary to make this much or there won't be enough water to boil for 10 minutes. The cabbage smell of this coloring increases over time, so I suggest discarding what you don't use and making fresh color each time you need it.

Icy Blue: Follow the instructions for purple coloring. Once cool, add a pinch of baking soda to create a blue hue. You can add more baking soda to make it a stronger color, but be careful not to add too much. Baking soda has a very strong flavor and will affect the taste of the icing. Blue coloring will fade over a couple of days, so eat up the treats quickly.

Icy Green: I've heard of people using spinach to make green coloring, but I personally have not had much success with it. I find that the color turns out too swampy-looking, and that the cooking process is too long. I prefer to use a small spoonful of the blue coloring described above, plus a pinch of turmeric. The blue and yellow combine to make a nice cool light green.

Metric Conversion Table

WEIGHT		VOLUME		OVEN TEMPERATURE		LENGTH	
⅛ oz	4 g	¼ tsp	1 mL	160°F	70°C	¼ inch	6 mm
½ oz	15 g	½ tsp	2 mL	275°F	135°C	½ inch	1.2 cm
1 oz	30 g	1 tsp	5 mL	300°F	150°C	¾ inch	2 cm
2 oz	60 g	1 Tbsp	15 mL	325°F	160°C	1 inch	2.5 cm
3 oz	85 g	1½ Tbsp	22 mL	350°F	175°C	1¼ inches	3 cm
4 oz/¼ lb	110 g	2 Tbsp	30 mL	400°F	200°C	1½ inches	4 cm
5 oz	140 g	3 Tbsp	45 mL	425°F	220°C	2 inches	5 cm
6 oz	170 g	¼ cup	60 mL	450°F	230°C	3 inches	8 cm
7 oz	200 g	⅓ cup	80 mL			4 inches	10 cm
8 oz/½ lb	225 g	½ cup	125 mL	CAN SIZES		5 inches	13 cm
12 oz/¾ lb	340 g	⅔ cup	160 mL	13.5 oz	398 mL	6 inches	15 cm
1 lb	450 g	¾ cup	185 mL	19 oz	540 mL	7 inches	18 cm
		1 cup	250 mL	26 oz	796 mL	8 inches	20 cm
		1¼ cups	310 mL			9 inches	23 cm
		1⅓ cups	330 mL			10 inches	25 cm
		1½ cups	375 mL			11 inches	27 cm
		2 cups	500 mL			12 inches	30 cm

Acknowledgments

Creating this cookbook has been a dream come true and an experience I'll cherish forever. Thank you so much to Kristin Cochrane and to Robert McCullough for believing in me and my vision for the book, and to the whole Appetite team for your incredible support. I'd especially like to thank my editor, Lesley Cameron. Your gentle persistence was exactly what I needed, and I'm lucky to have had you in my corner.

To the uber-talented Janis Nicolay, who is responsible for all the gorgeous photography in this book: I can't thank you enough for your generosity with your time and ideas, and for your patience when working with me, a cookbook first-timer. You've been so much more than a photographer on this project and I feel so fortunate that I've had the chance to work with you.

A few shots in this book needed reinforcements (who knew it would be so hard to make a roast chicken look pretty?). Thank you, Becky Paris Turner, for your beautiful food styling, and thank you, Nicole Sjostedt, the prop stylist who helped make the cover so fabulous. I'm also grateful to North Arm Farm for generously allowing us to shoot all the outdoor shots, including the cover, at their beautiful organic farm in Pemberton, BC. It's one of my favorite places to take my children in summer—and we all enjoy eating their produce all summer long. In fact, thank you to all organic farmers for your high professional standards and passion for what you do. Your work is so important for all of us and our planet.

While I was busy on *It All Begins with Food*, I was lucky to have a great team keeping things afloat at Love Child Organics. Thank you so much to the Love Child and GreenSpace Brands team for your genuine enthusiasm and support for this project, and for your understanding when I missed yet another meeting because I was too busy writing or working in the kitchen.

Getting these recipes exactly right wasn't always easy. Many thanks go to an array of friends, family, and colleagues who tasted and tested recipes, gave advice, and, most importantly, encouraged me when the challenges felt insurmountable.

My children were just that little bit too grown up to be photographed for the baby sections of this cookbook. Luckily, two of my oldest friends stepped in to help. Thank you, Kira and Molly, for lending me your babies, Lucy and Kiefer. I love seeing their little faces in this book.

Over the last few years, I've been fortunate to become acquainted with some really special children's brands. Two of them were kind enough to provide some of the gorgeous children's clothes you see on the babies and my two kids. Thank you so much to VONBON Apparel and WHEAT Canada.

A huge thank-you, Mom and Dad, for your never-ending love and support, particularly when I had the crazy idea to become an entrepreneur and put everything I had into Love Child Organics. Dad, I get my entrepreneurial spirit from you; Mom, my love of cooking and good food is without a doubt down to you. Way back when, as you fed your young family, you knew that It All Begins with Food.

And to the rest of my extended food-loving family, including my sister, Ashley, who is an incredible cook, and my aunts, who are about as passionate about fresh organic produce as one could be: I love having such a food-obsessed family. Thank you for inspiring me in so many ways as I wrote this book.

And now for my own little family. To my husband, John: thank you so much for your love and unfailing belief in me. Your understanding when I was unavailable evenings and weekends for months at a time as I wrote this book did not go unnoticed and was appreciated more than I can say. I love you, despite your inability to cook more than one dish. Poppy and Cam, I'll never forget your earnest little faces as you'd say to me, "Mommy, this recipe should definitely, definitely be in The Cookbook." Thank you for being excited about "The Cookbook," as you call it, even though it meant your mommy spent too much time away from you while writing it. You truly are my inspiration for creating clean, delicious food kids love to eat, and I love you both more than anything.

And finally, thank you to all the families who have brought Love Child Organics into your homes. It's such a privilege to have helped you feed your babies. And now, with this cookbook in your kitchen, I hope you're inspired to cook nourishing and delicious food for your family for many years to come.

Index